Alexandre Vatimbella

Twenty First Century
New Yorkers

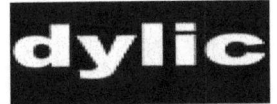

Foreword

All the pictures of this book were shooted in New York City for ten years between 2007 et 2016.

There was no particular plan as I was looking for situations that I thought were interesting or were surprising me.

So I carried my camera with me everywhere I was going in NYC, in all the boroughs, often aimlessly, just like a bashful lover of this city looking all around him, to discover once more its unique power and shooting the scenes which were proposed to me.

So, in my view, it's not an artwork, it's just a way to testify of what I saw, more a work of a journalist, of a witness of his time, than a work of an artist. My will was to make a patchwork of all these people who populate the streets of NYC.

These pictures must be understood like pieces of evidence of people who live and visit this fascinated megalopolis.

So the real heroes of the book are all these people my camera met.

Alexandre Vatimbella

Avant-propos

Toutes les photos de cet ouvrage ont été prises à New York pendant dix ans, de 2007 à 2016.

Je n'avais pas de plan particulier, je recherchais juste des situations intéressantes ou qui pouvaient me surprendre.

J'ai emmené mon appareil photo avec moi partout où j'allais dans New York, dans tous les boroughs, souvent au hasard, comme un amoureux transi de cette ville regardant autour de moi pour découvrir encore une fois sa puissance unique et photographiant les scènes qui se proposaient à mon regard.

C'est pourquoi, selon moi, ce n'est pas une œuvre d'art que j'ai réalisé, juste une manière de témoigner ce que j'ai vu, plus un travail de journaliste, d'un témoin de son temps, qu'un travail d'un artiste. Ma volonté était de faire patchwork de tous ces gens qui peuplent les rues de New York.

Ces photos doivent être comprises comme des témoignages de ces gens qui vivent ou visitent cette mégalopole fascinante.

Ainsi, les vrais héros de ce livre sont tous ces gens que mon appareil photo a rencontrés.

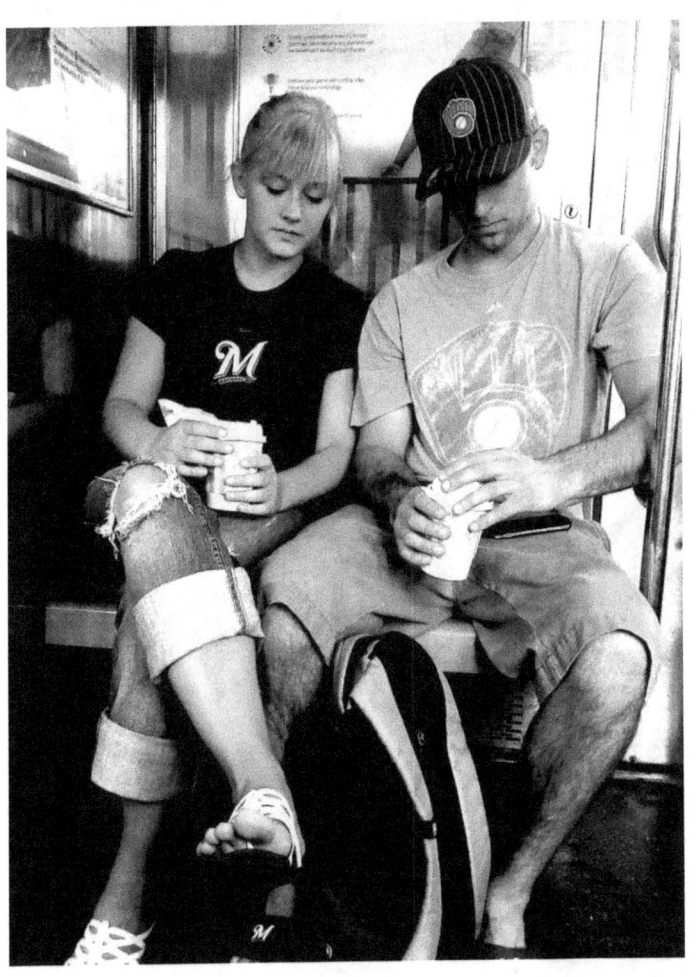

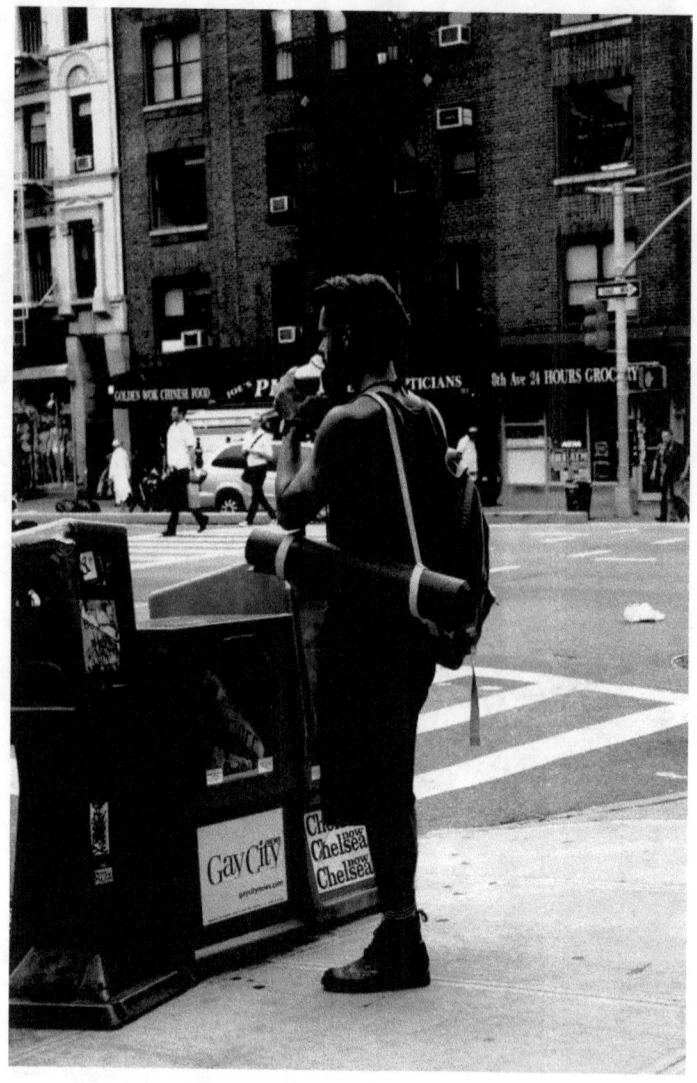

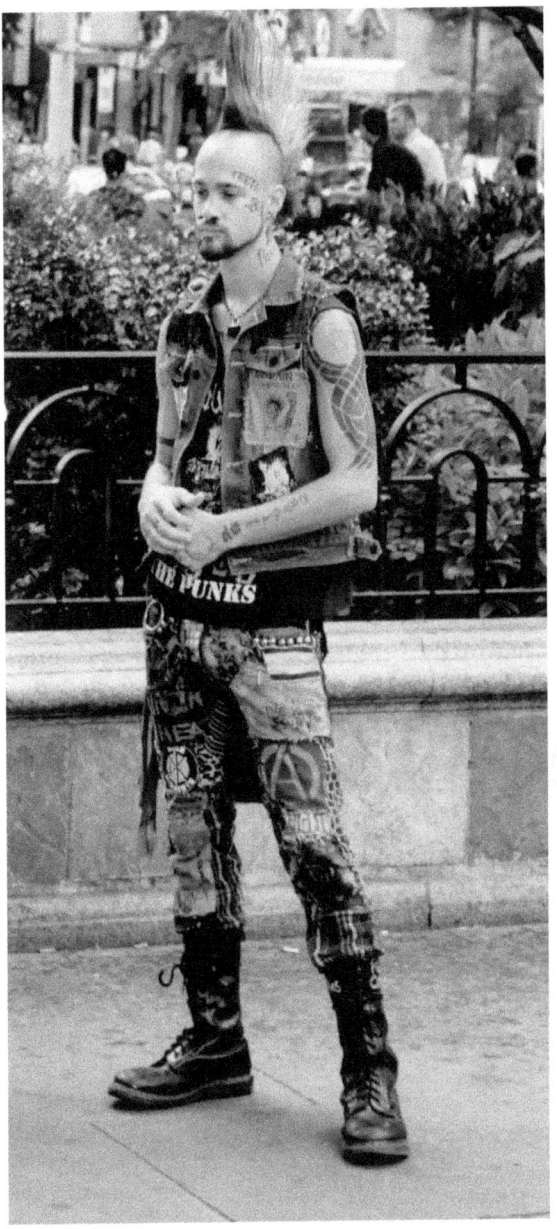

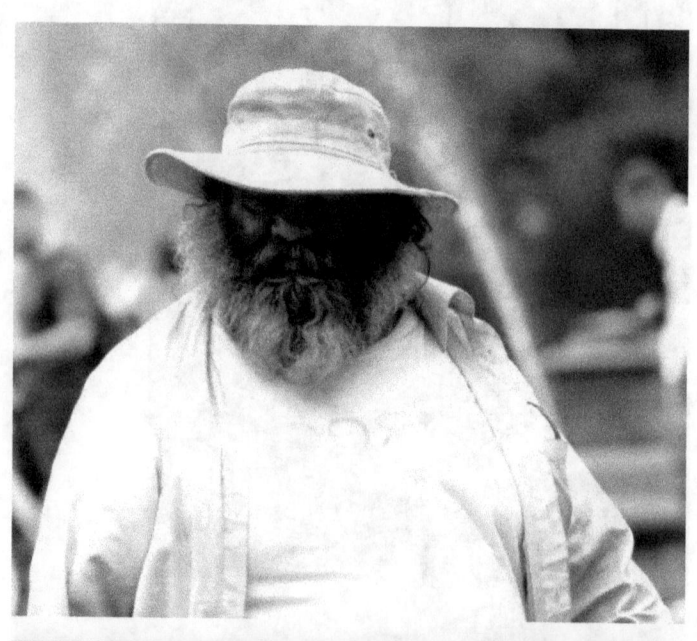

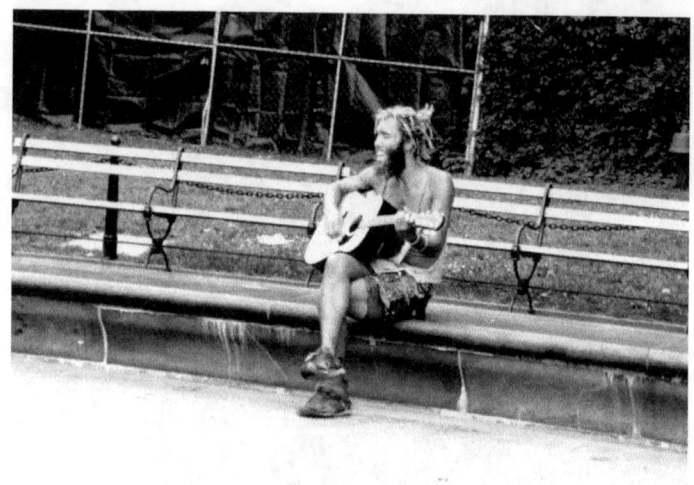

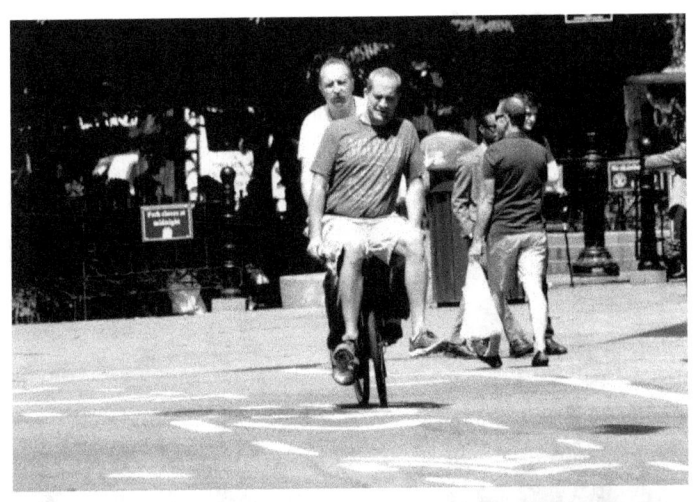

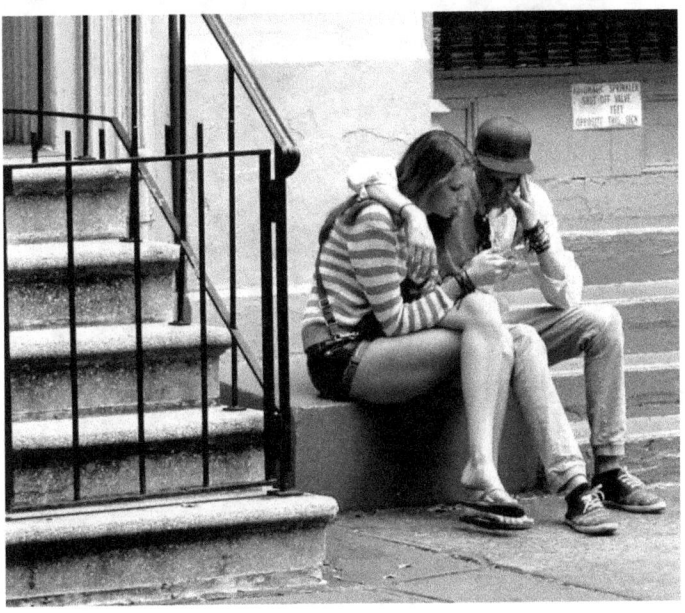

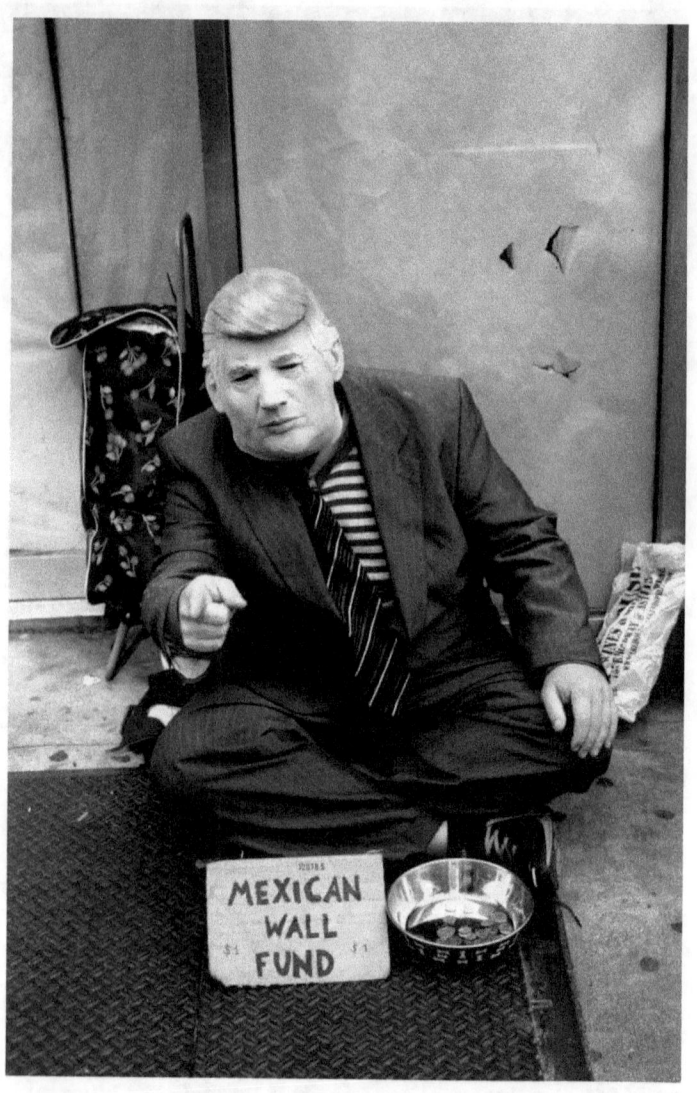

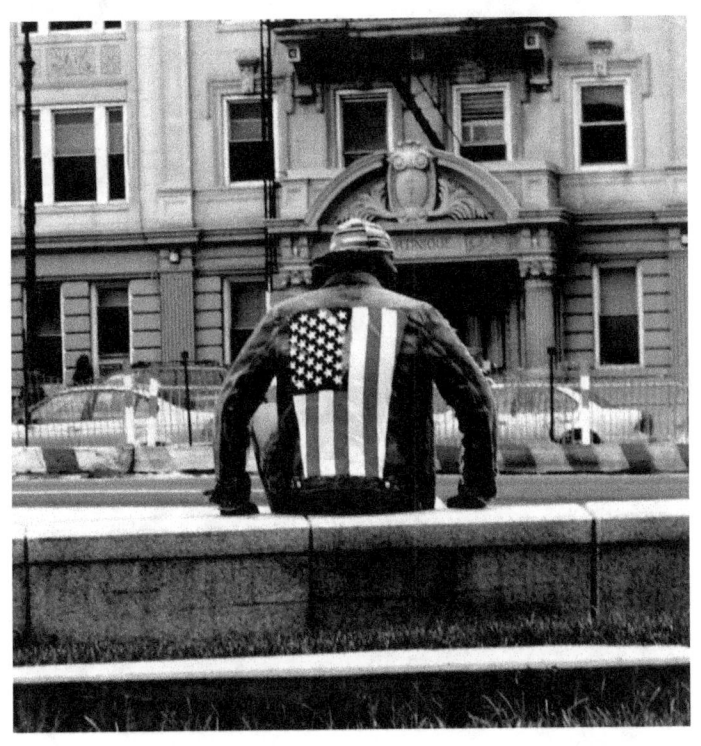

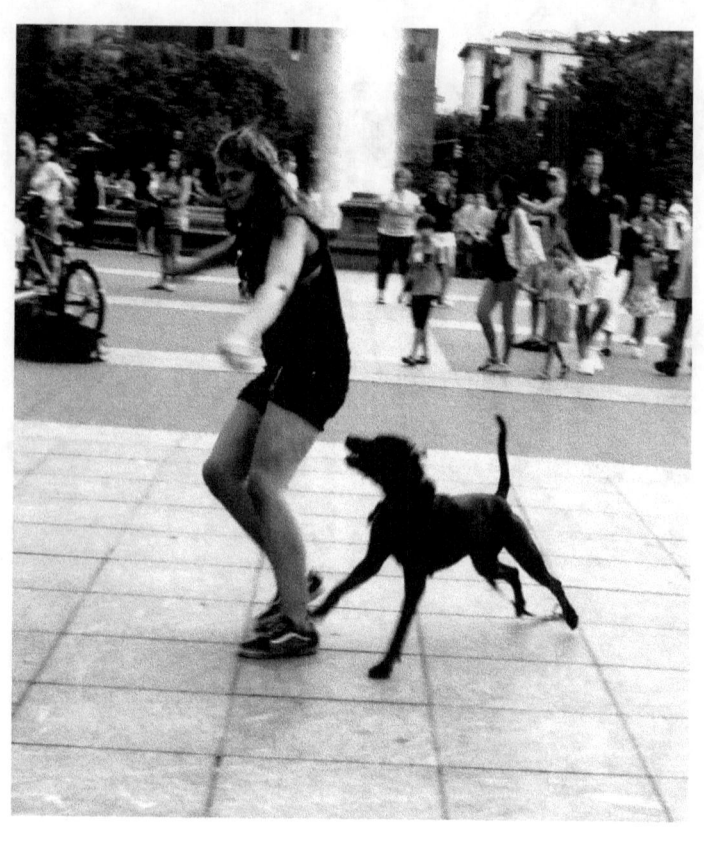

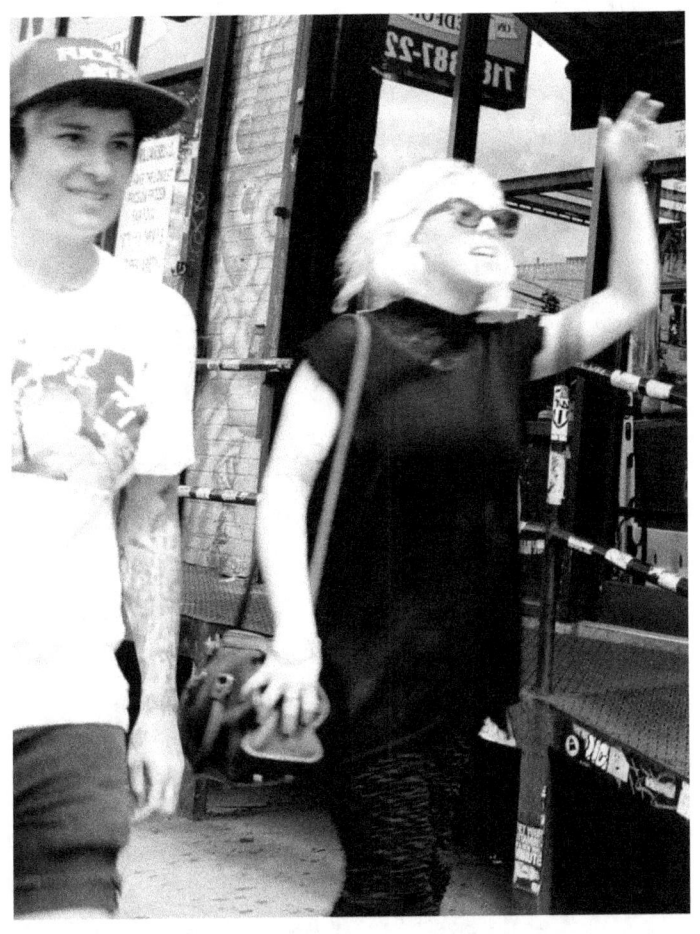

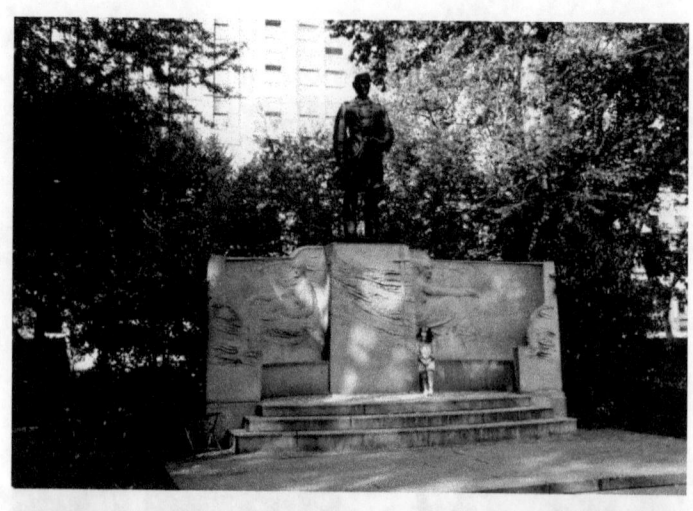

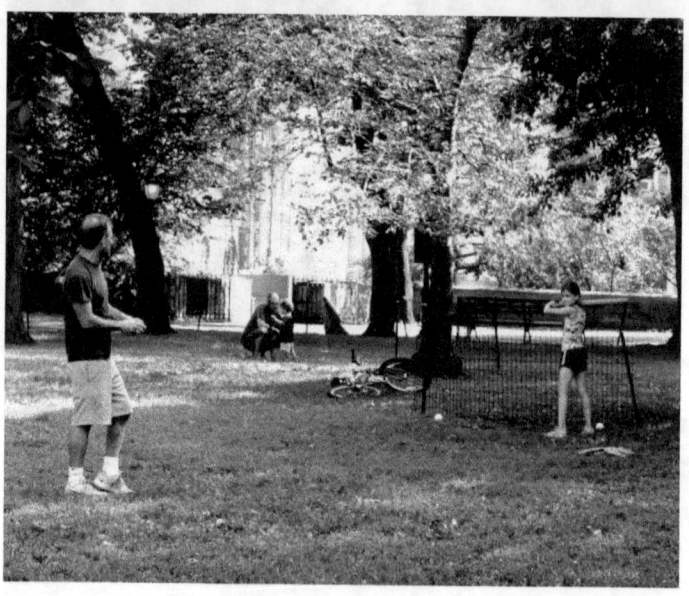

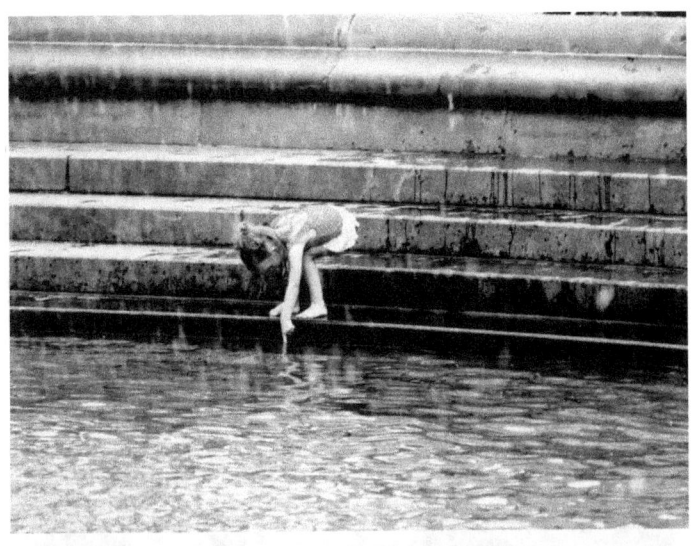

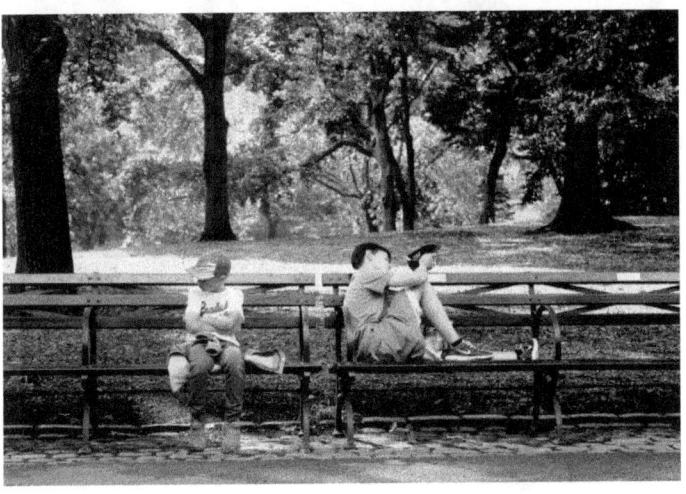

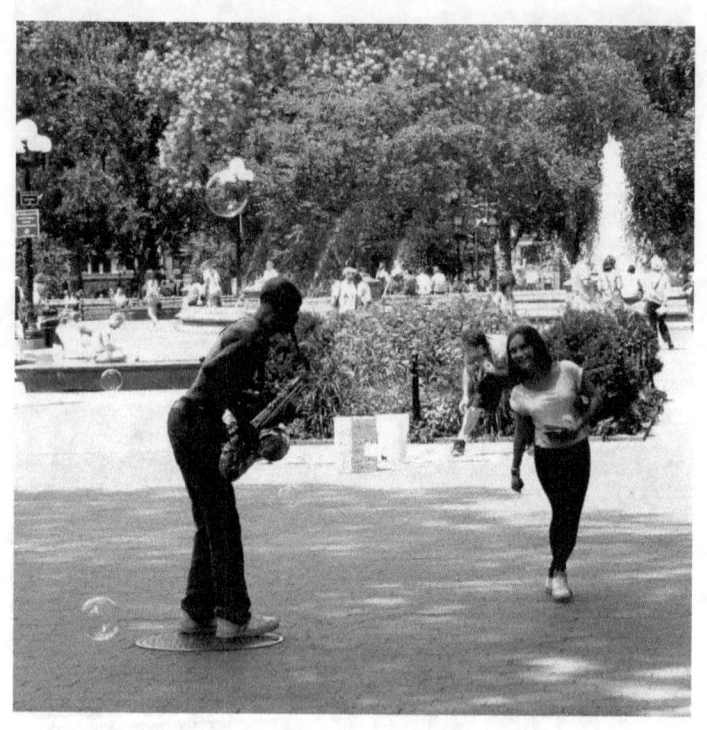

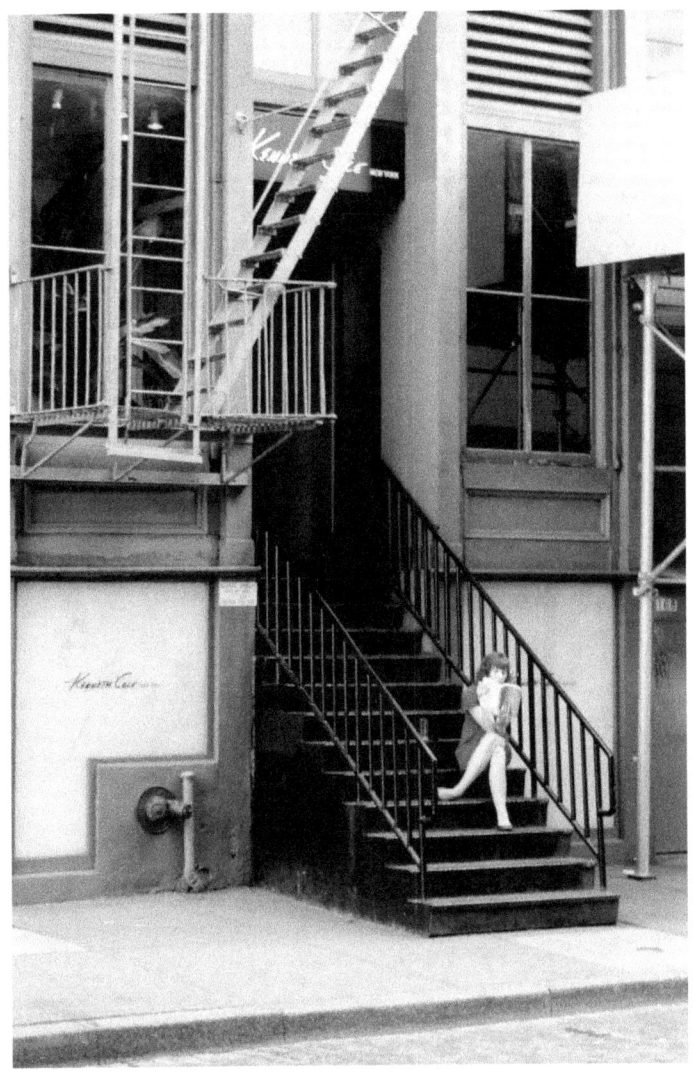

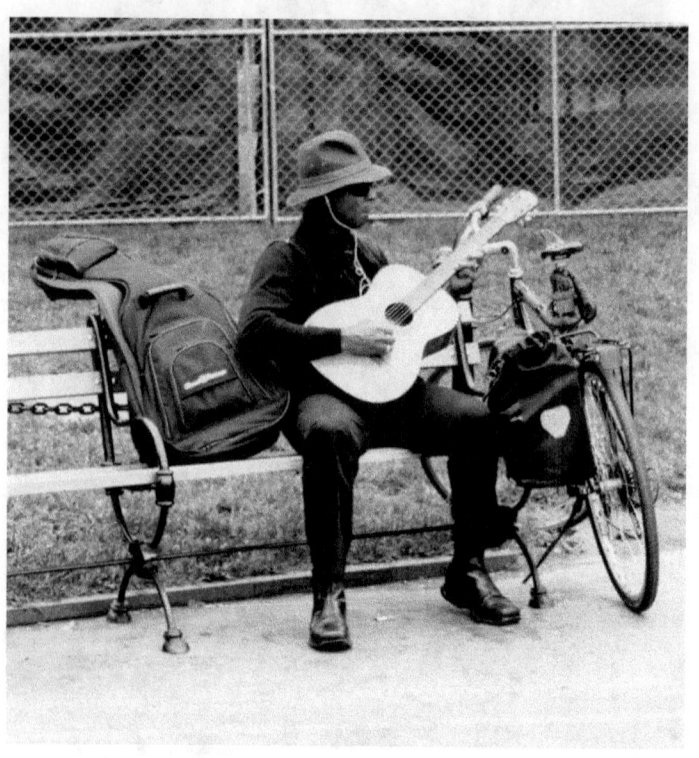

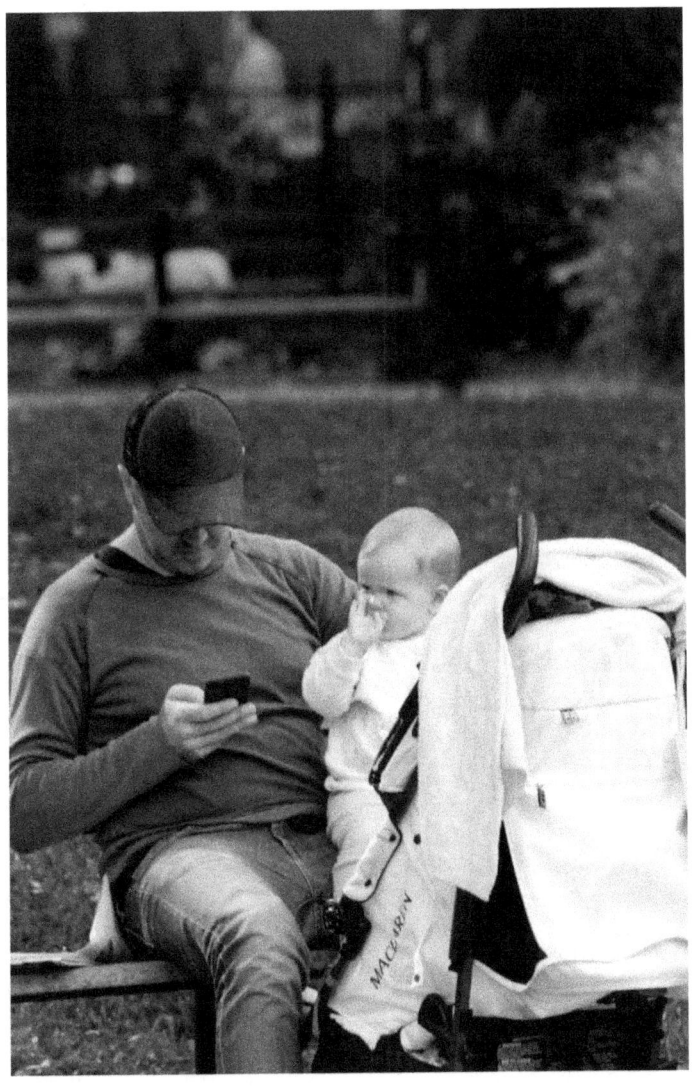

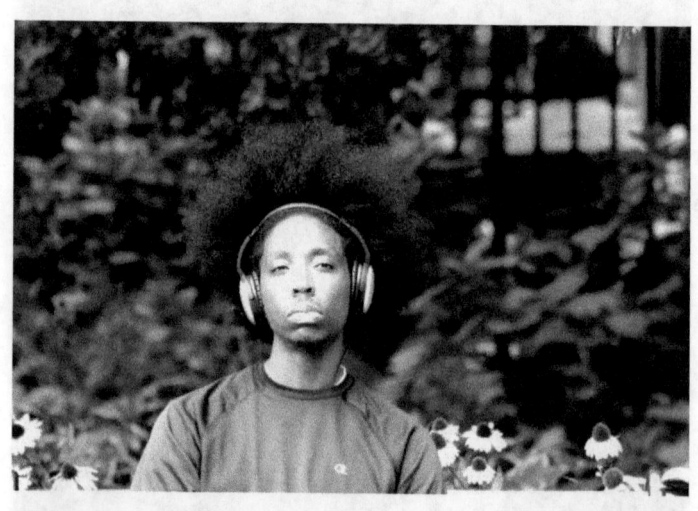
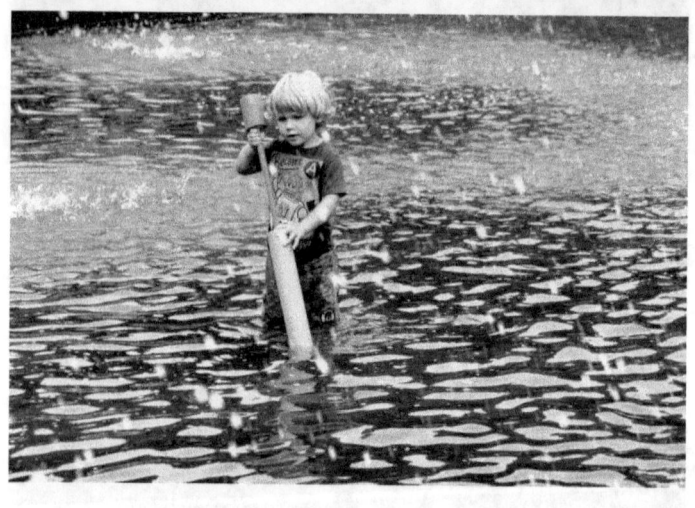

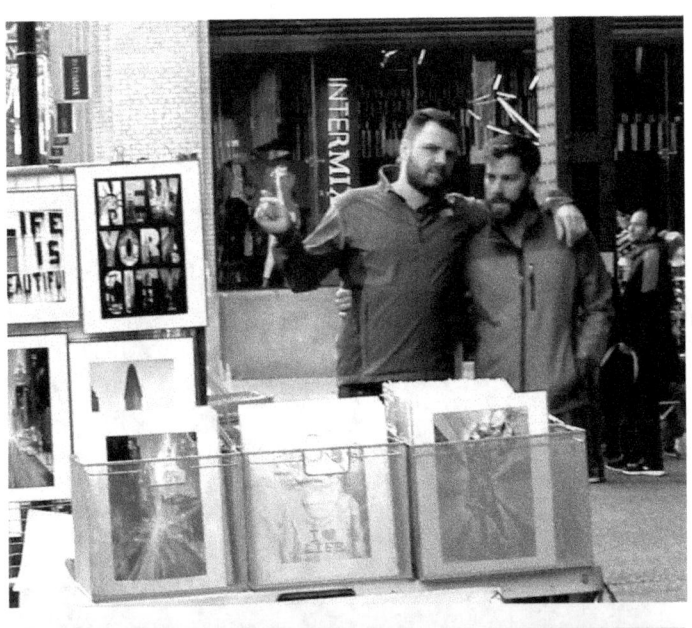

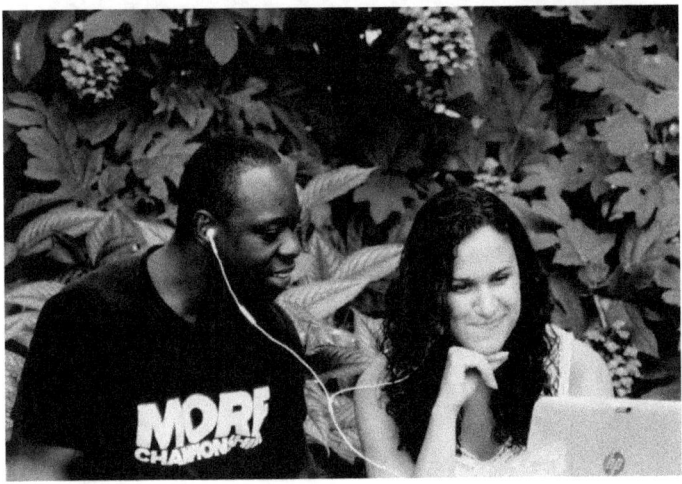

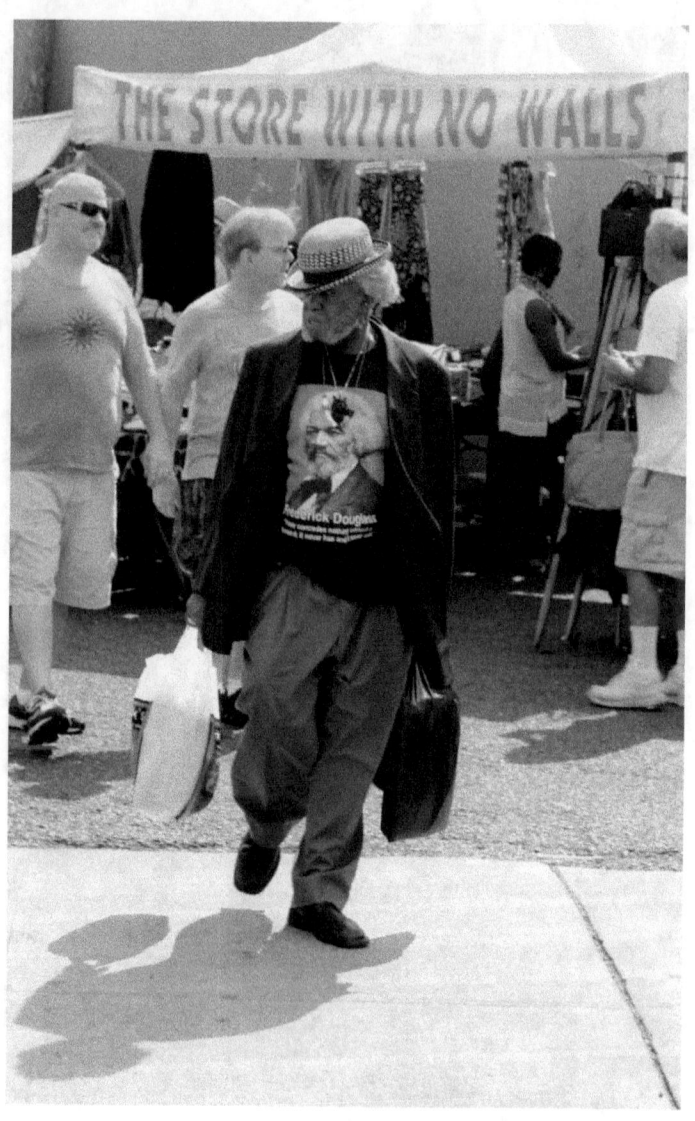

24

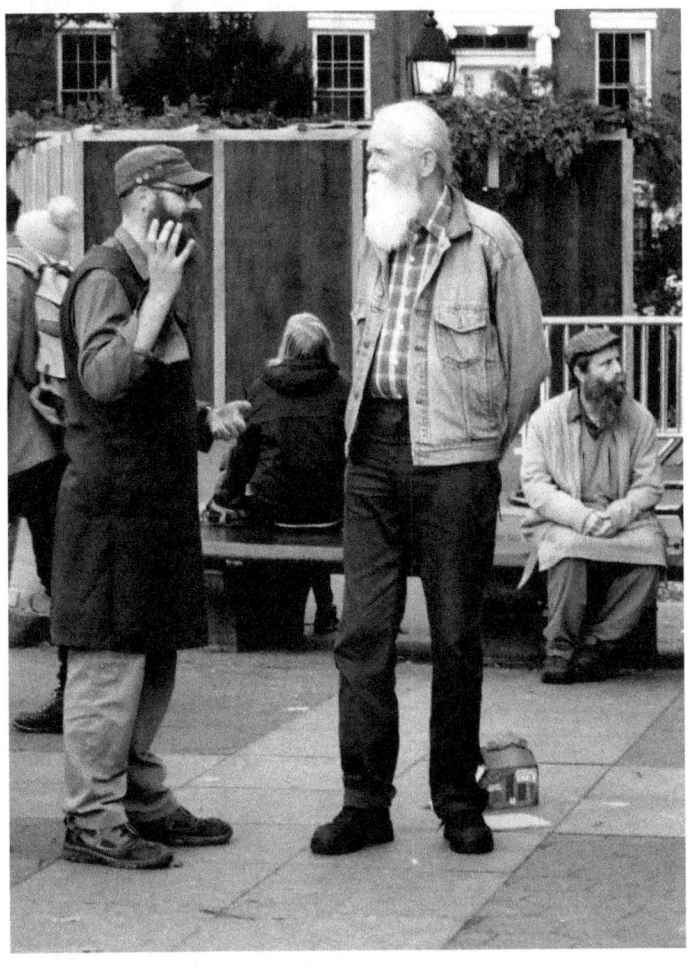

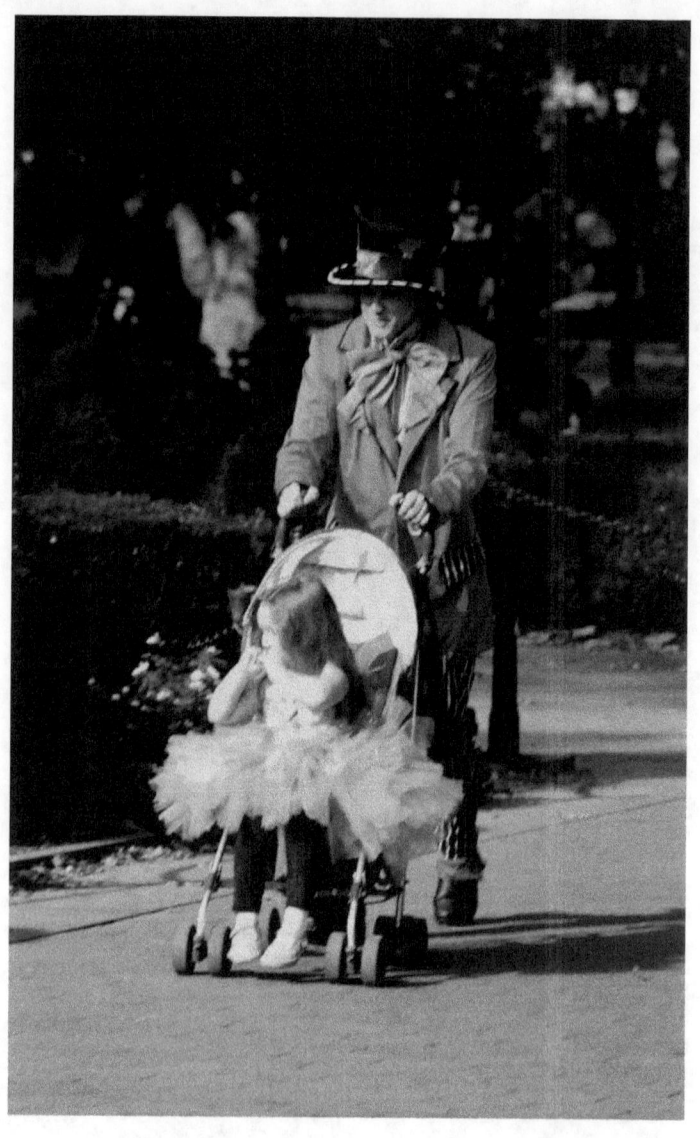

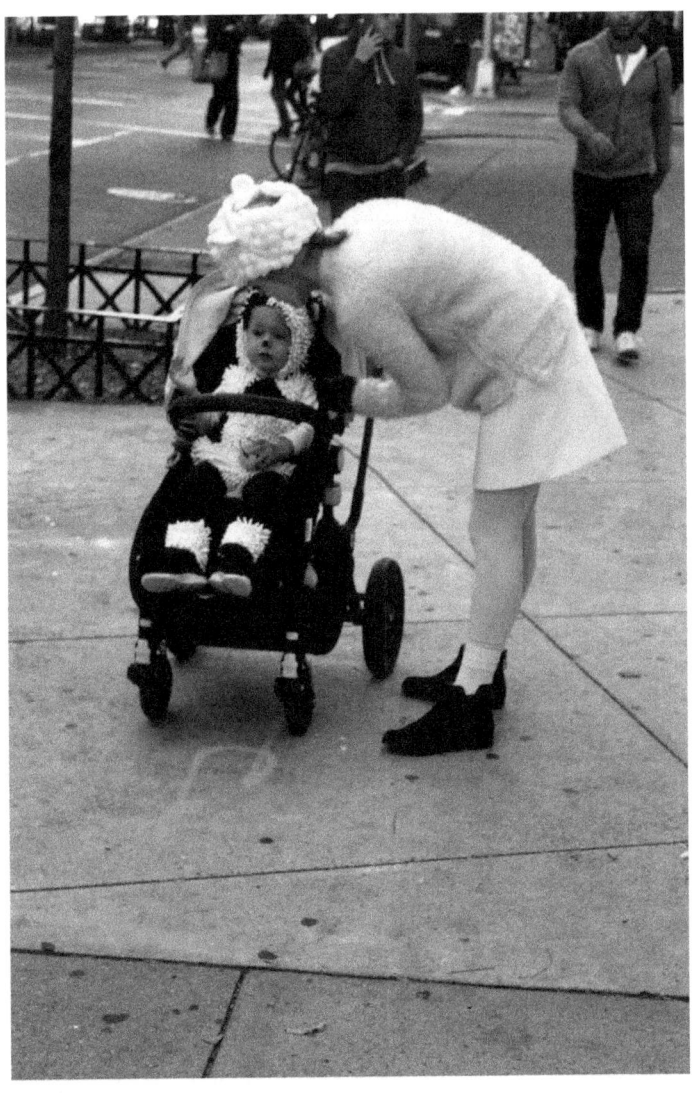

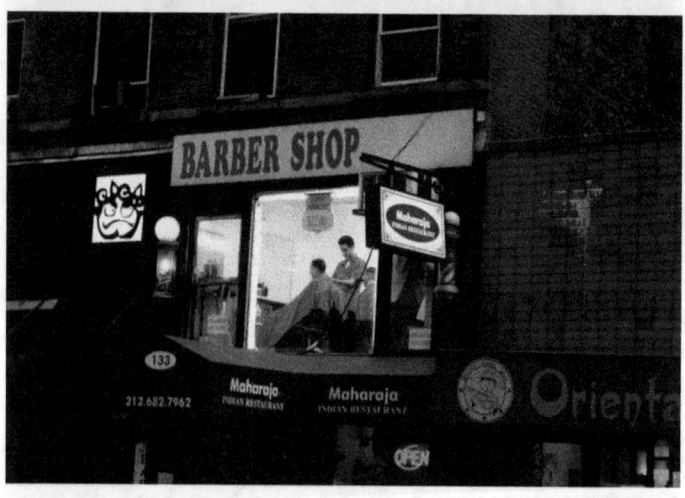

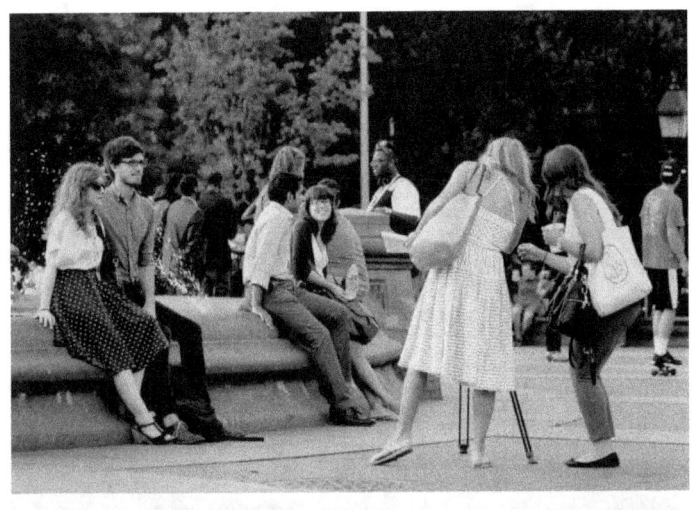

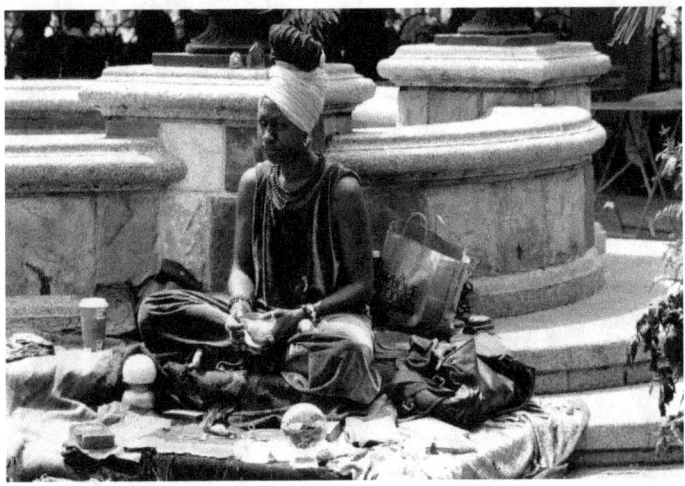

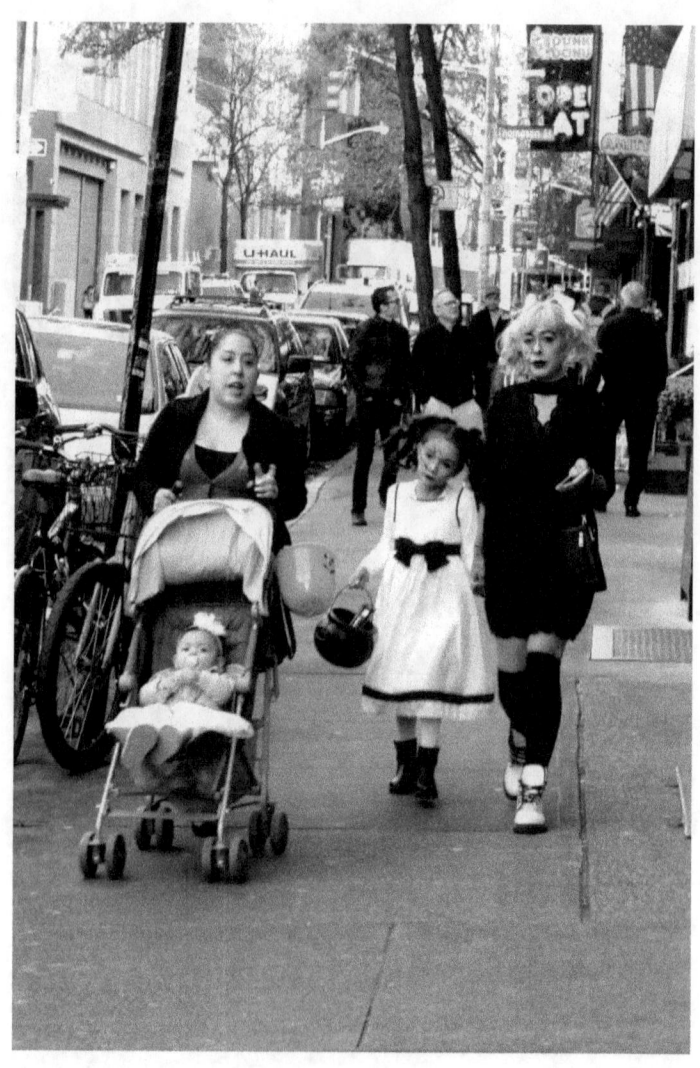

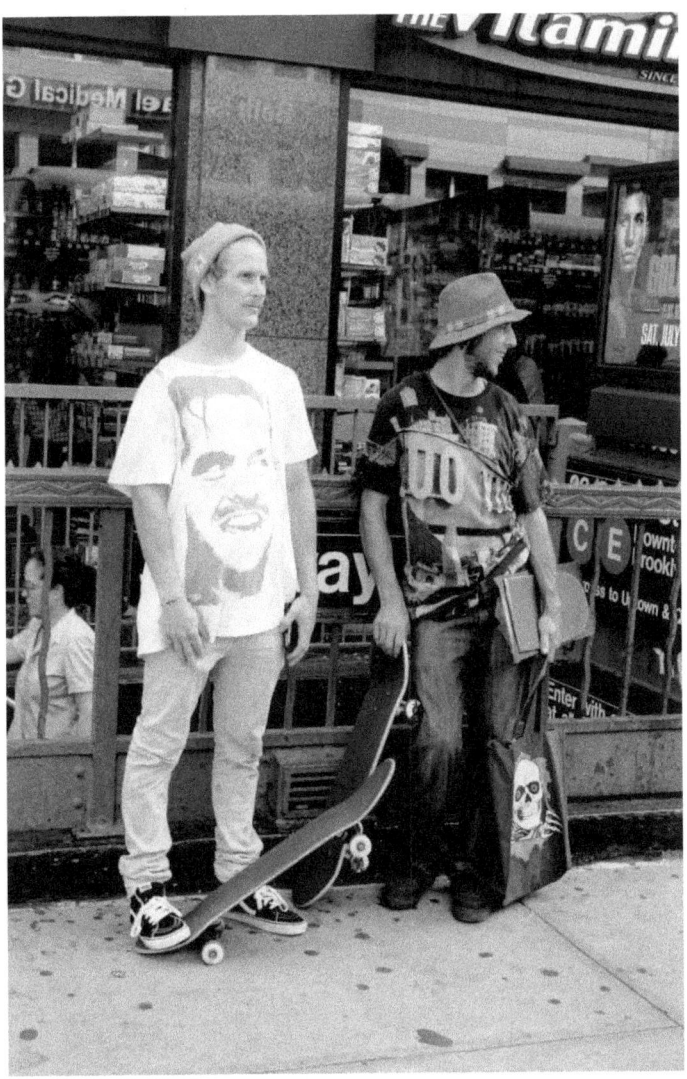

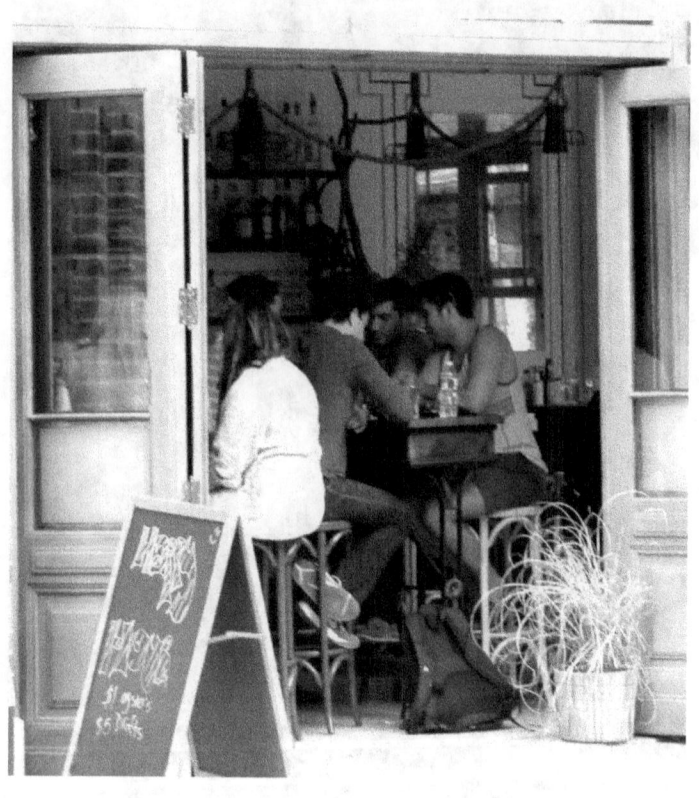

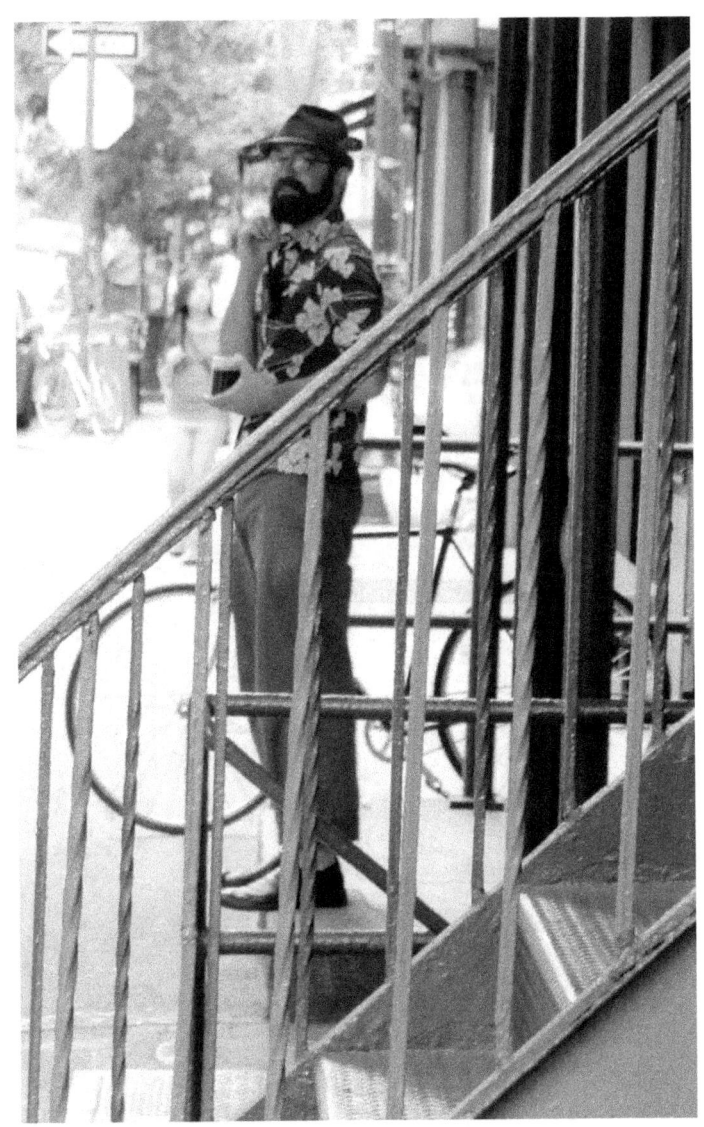

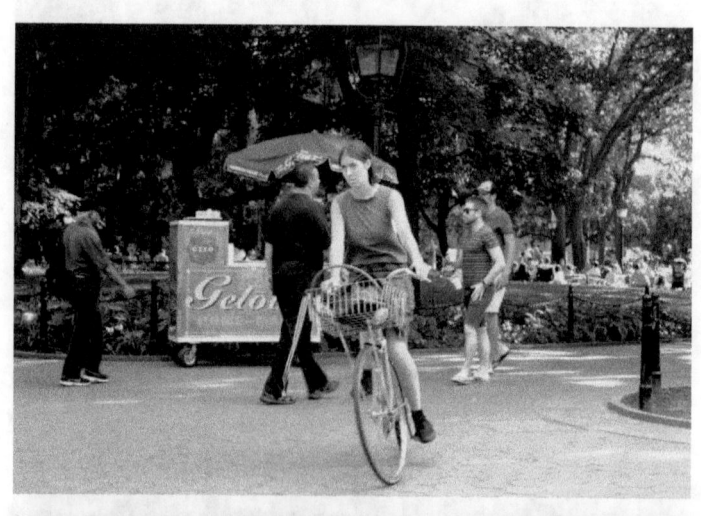

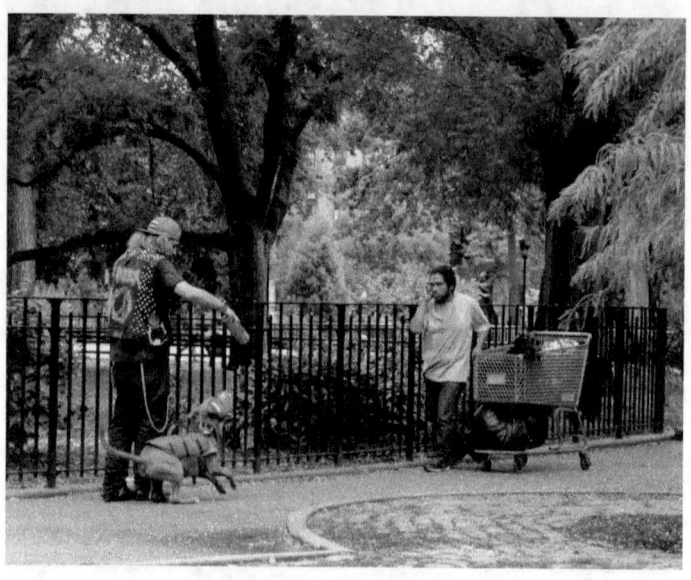

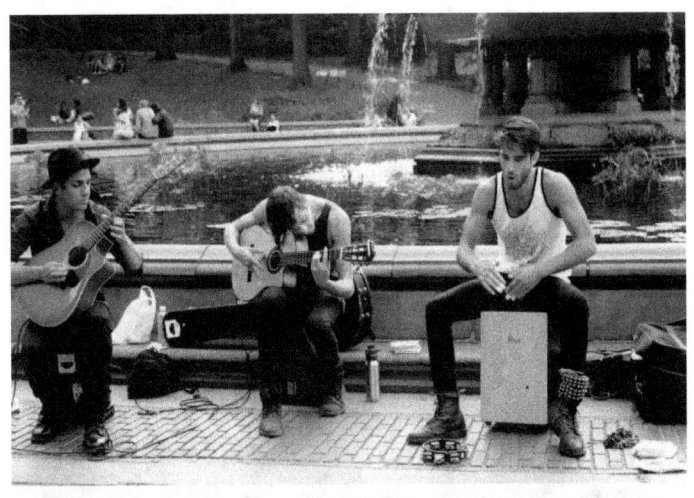

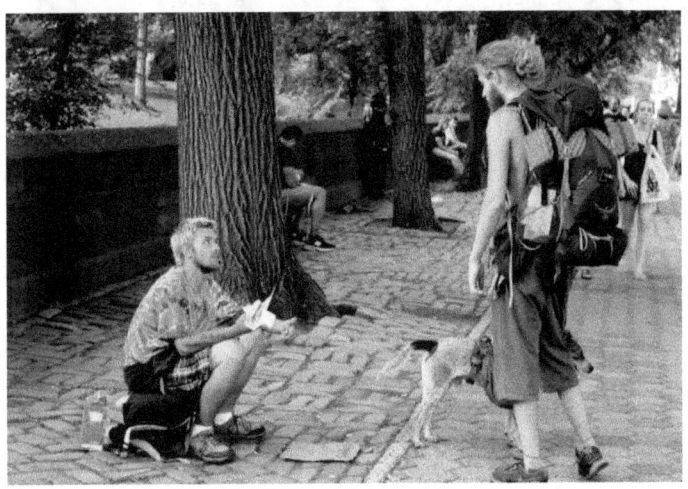

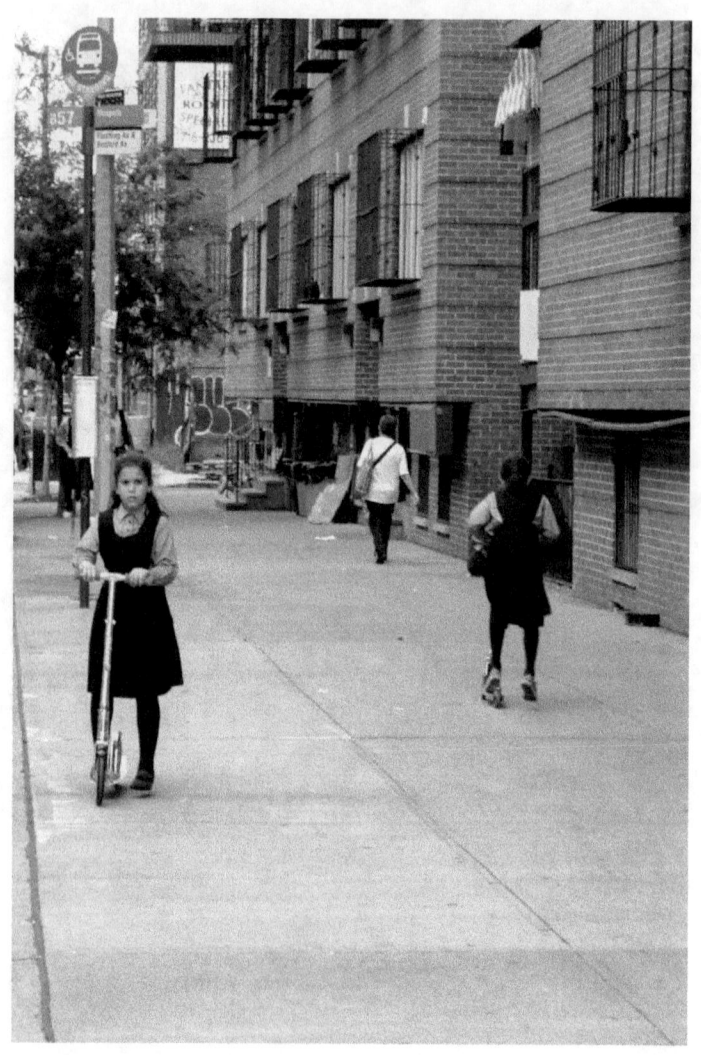

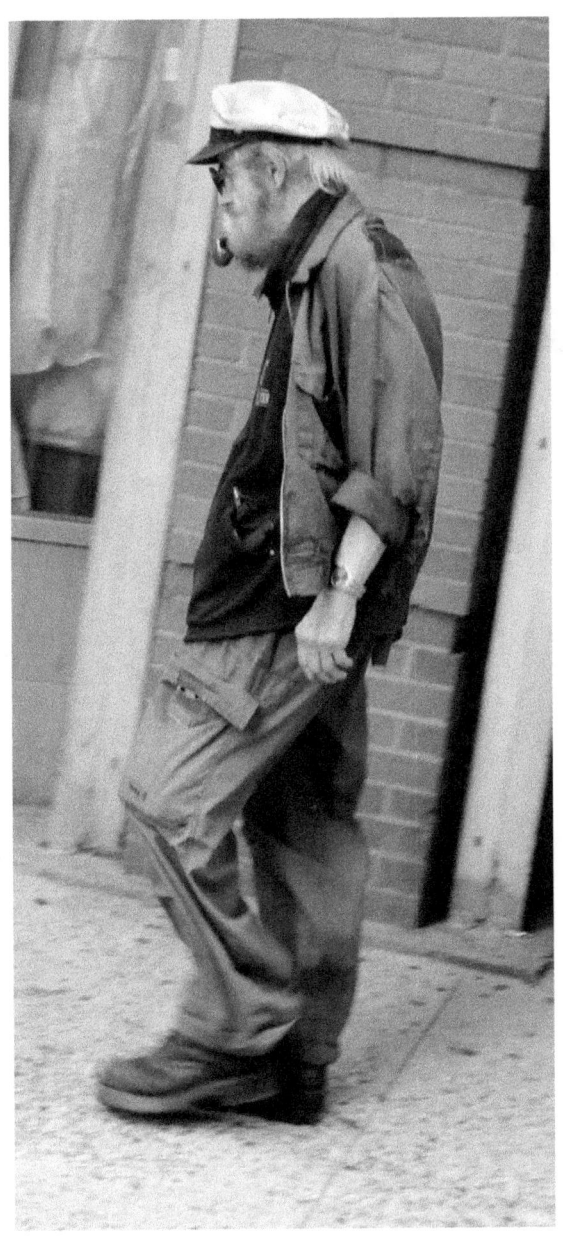

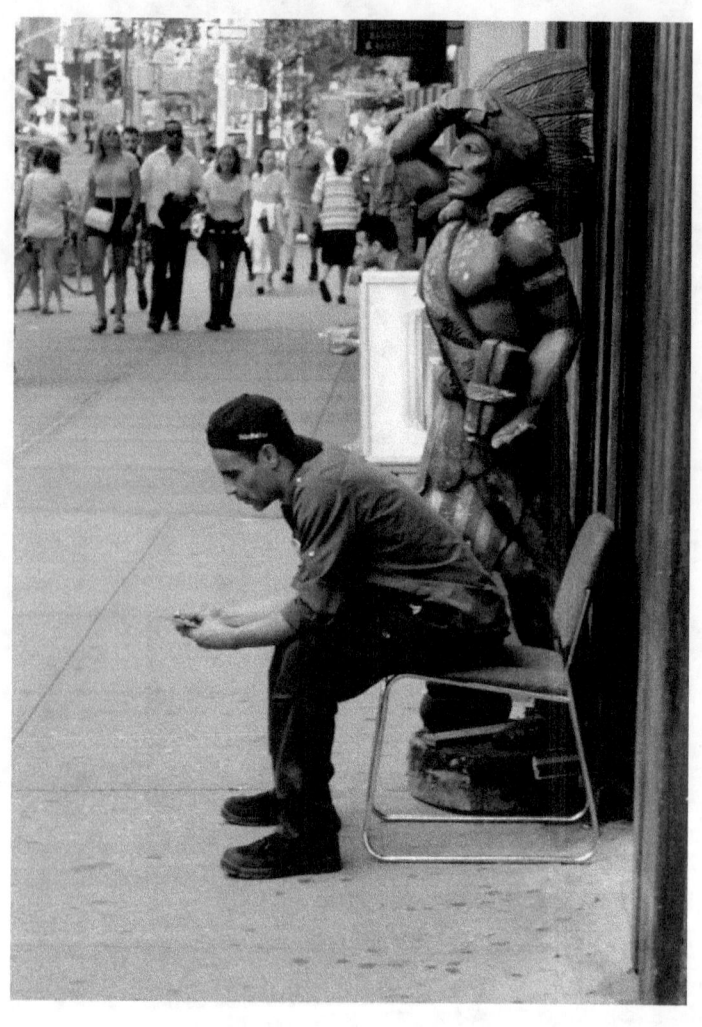

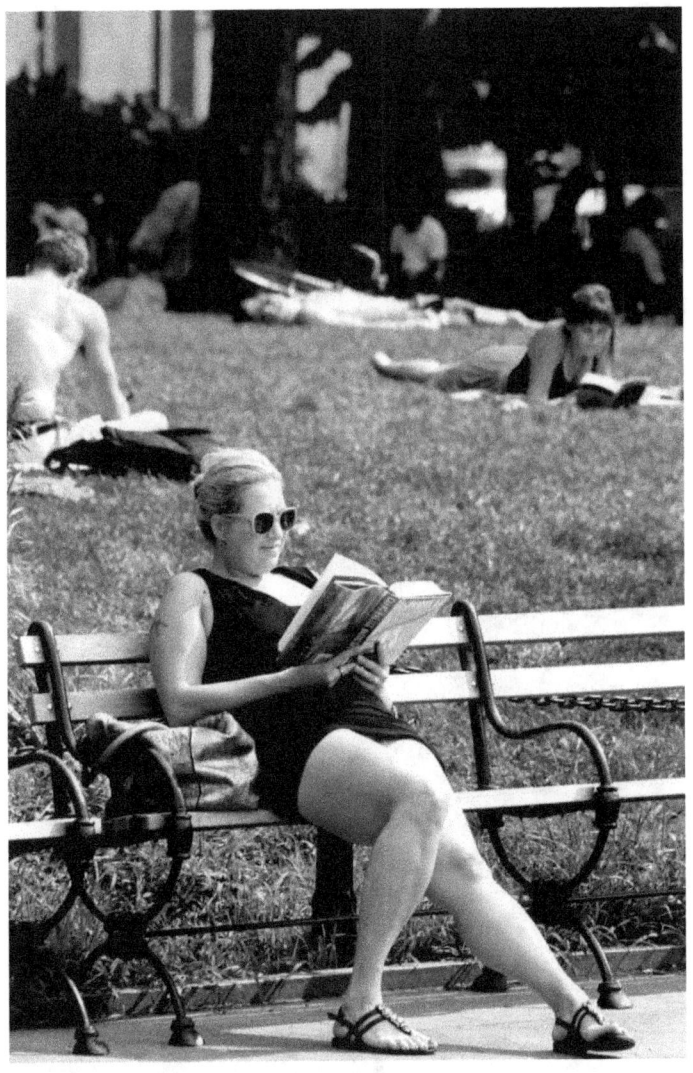

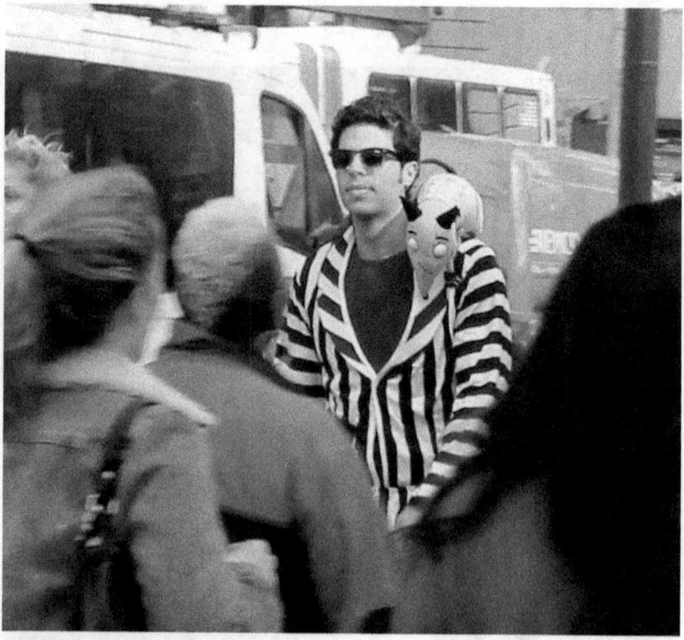

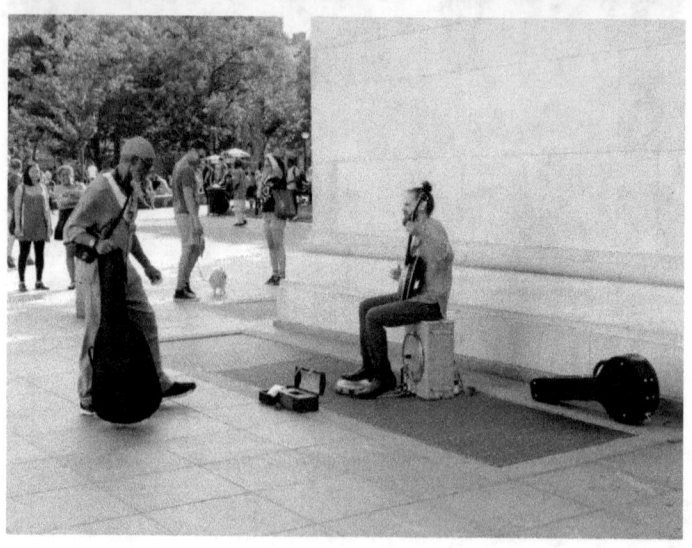

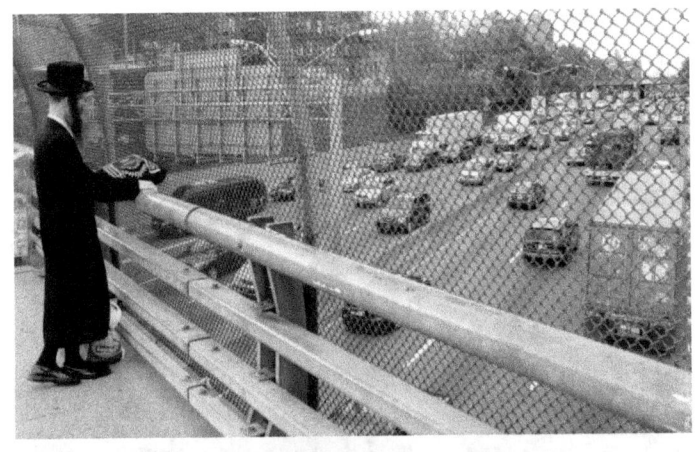

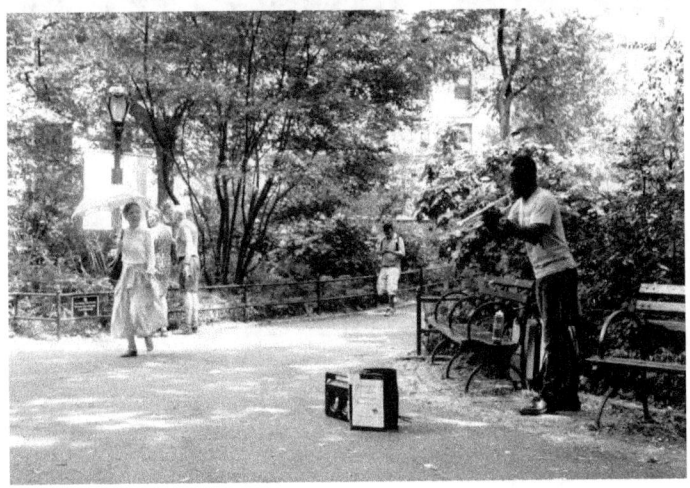

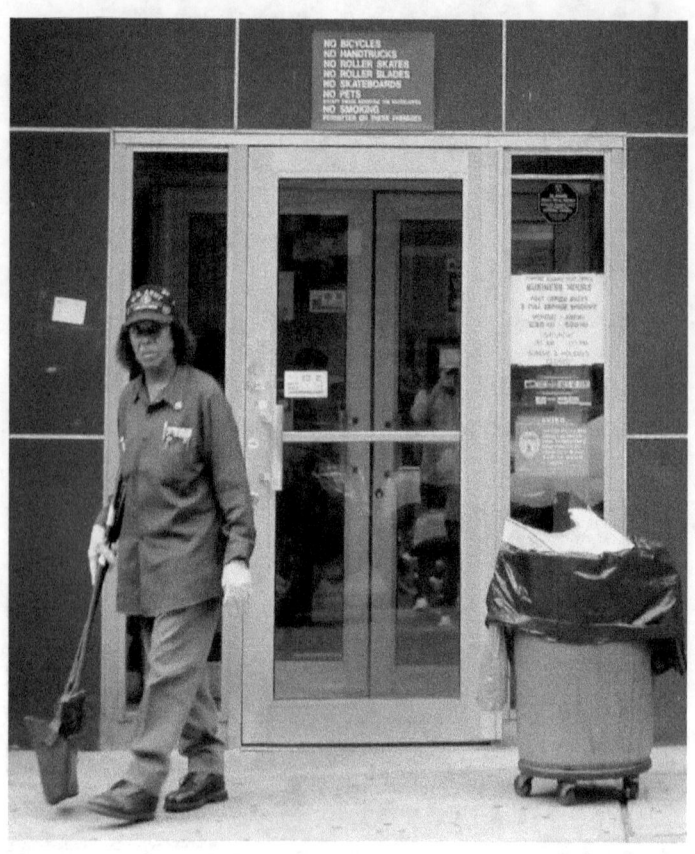

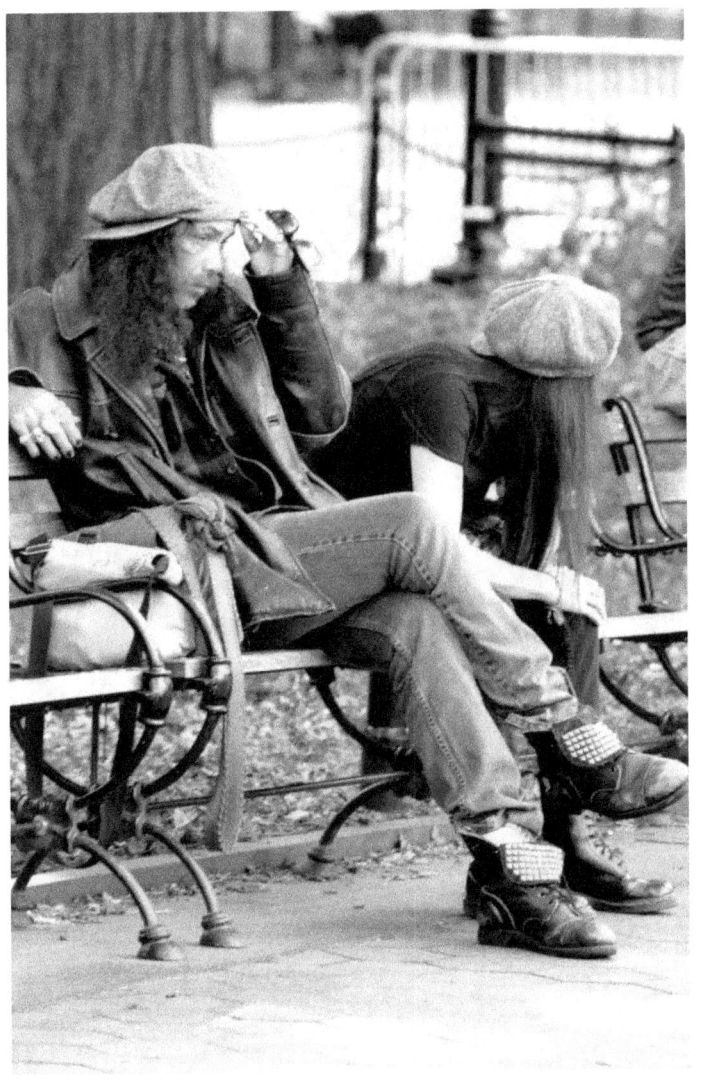

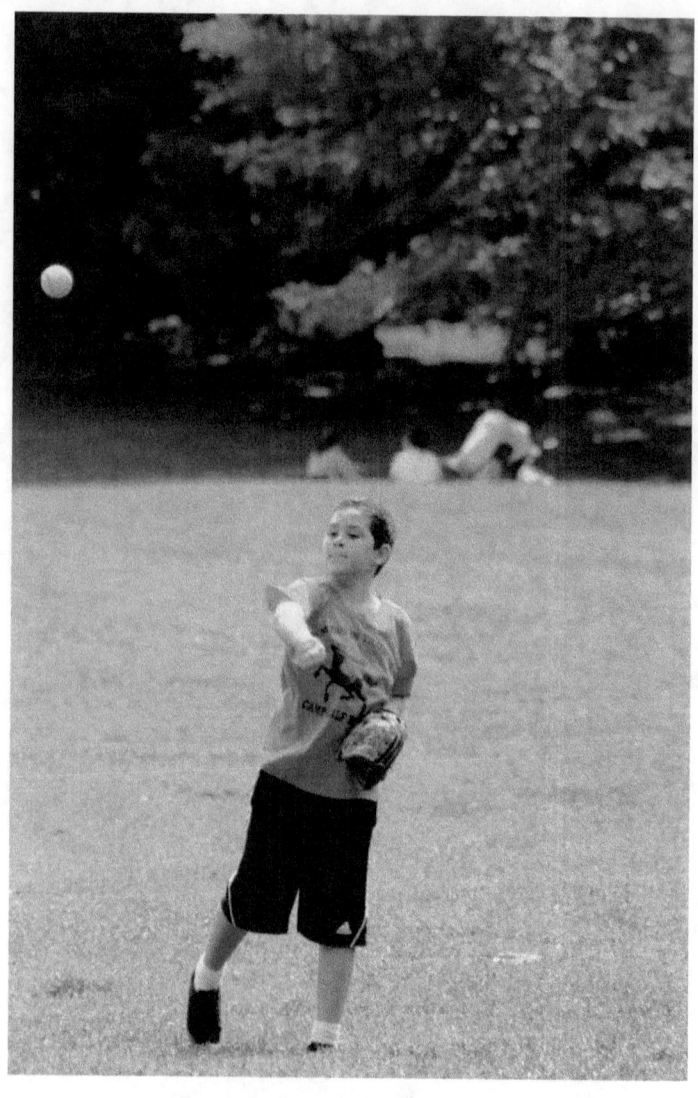

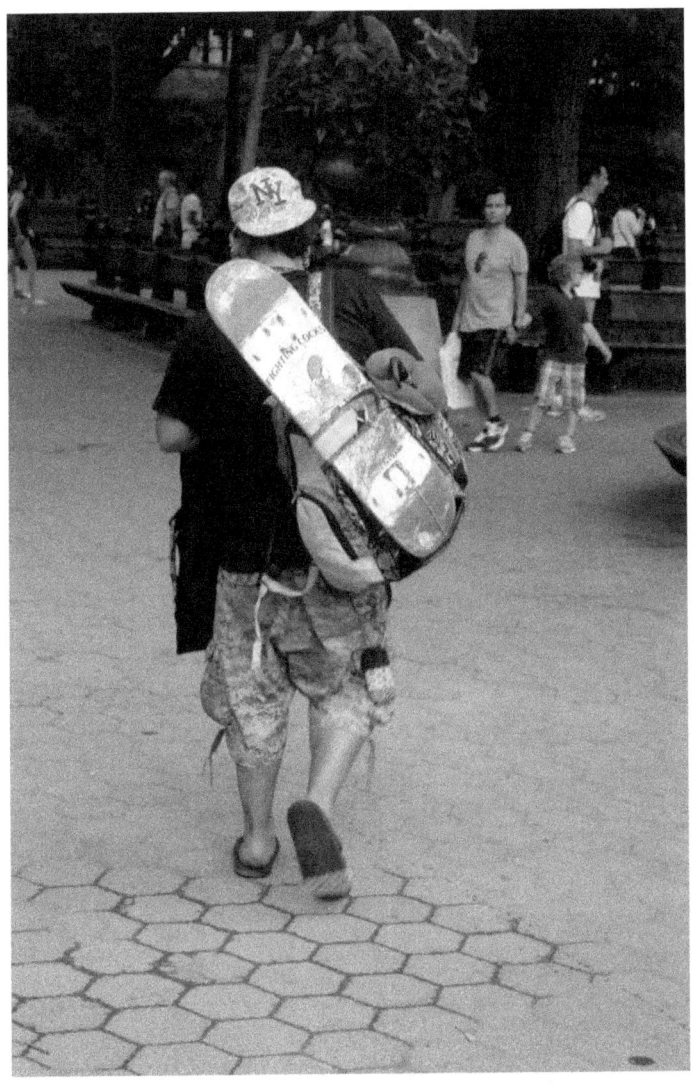

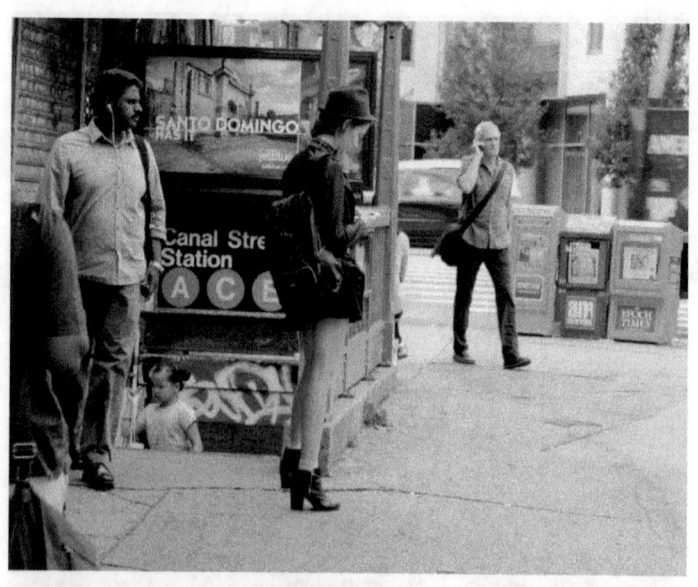

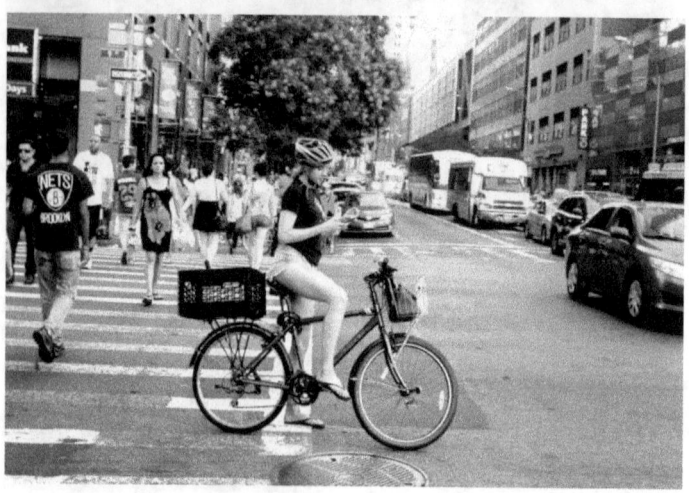

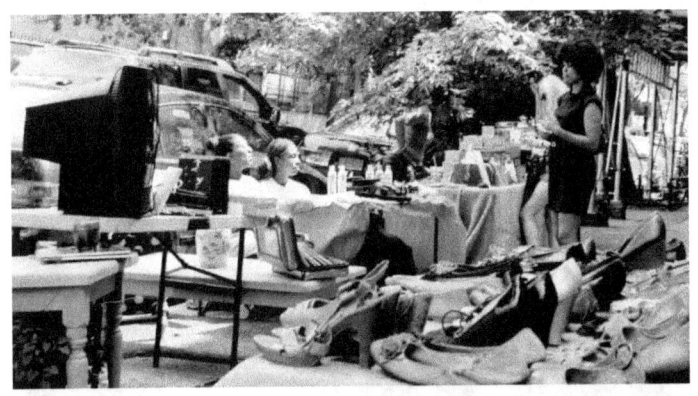

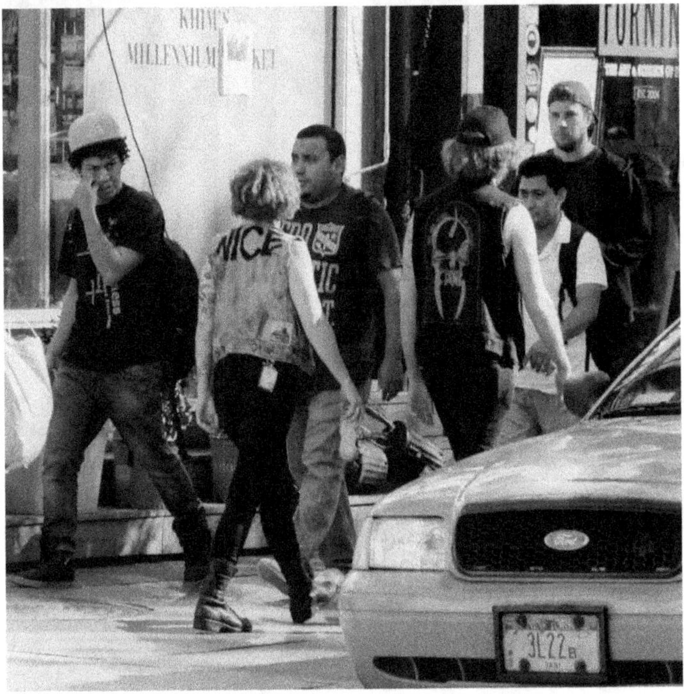

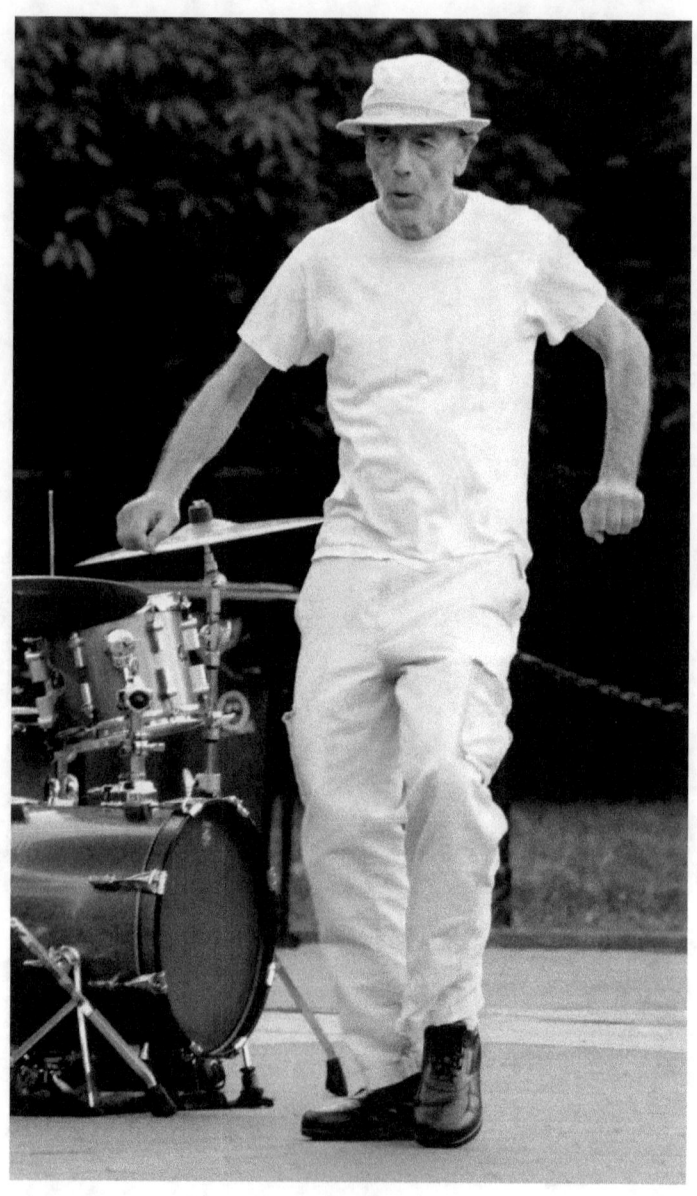

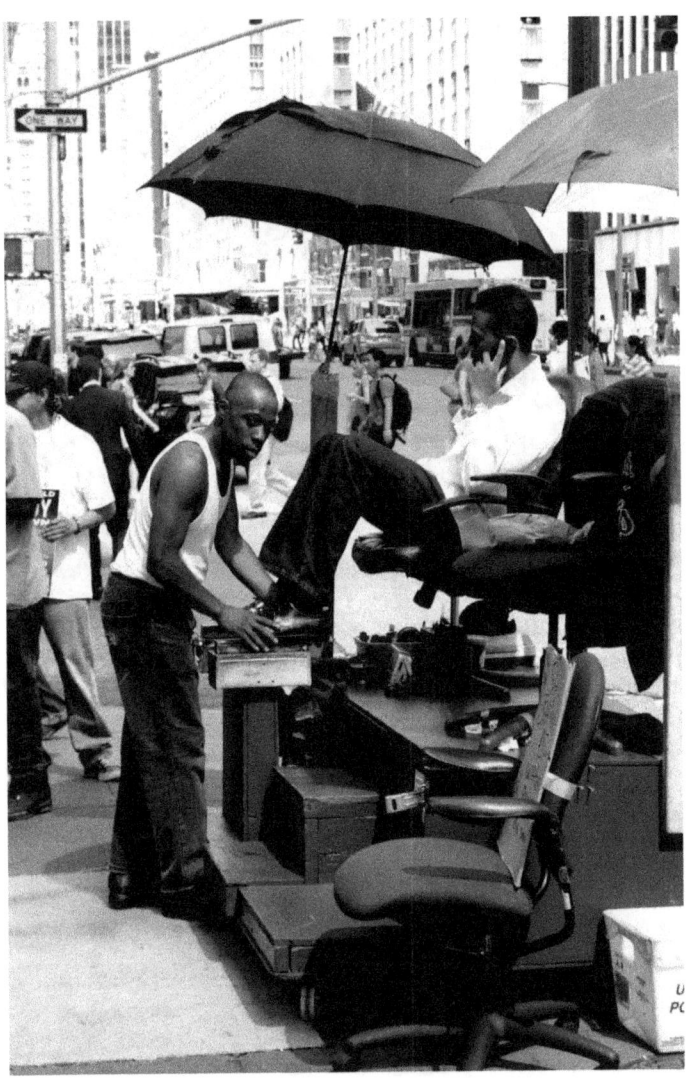

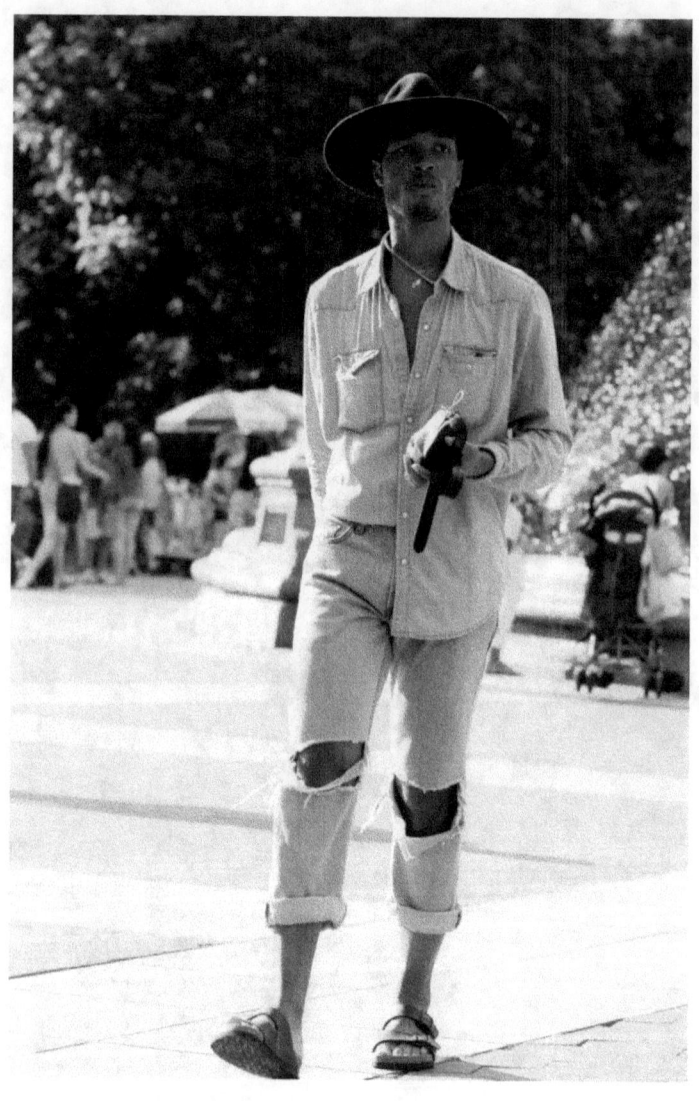

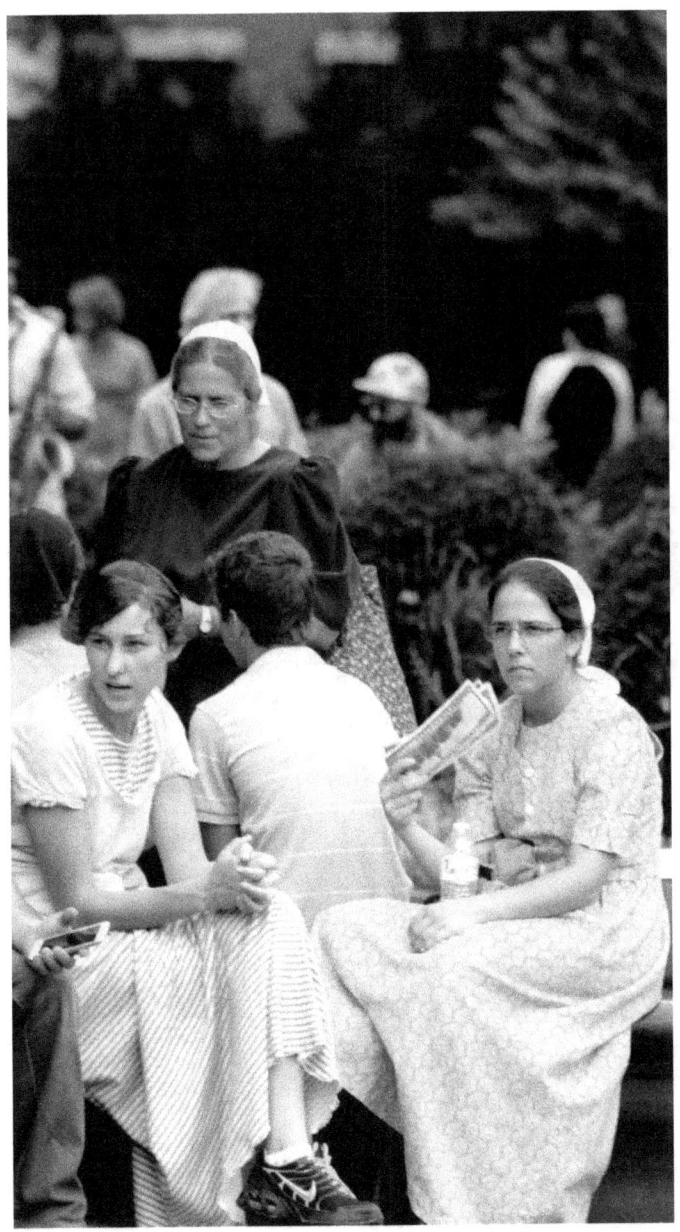

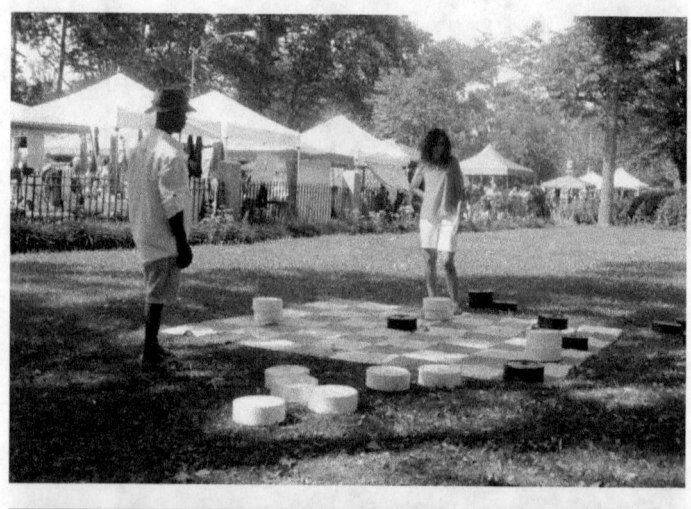

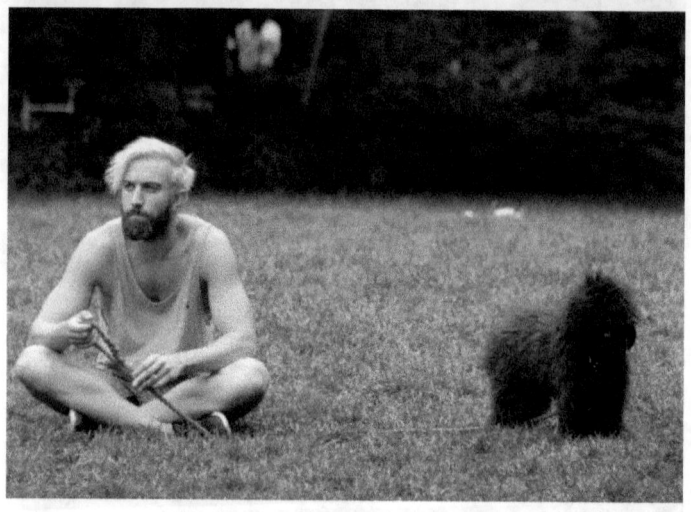

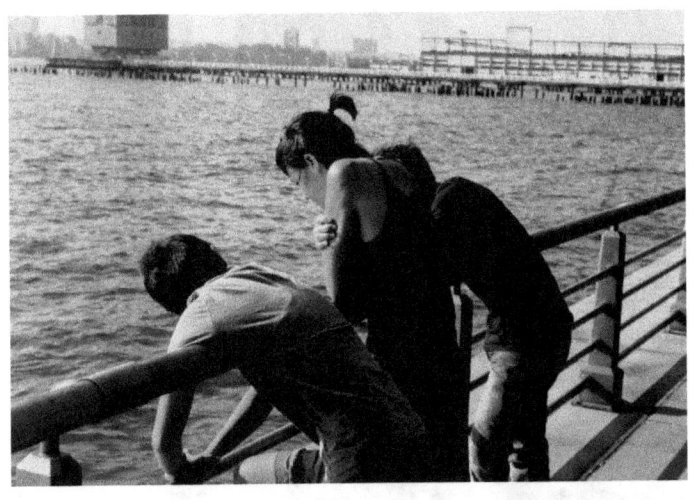

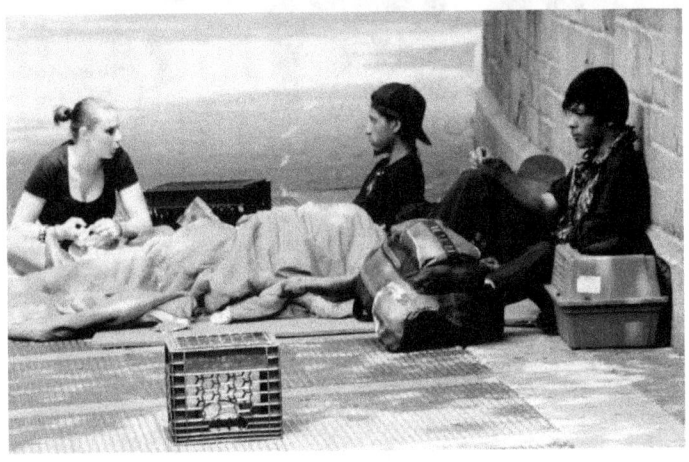

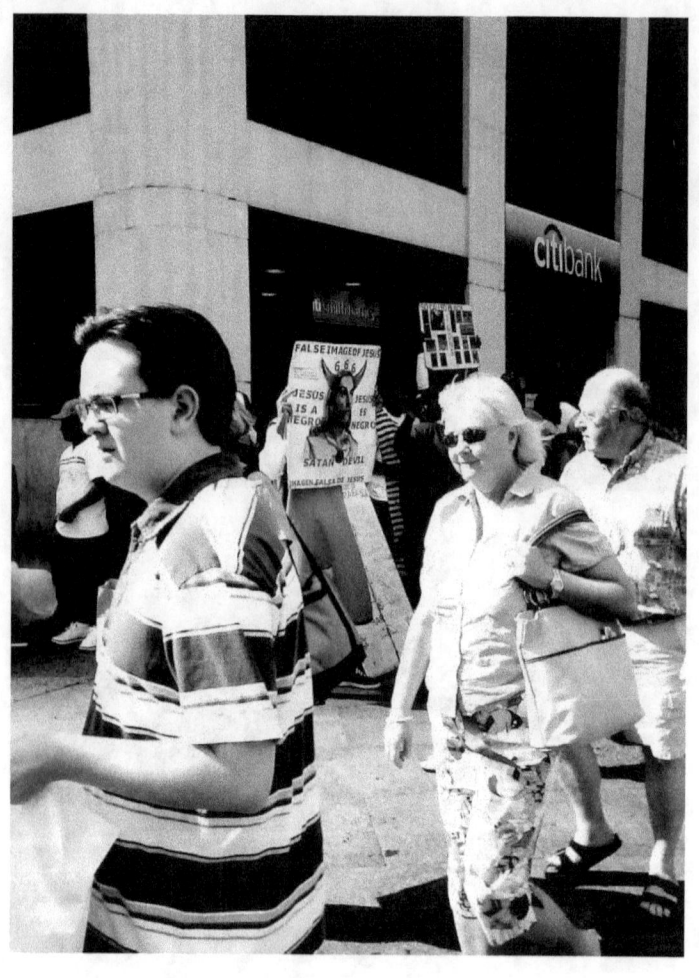

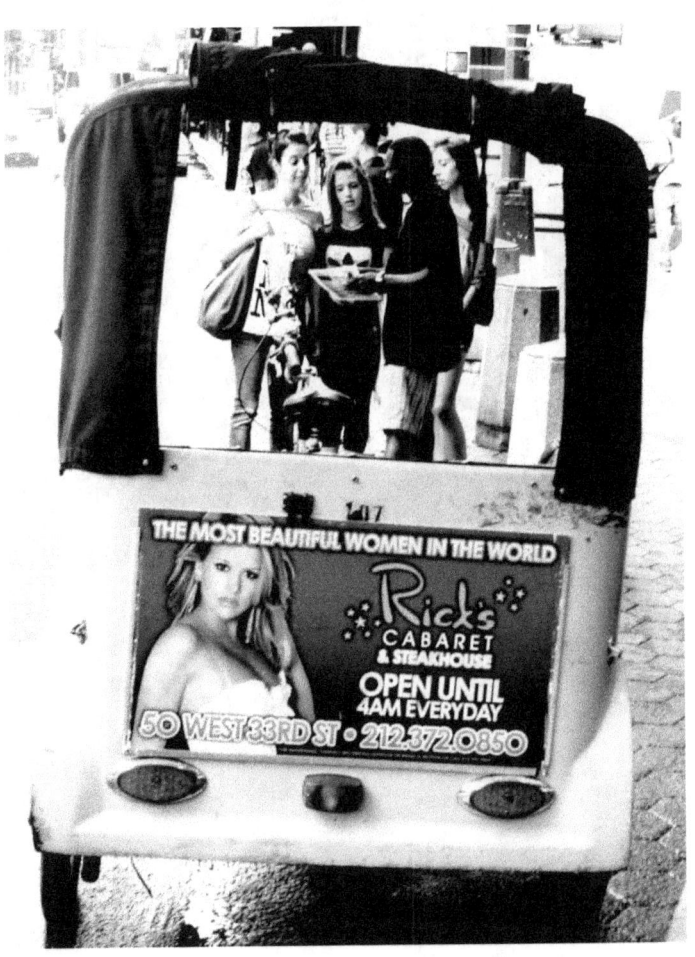

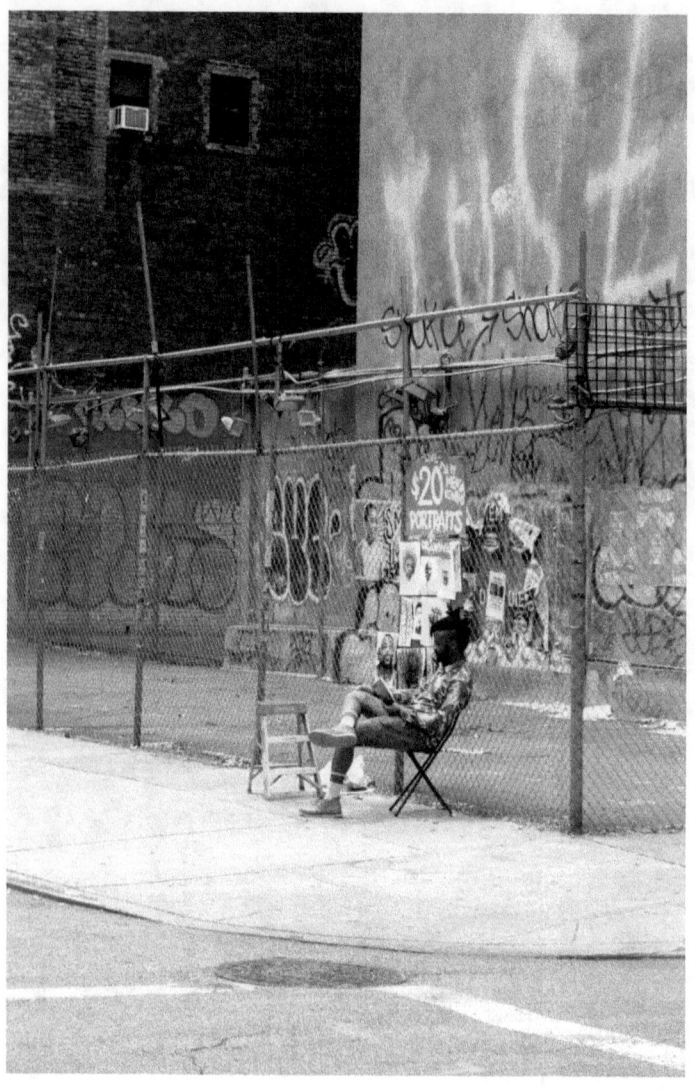

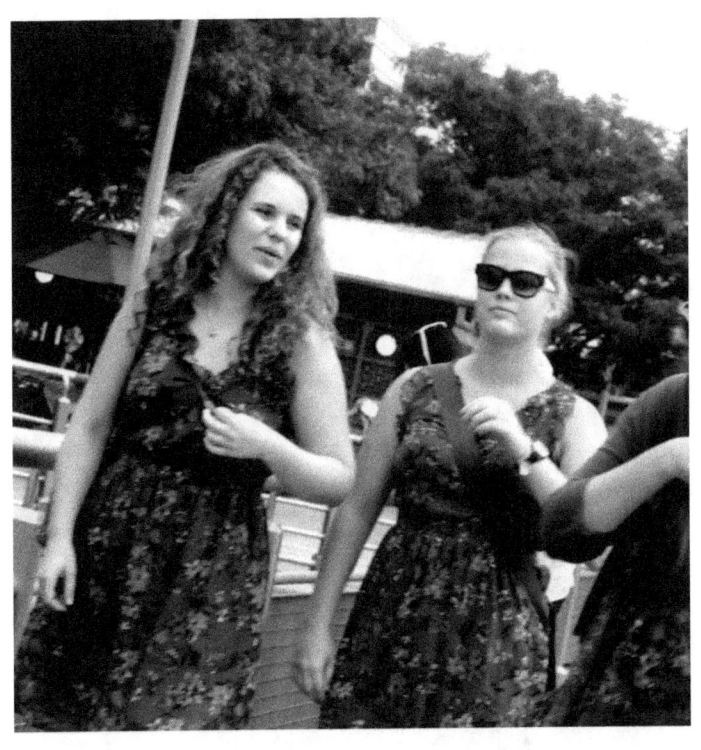

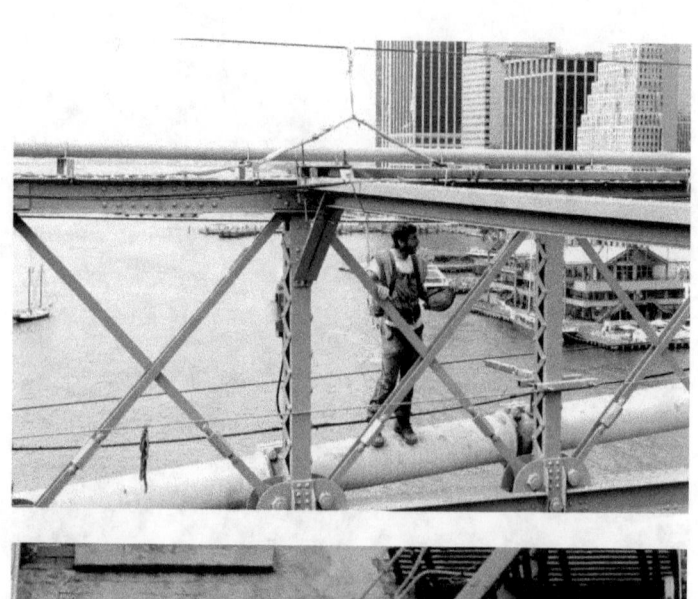

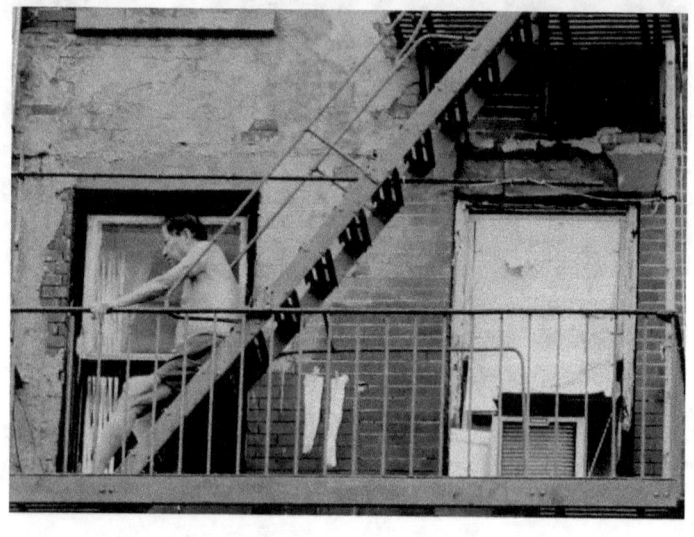

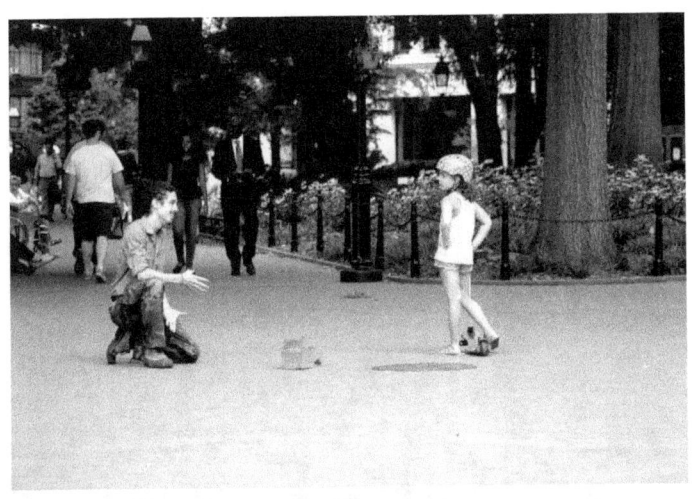

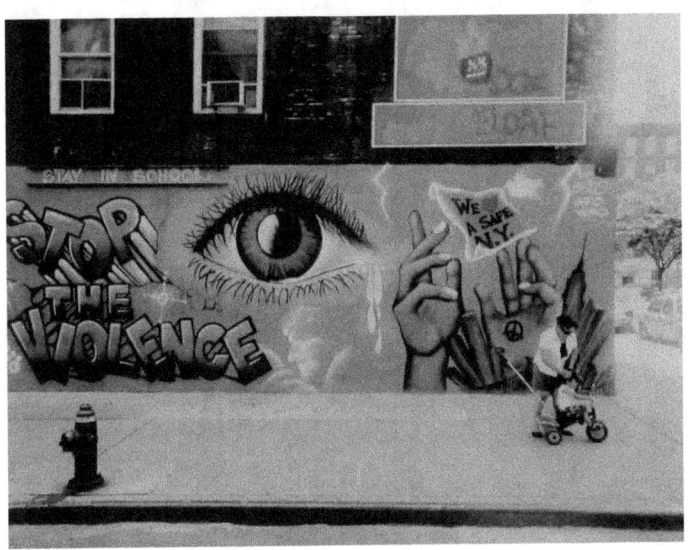

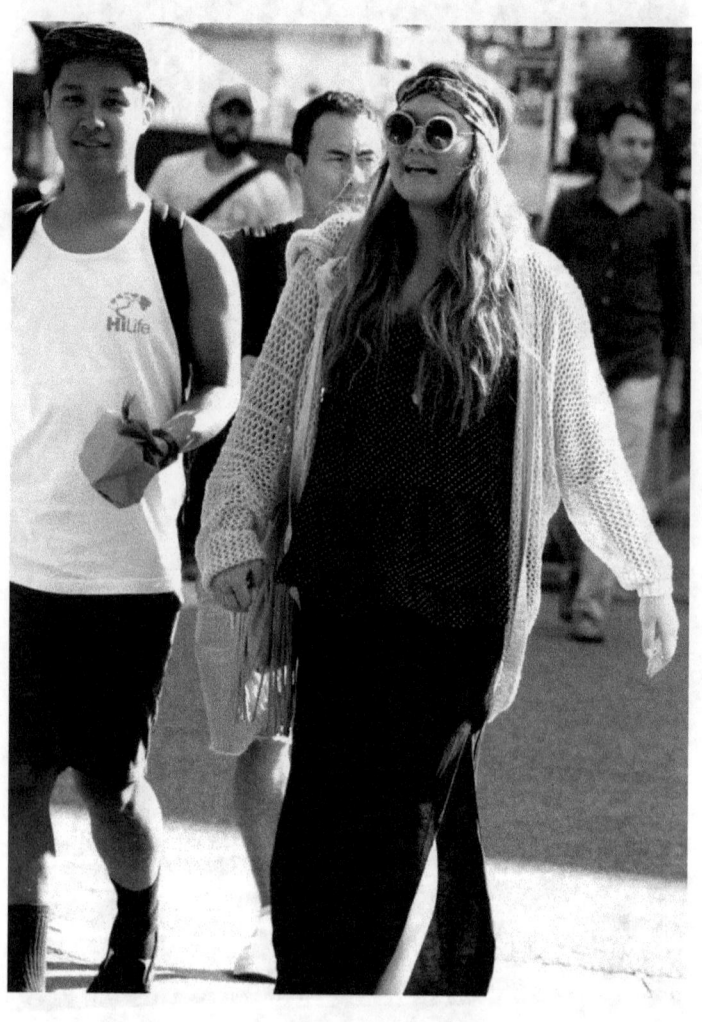

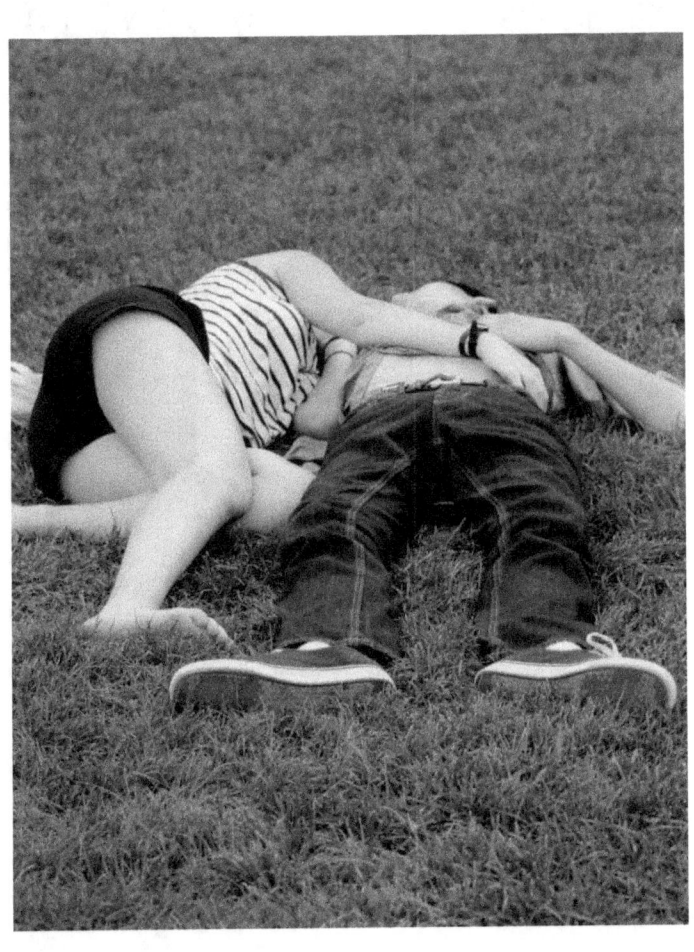

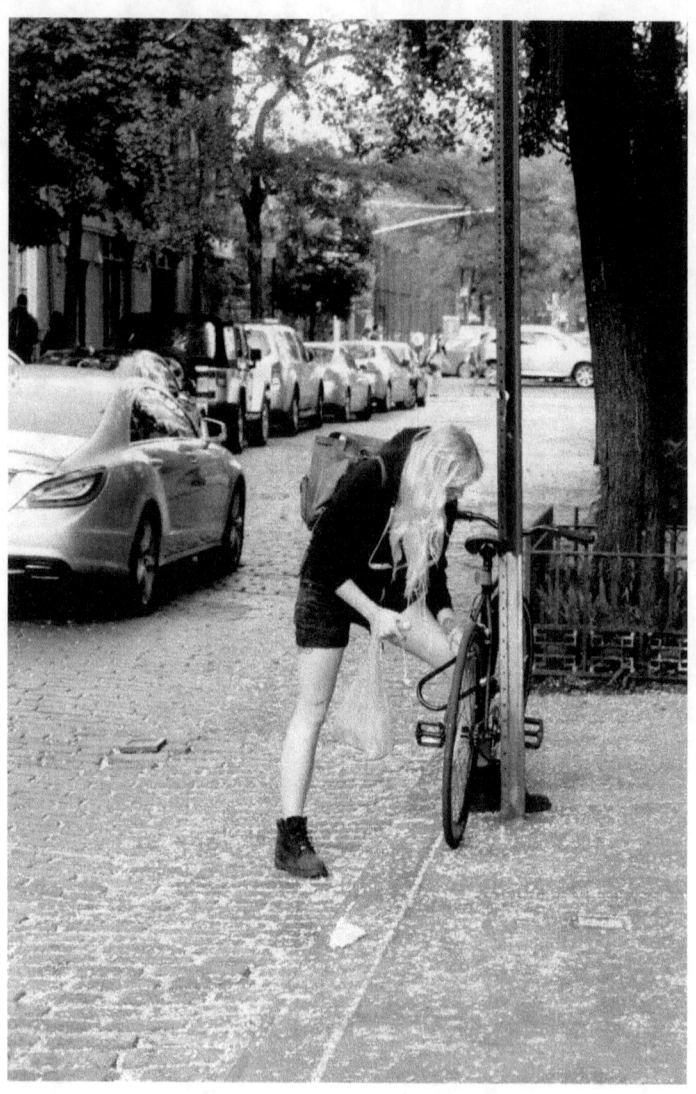

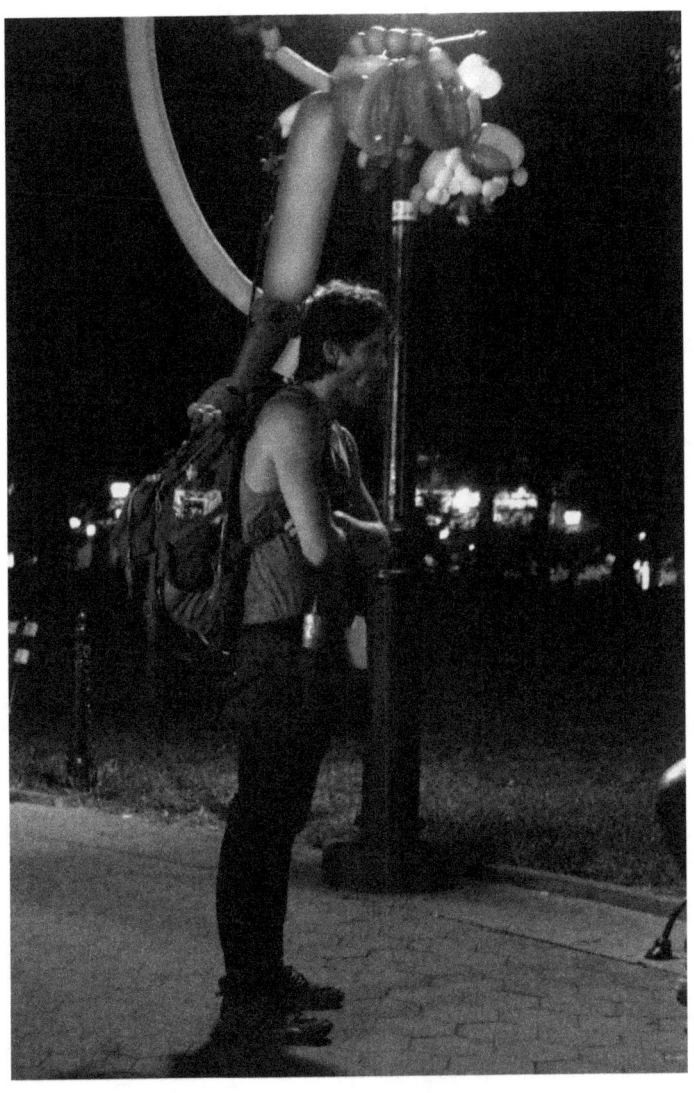

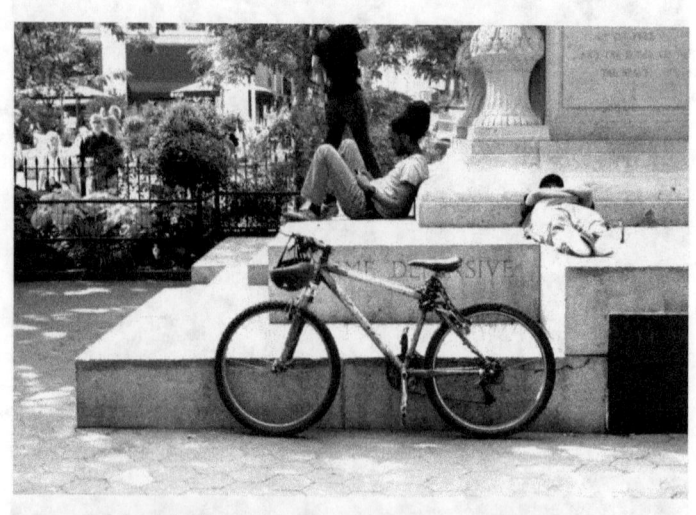

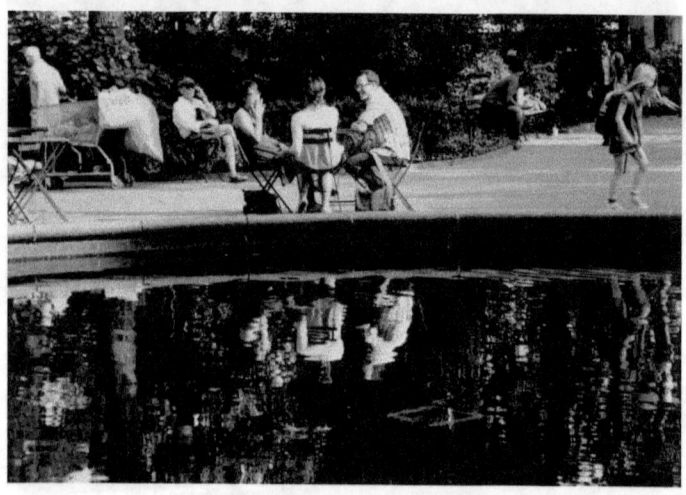

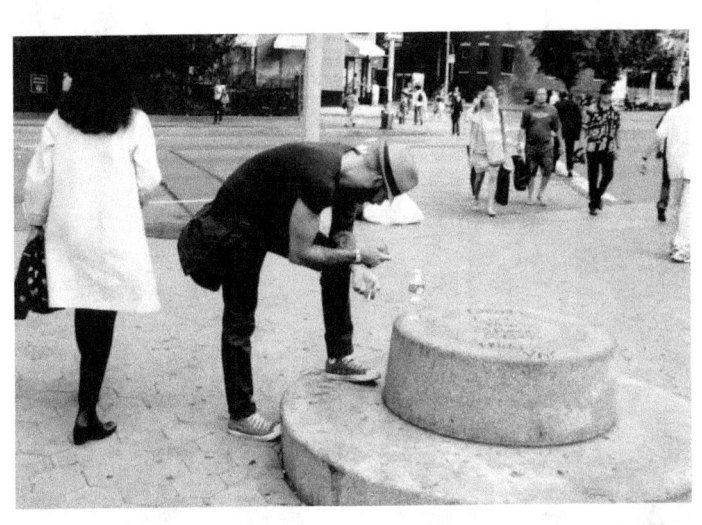

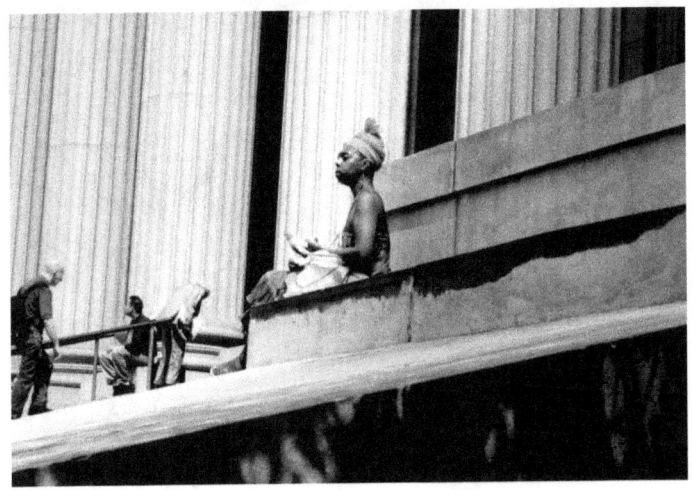

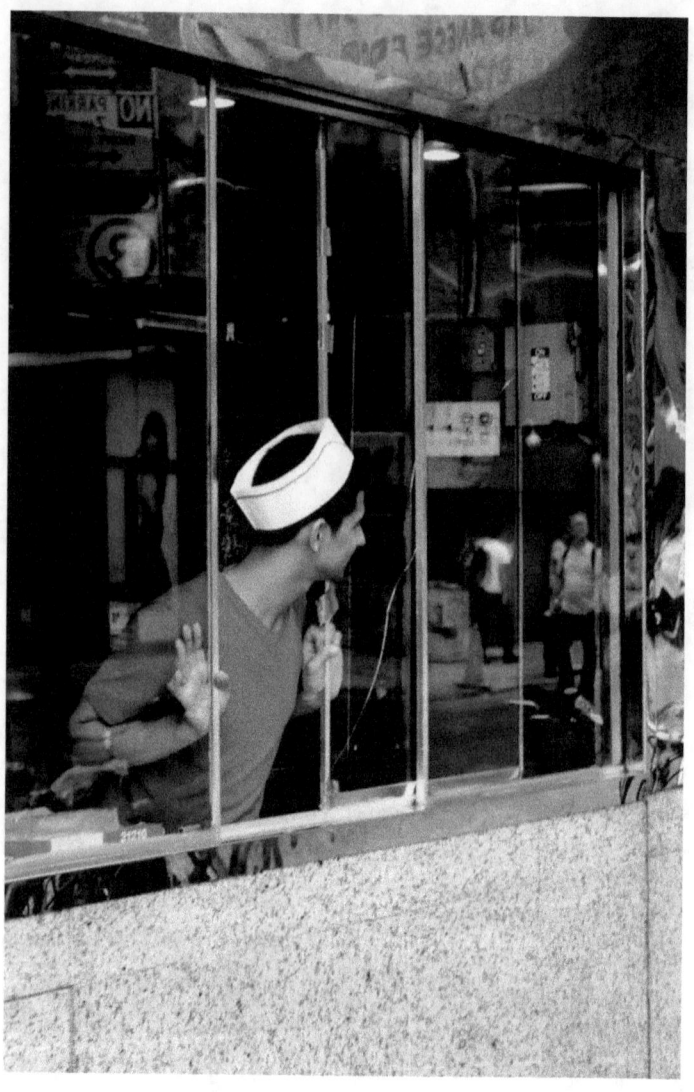

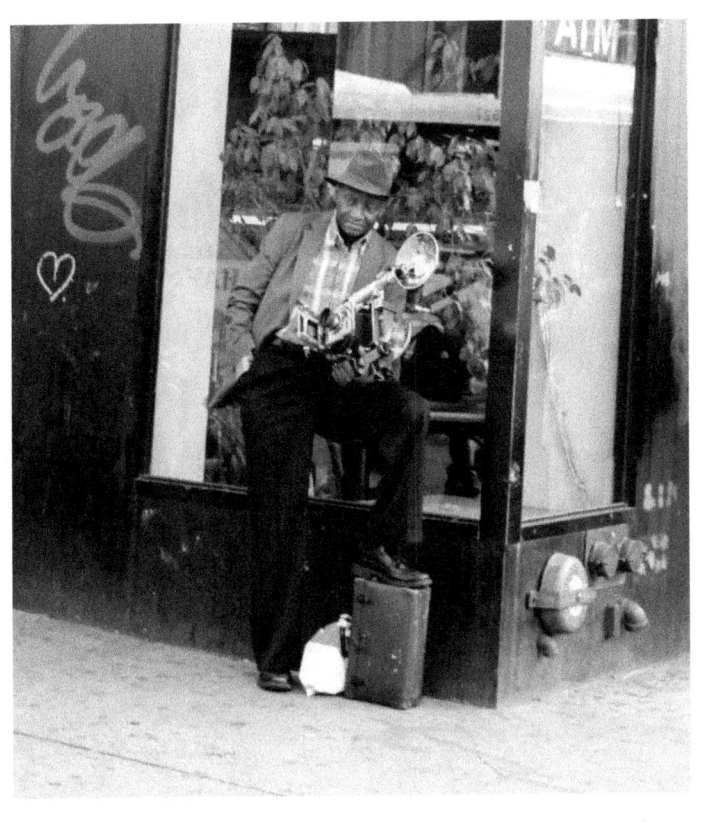

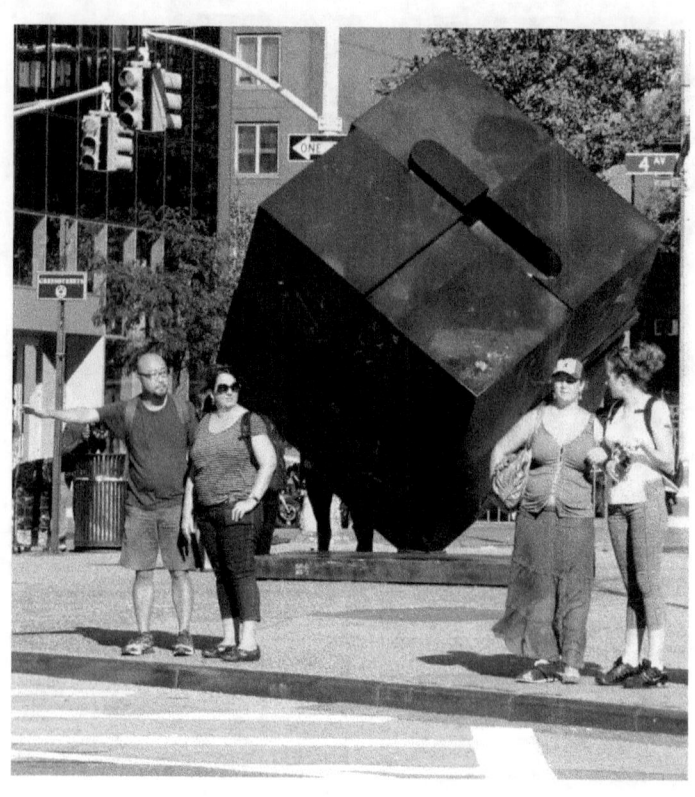

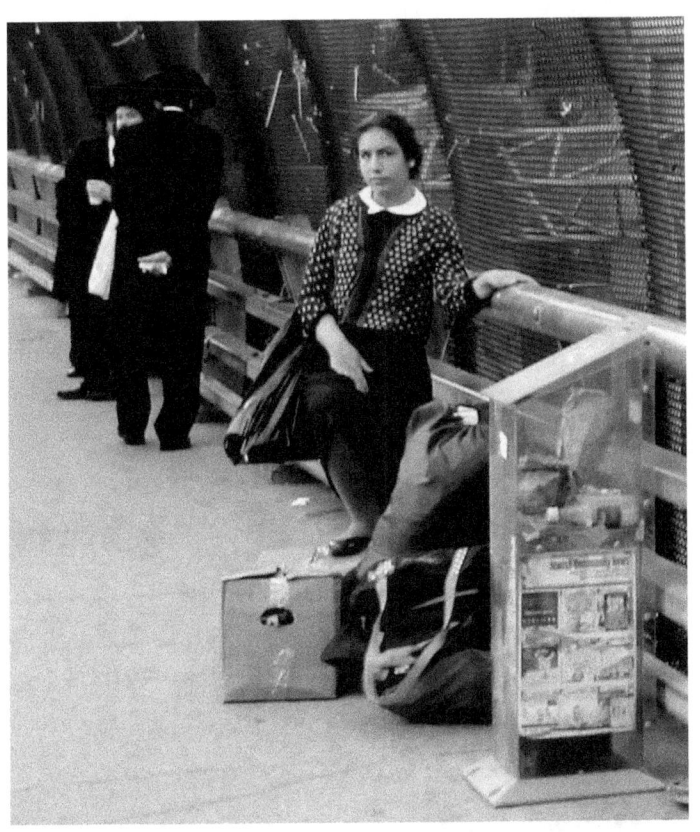

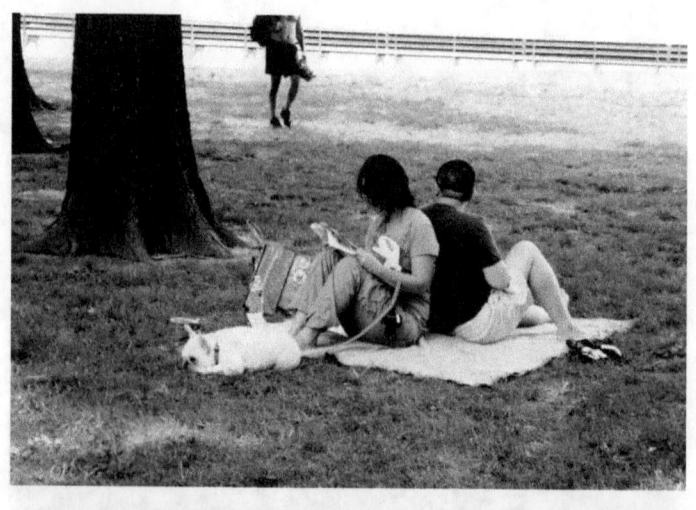

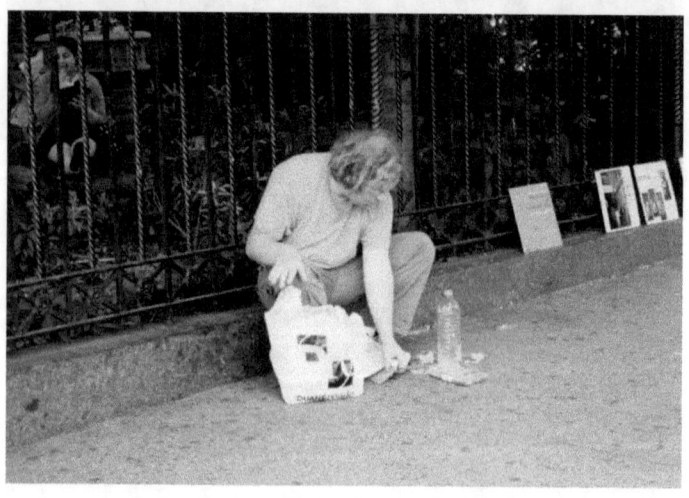

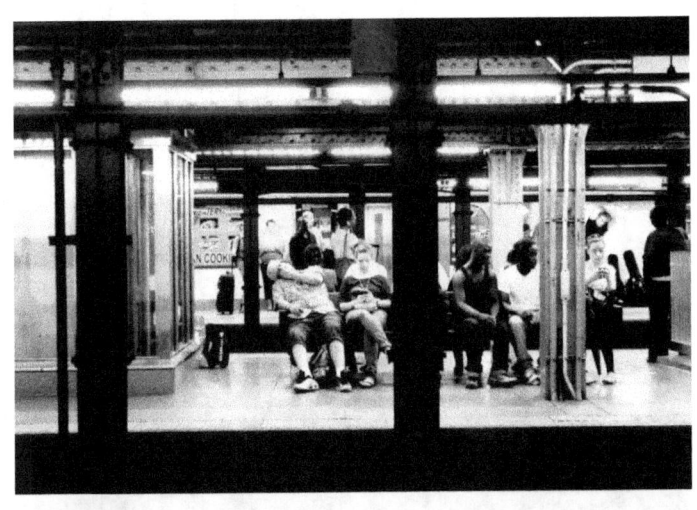

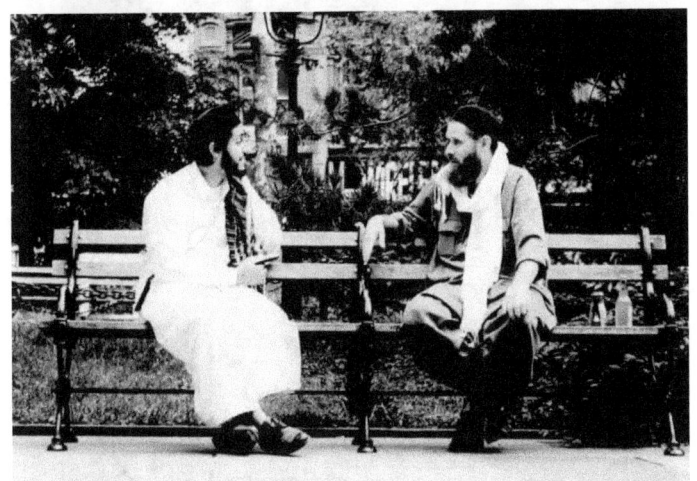

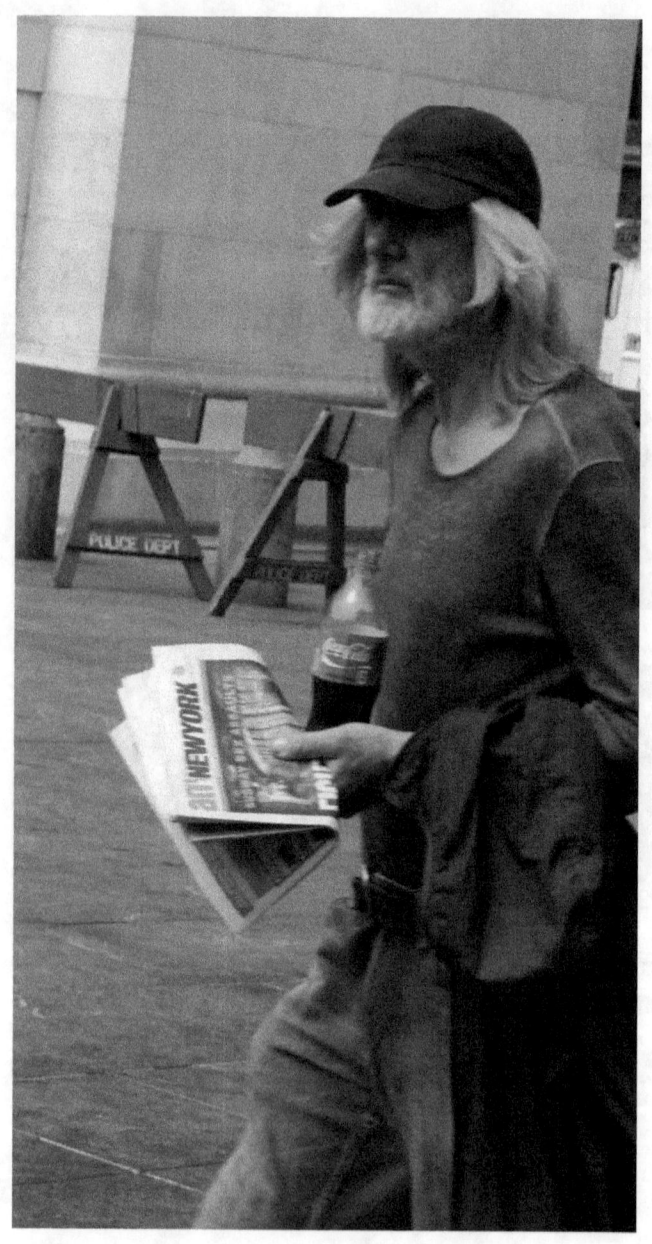

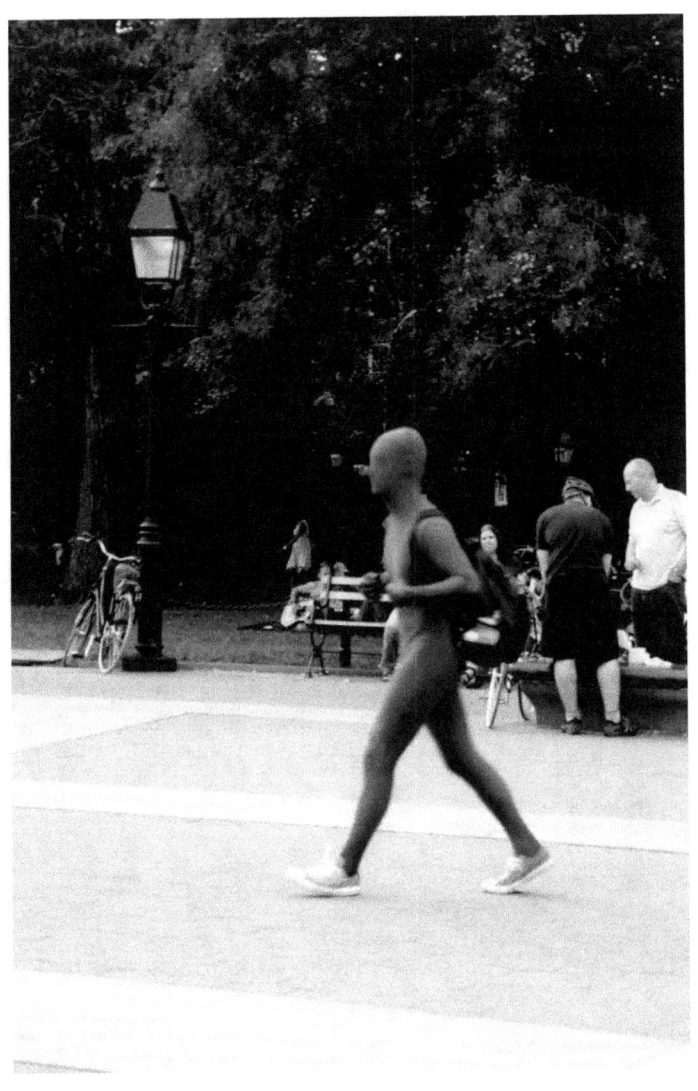

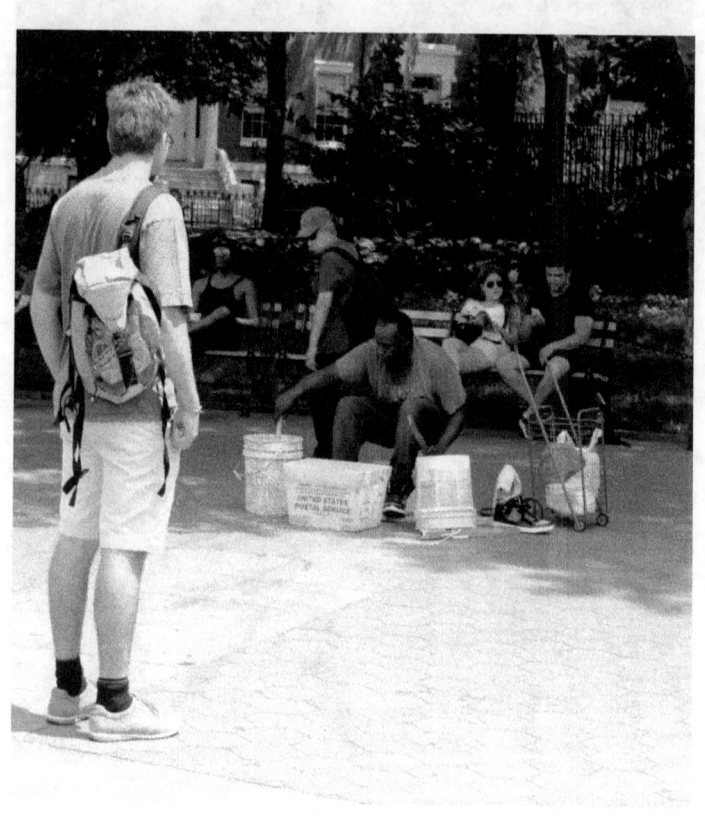

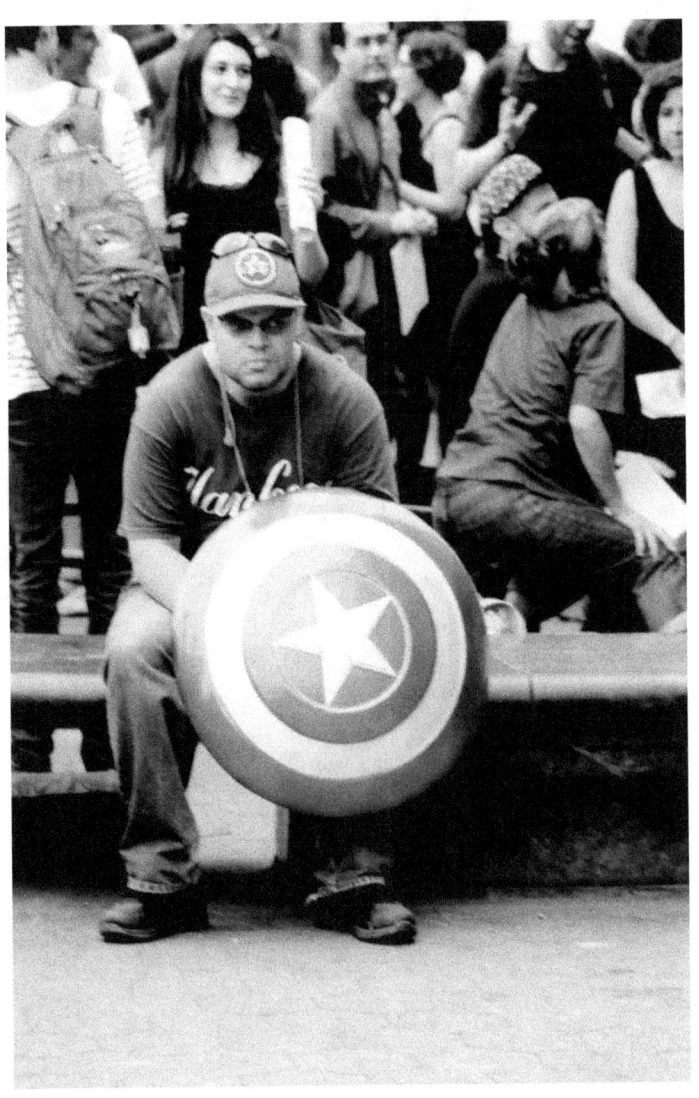

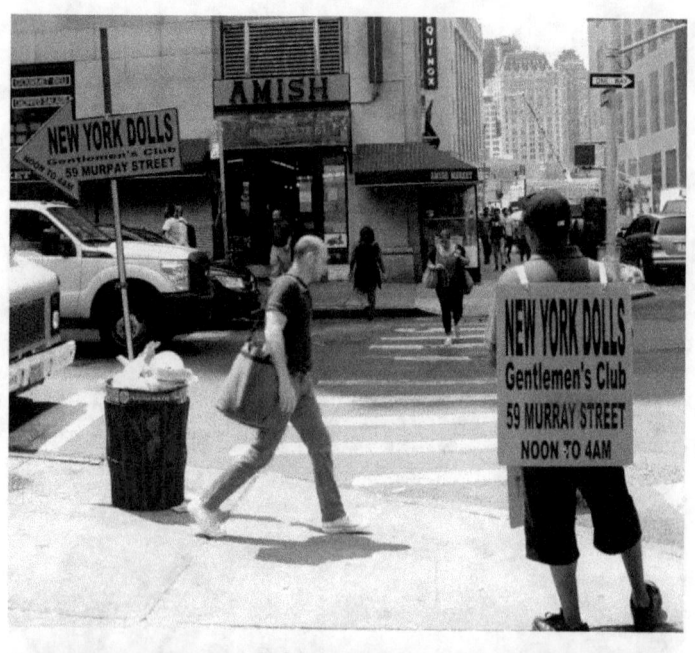

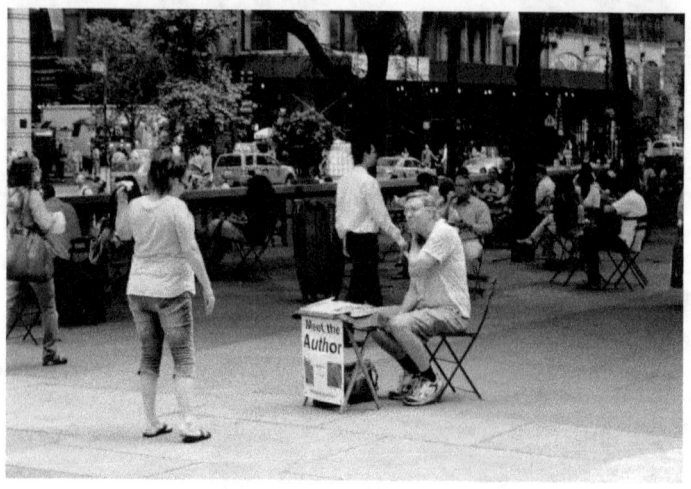

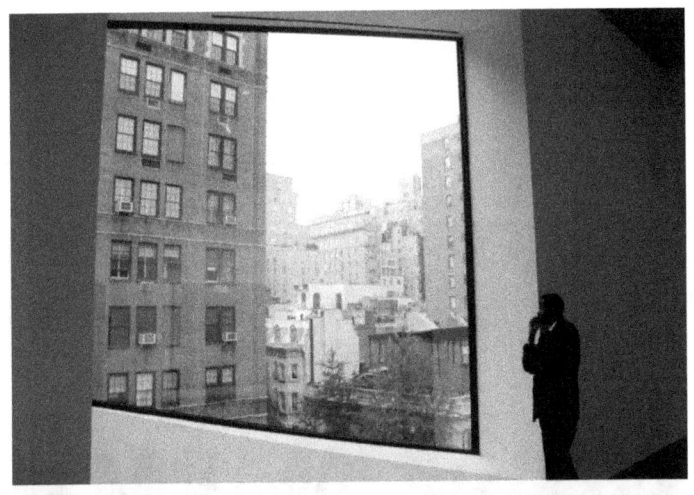

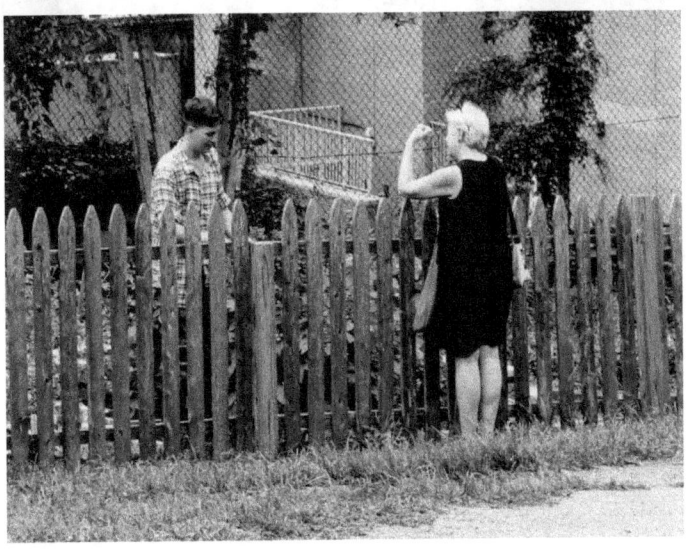

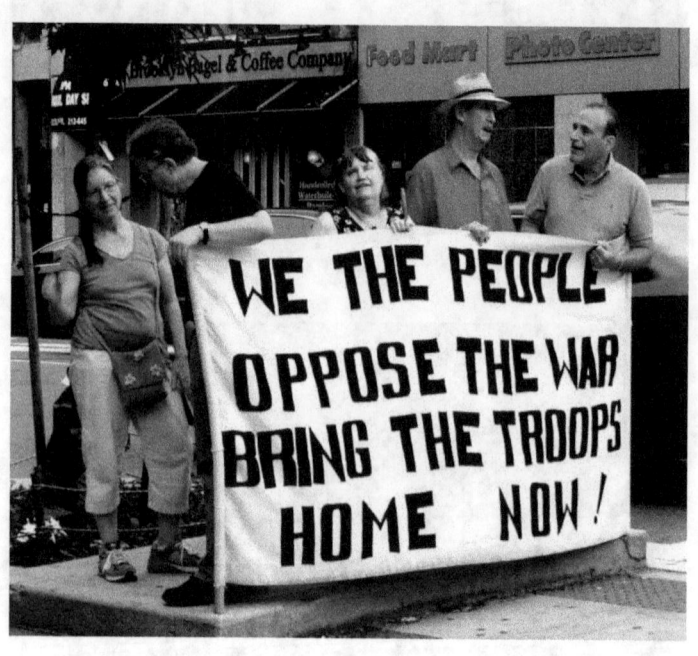

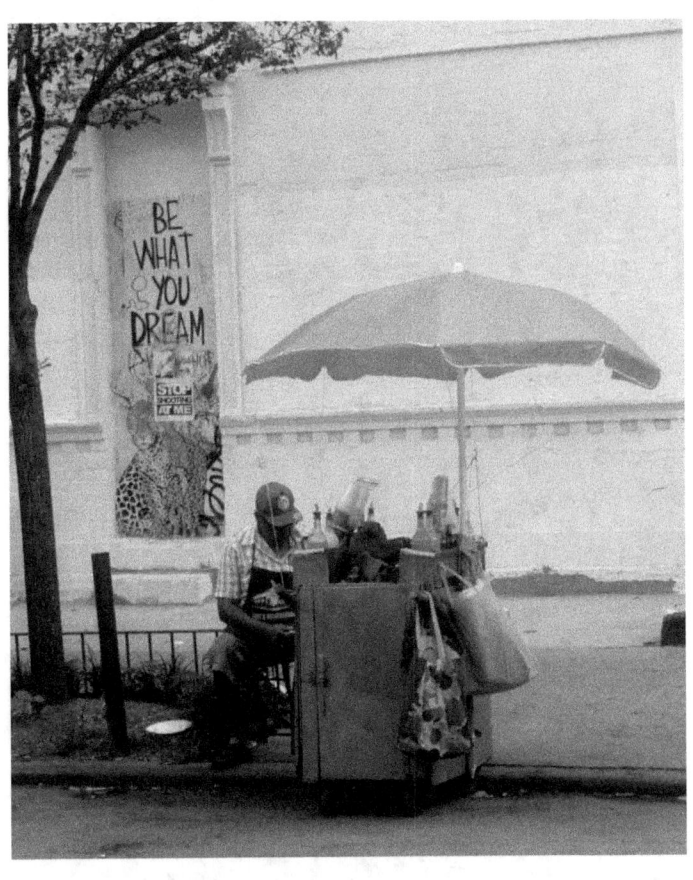

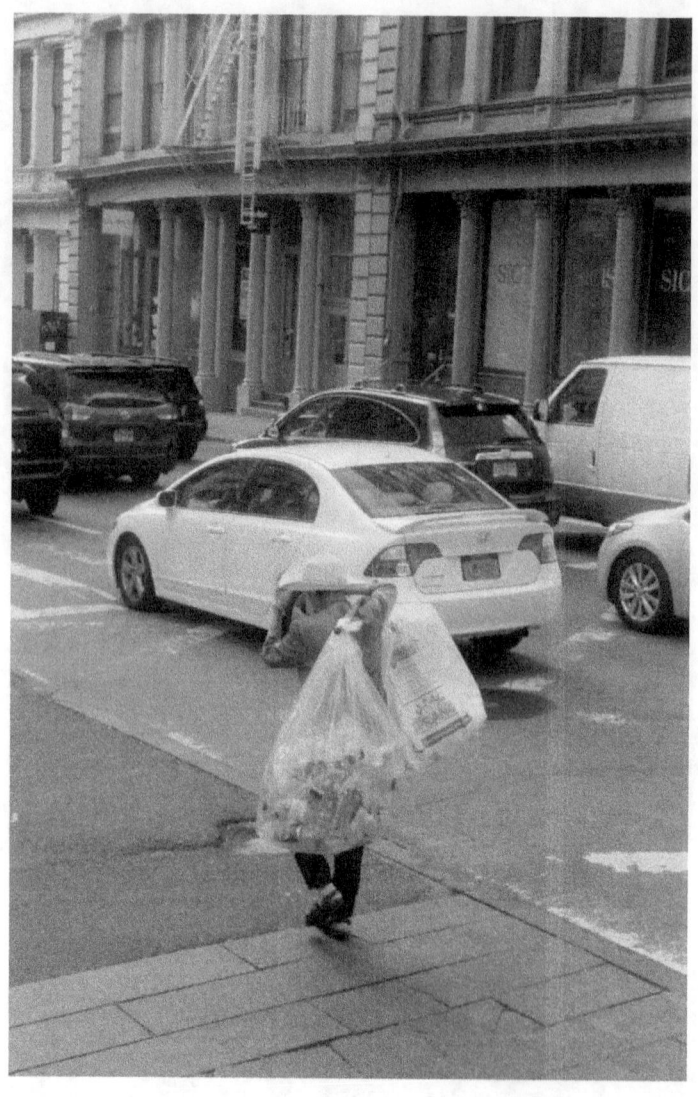

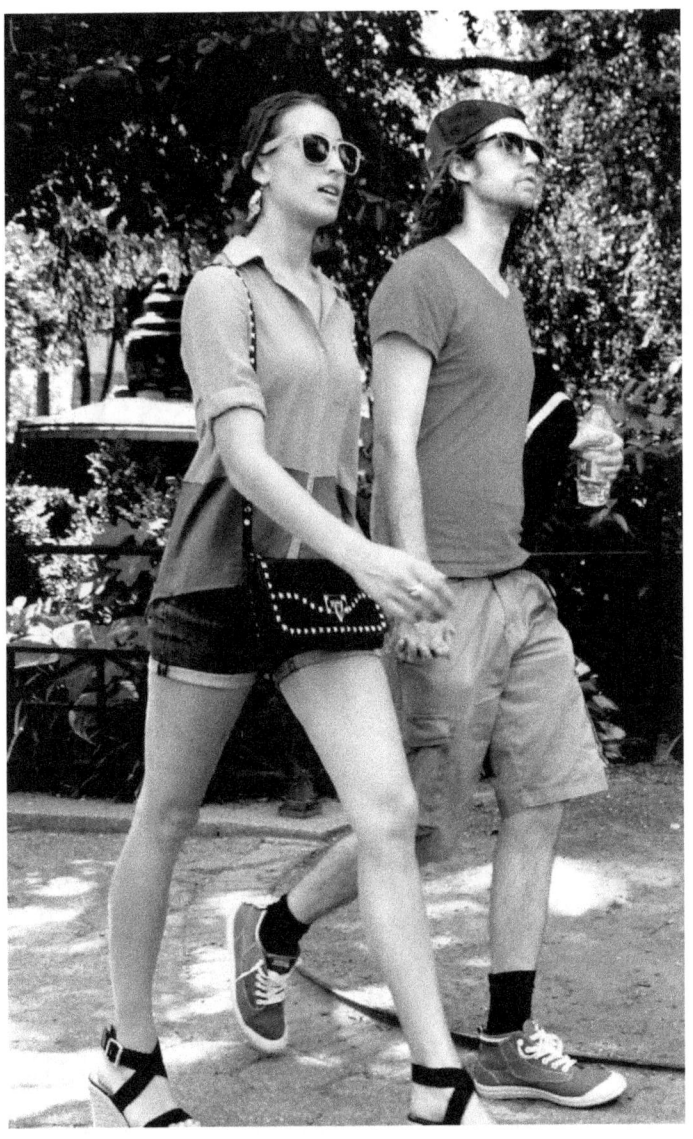

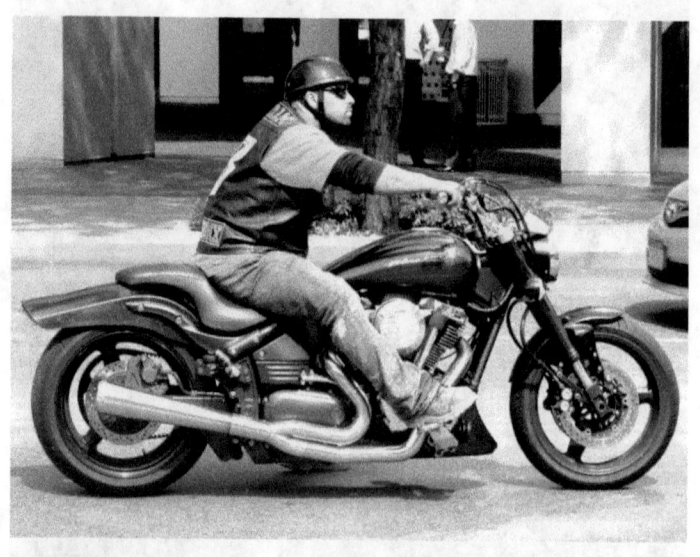

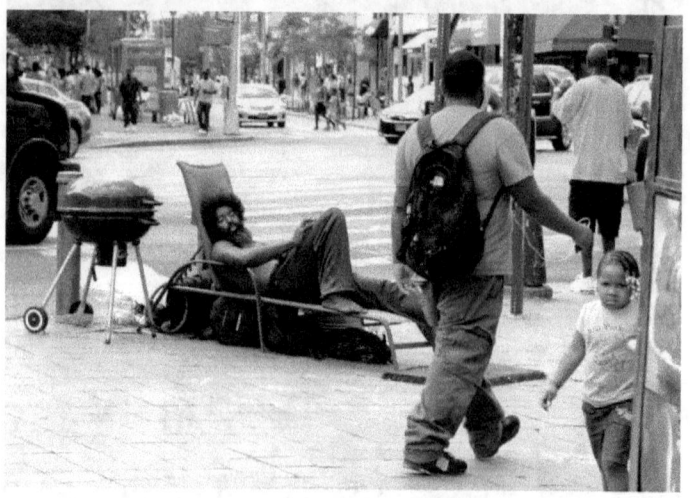

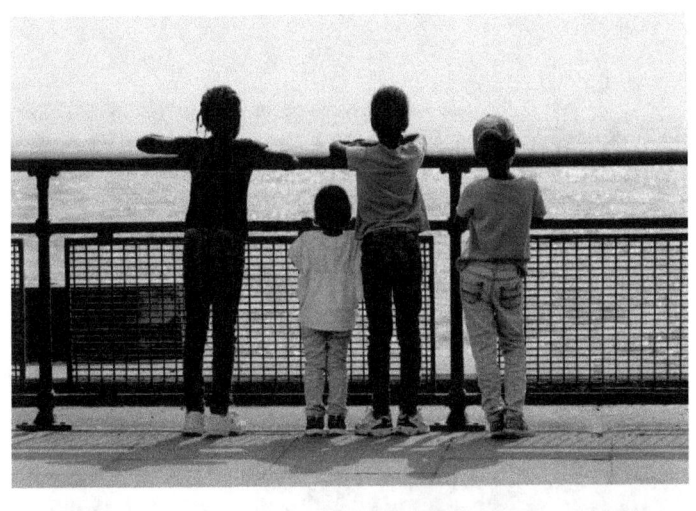

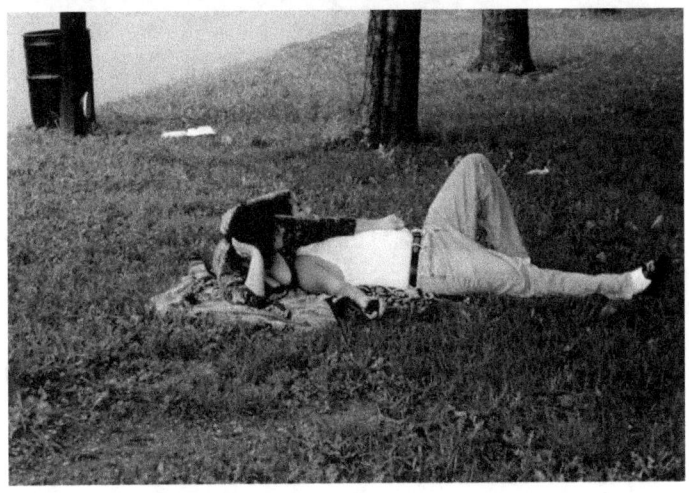

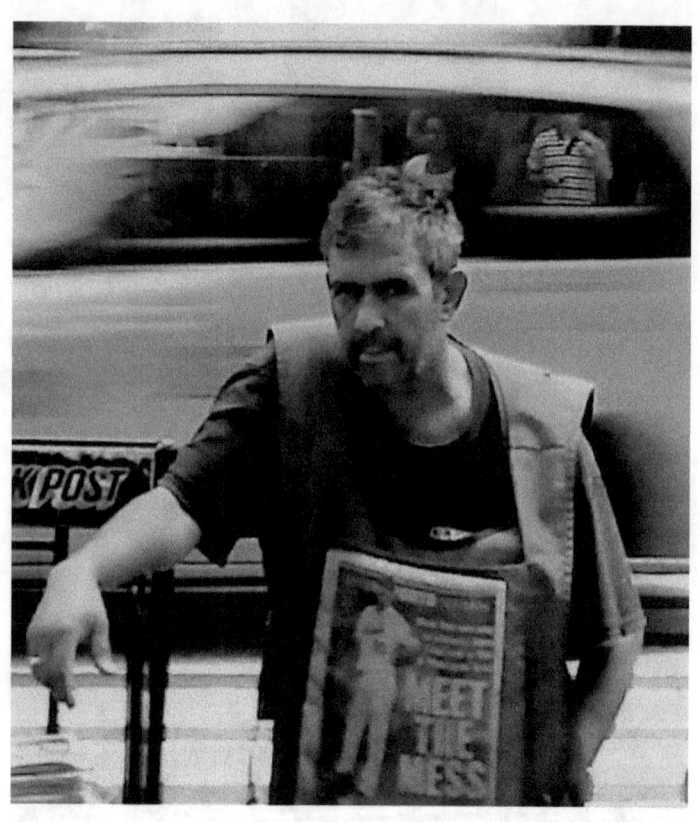

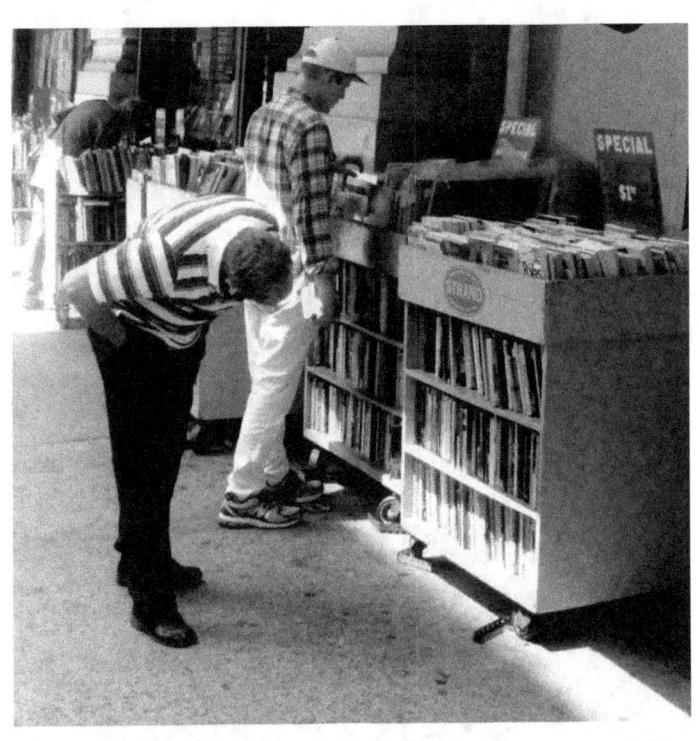

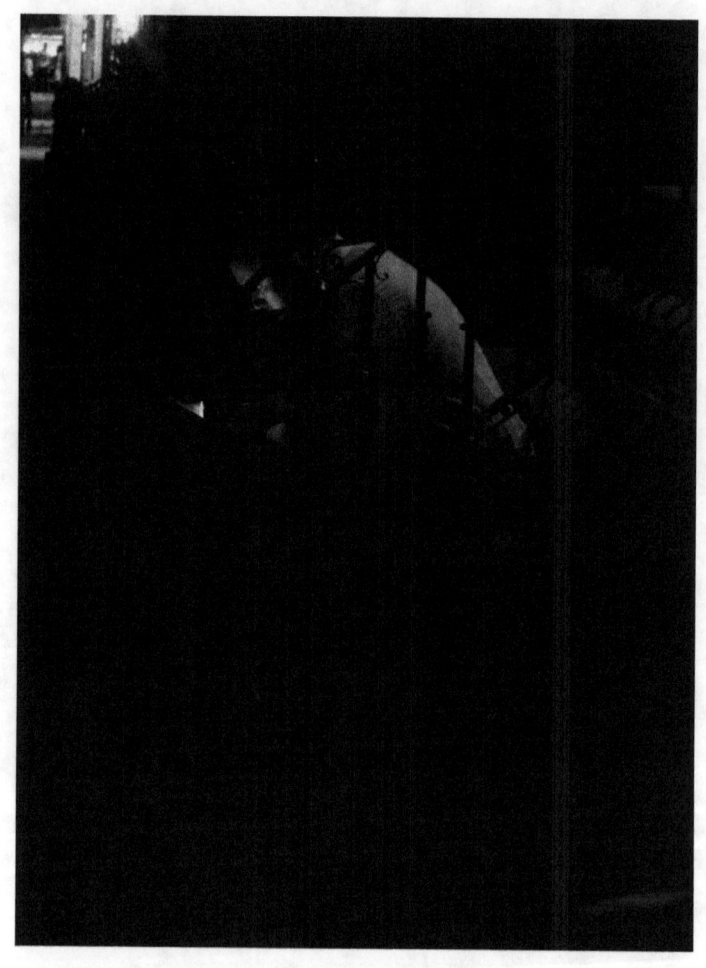

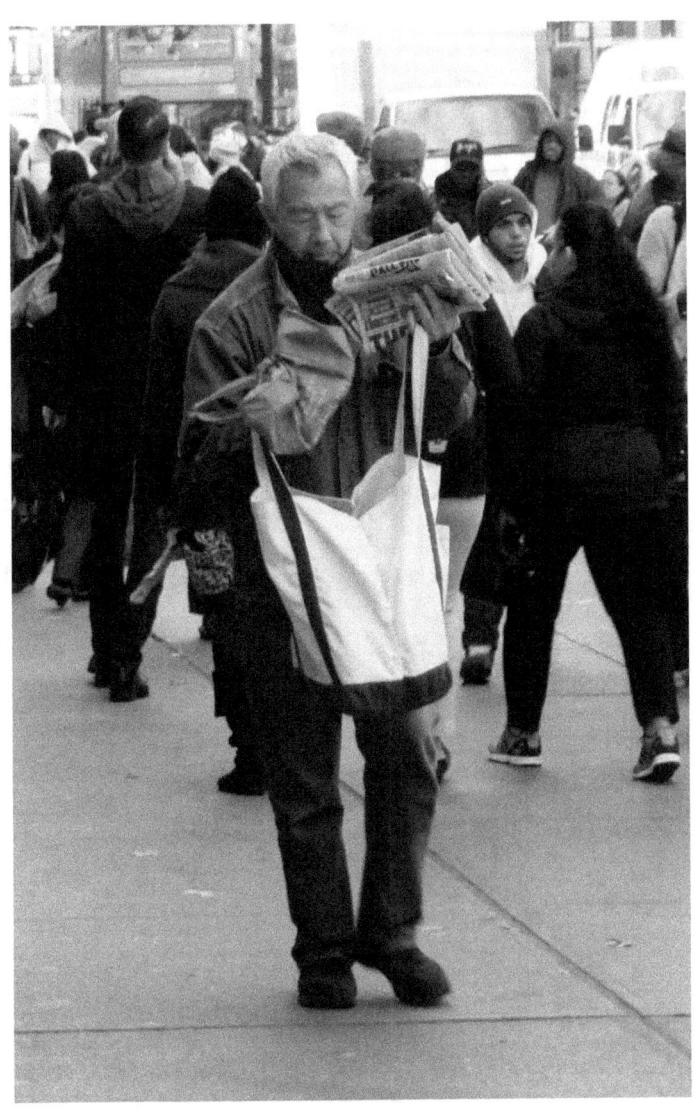

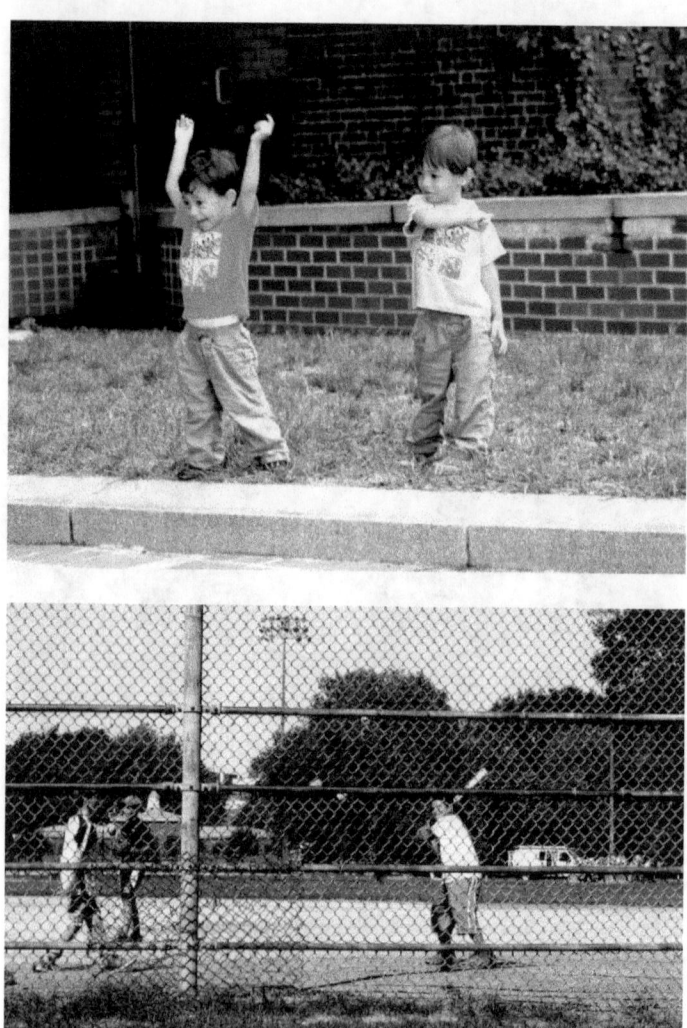

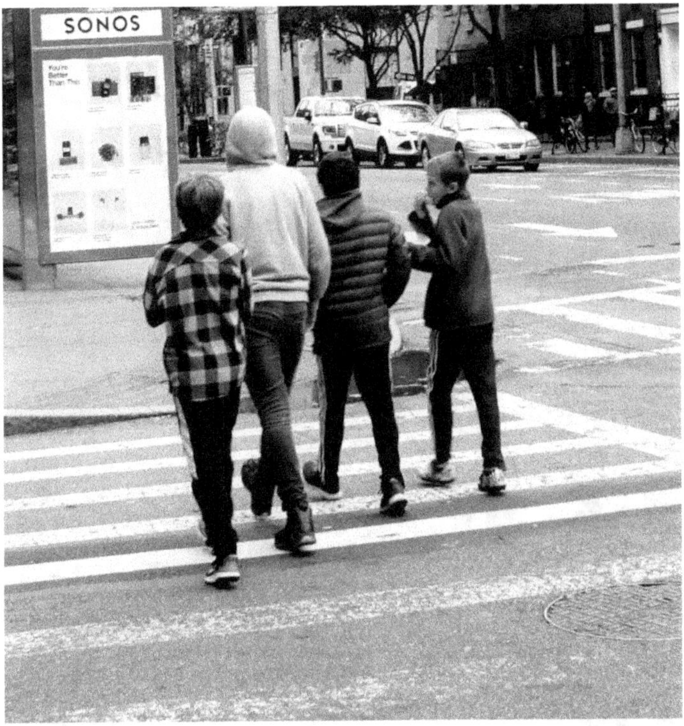

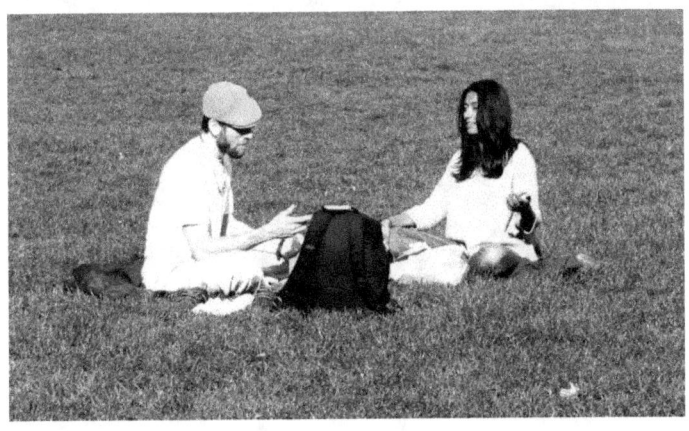

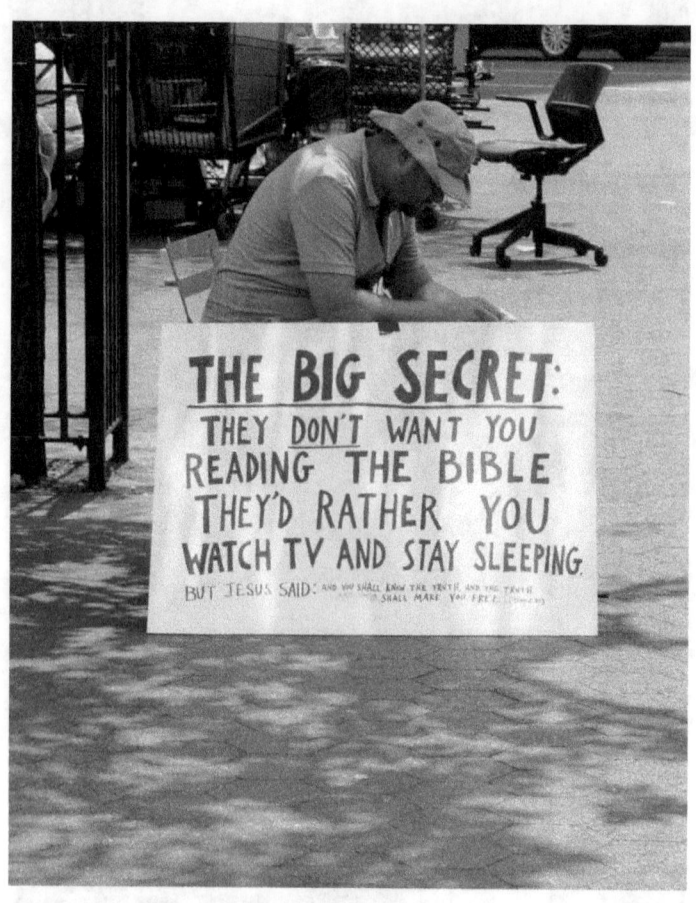

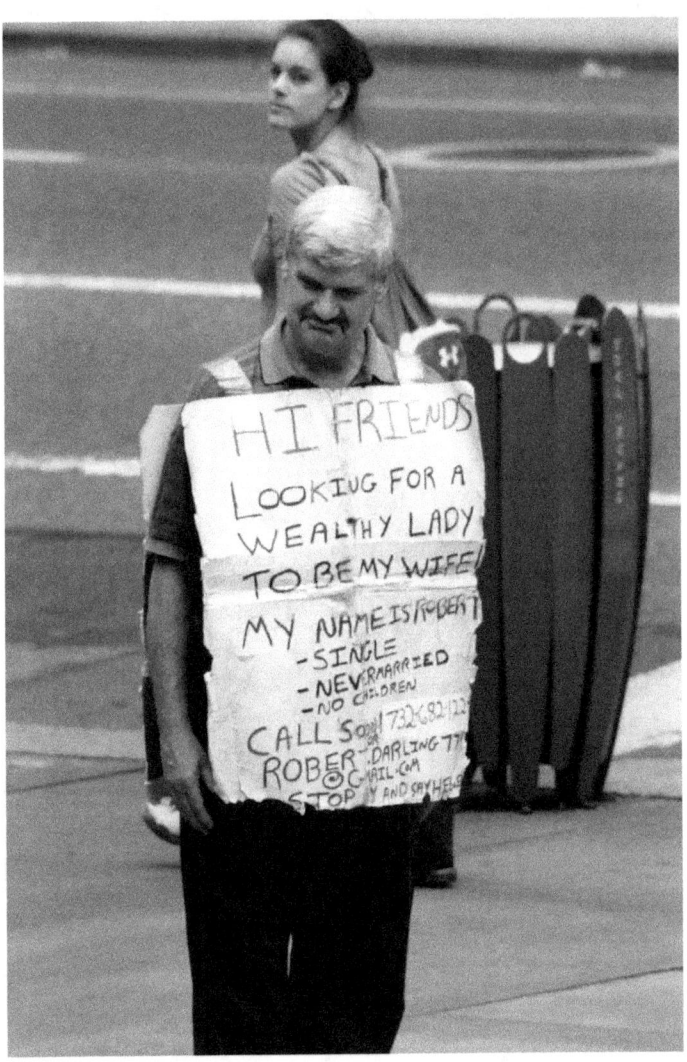

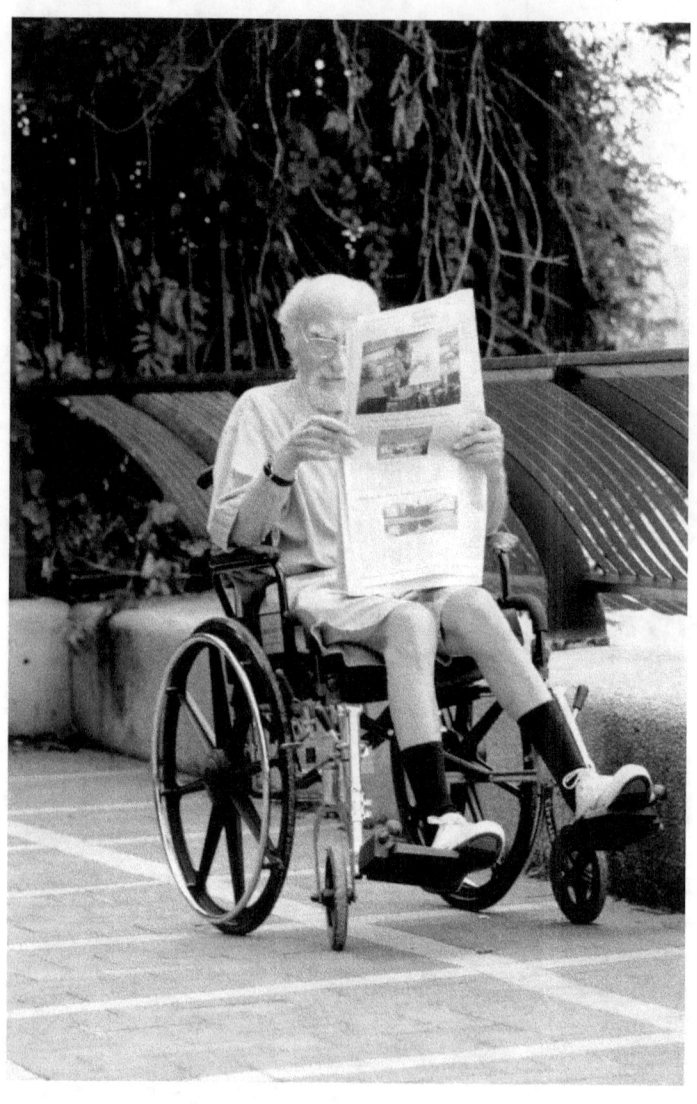

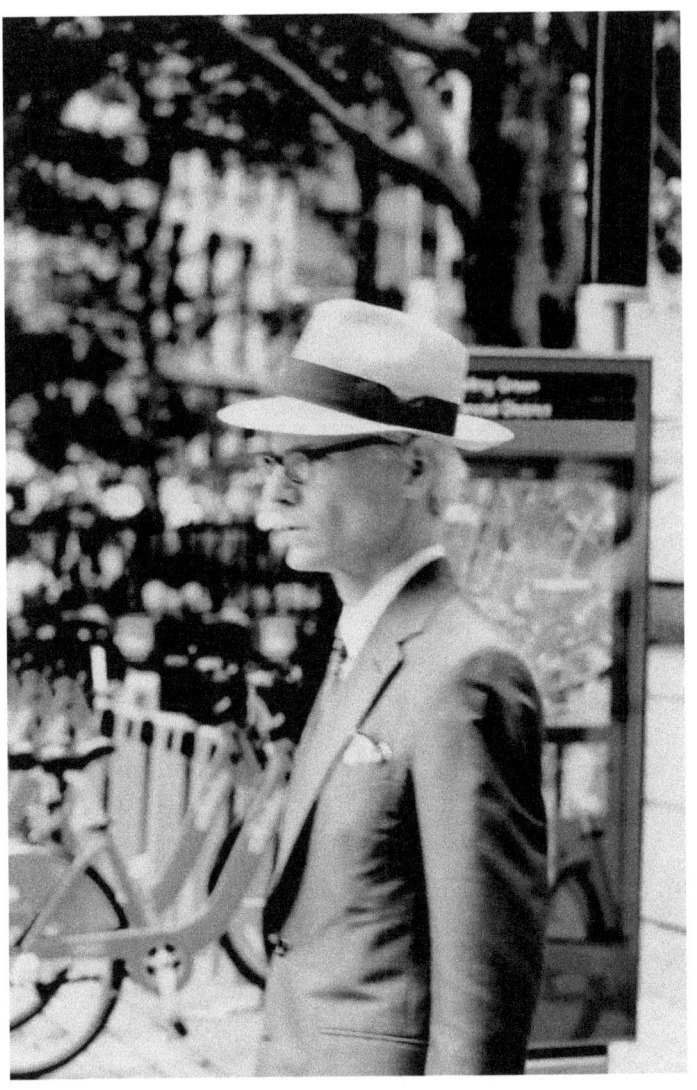

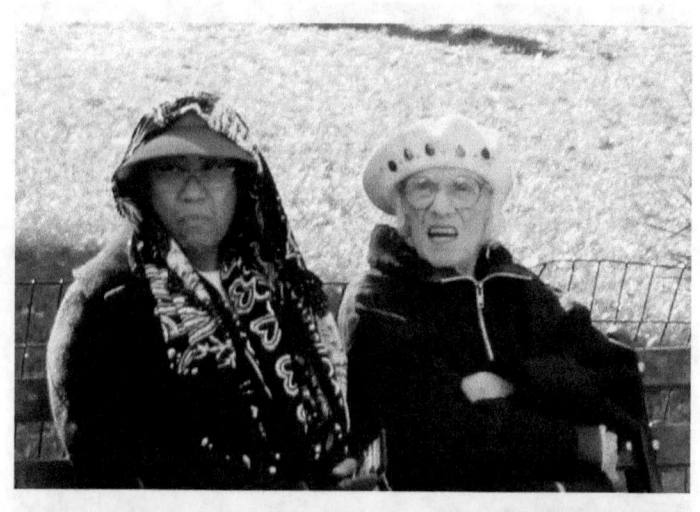

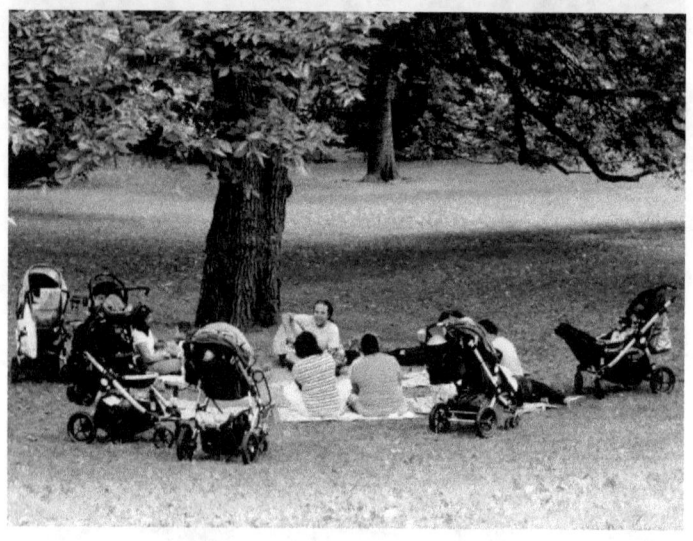

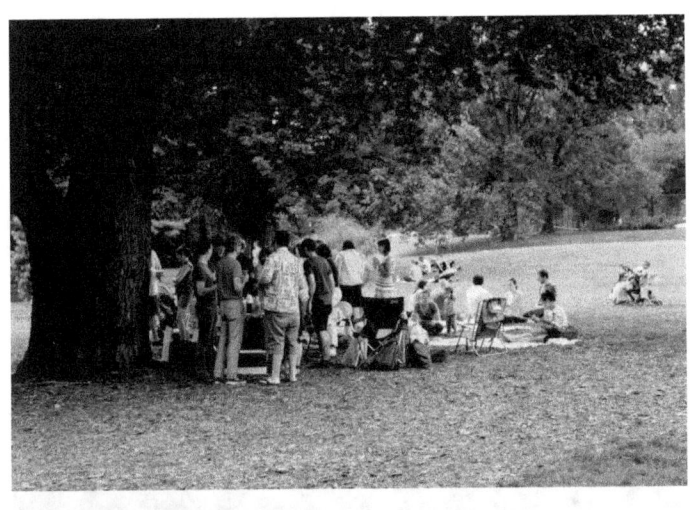

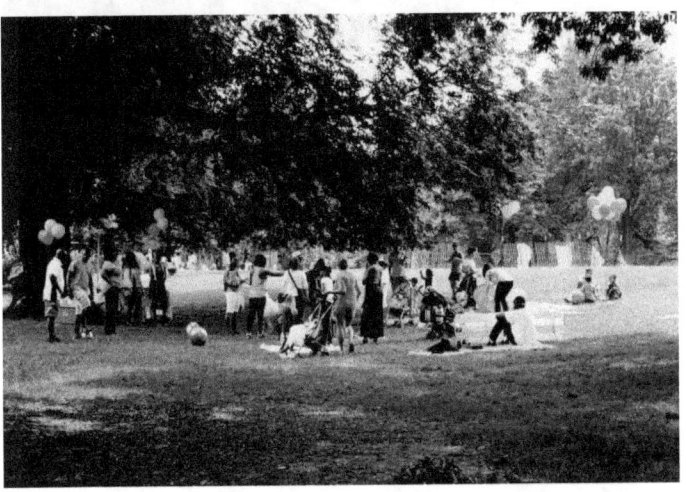

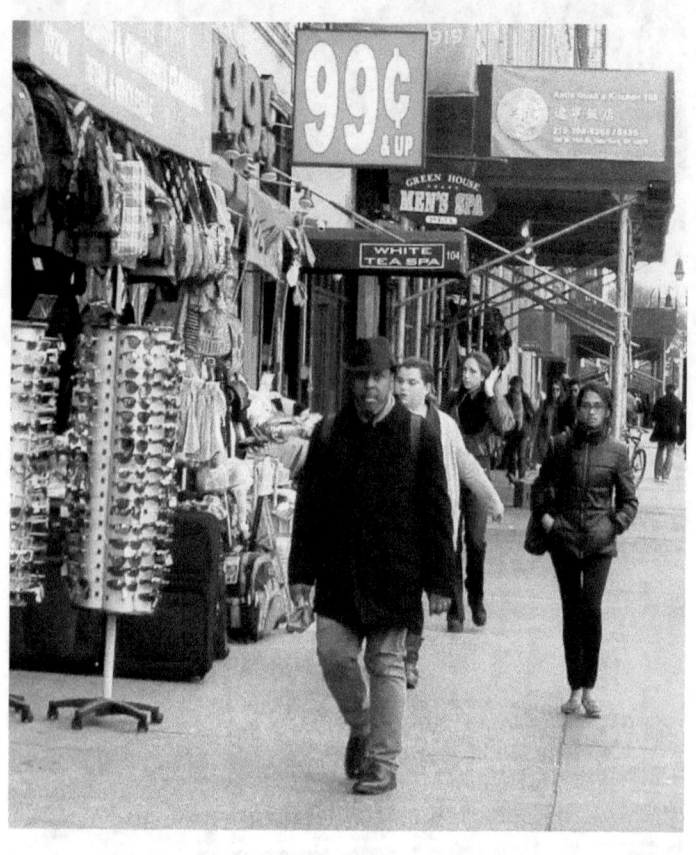

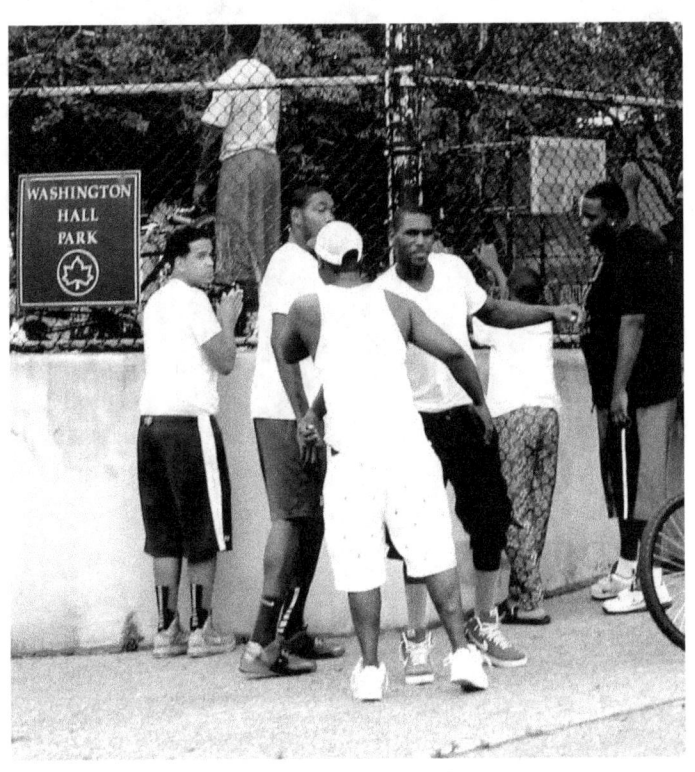

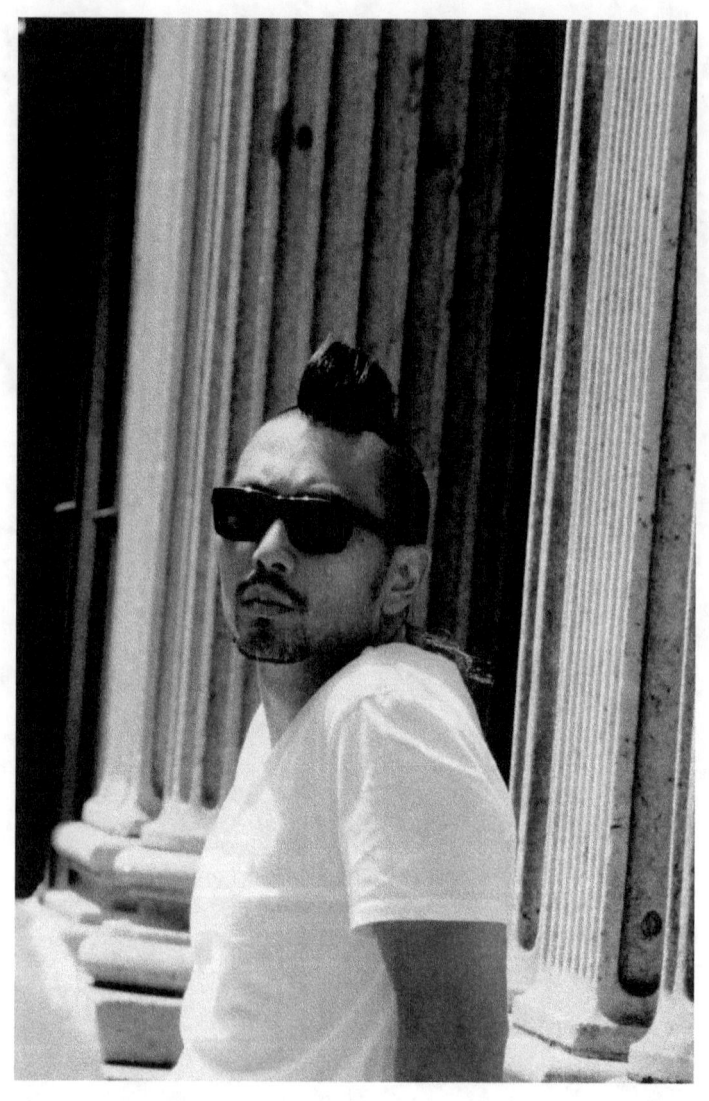

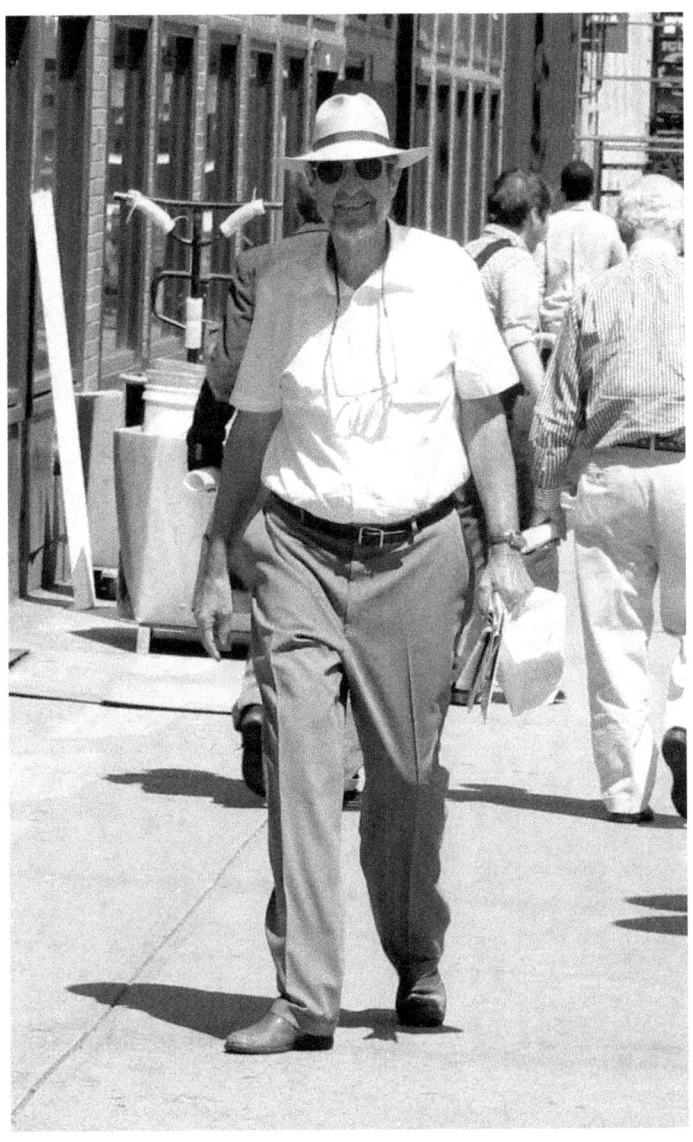

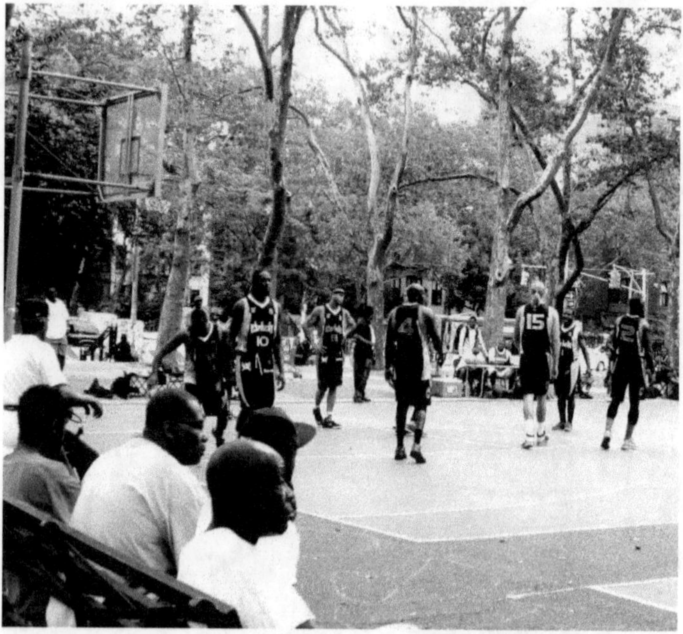

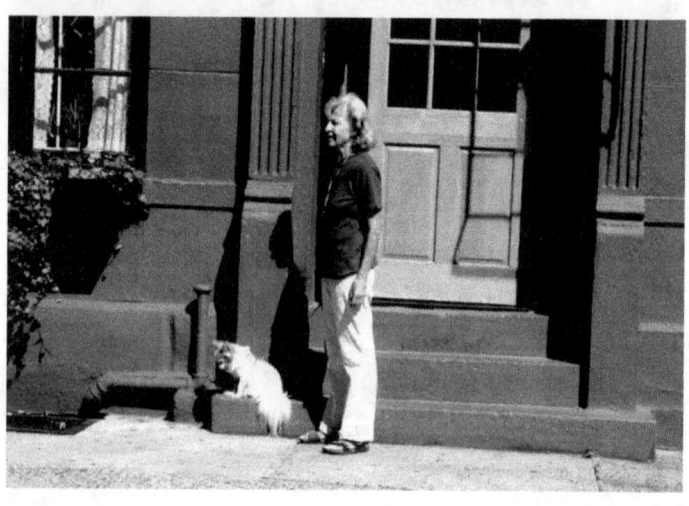

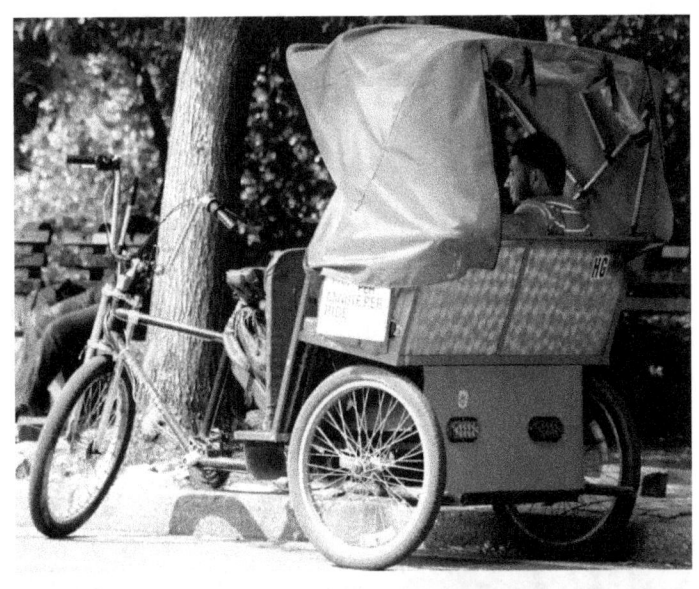

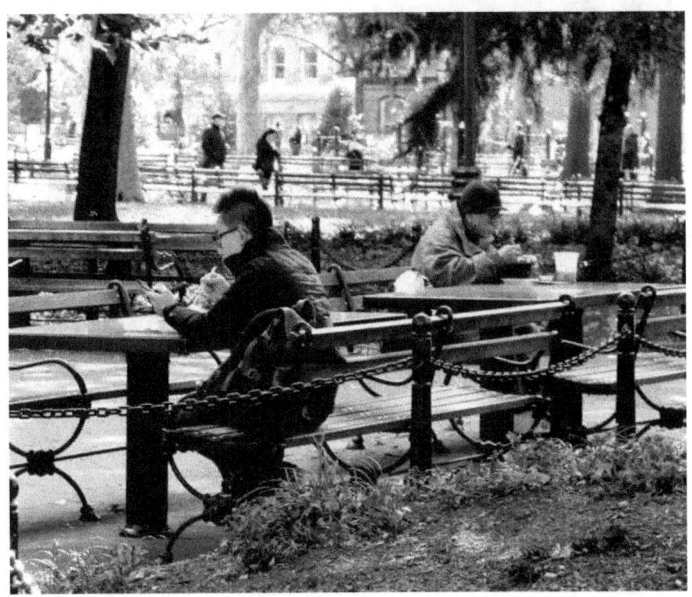

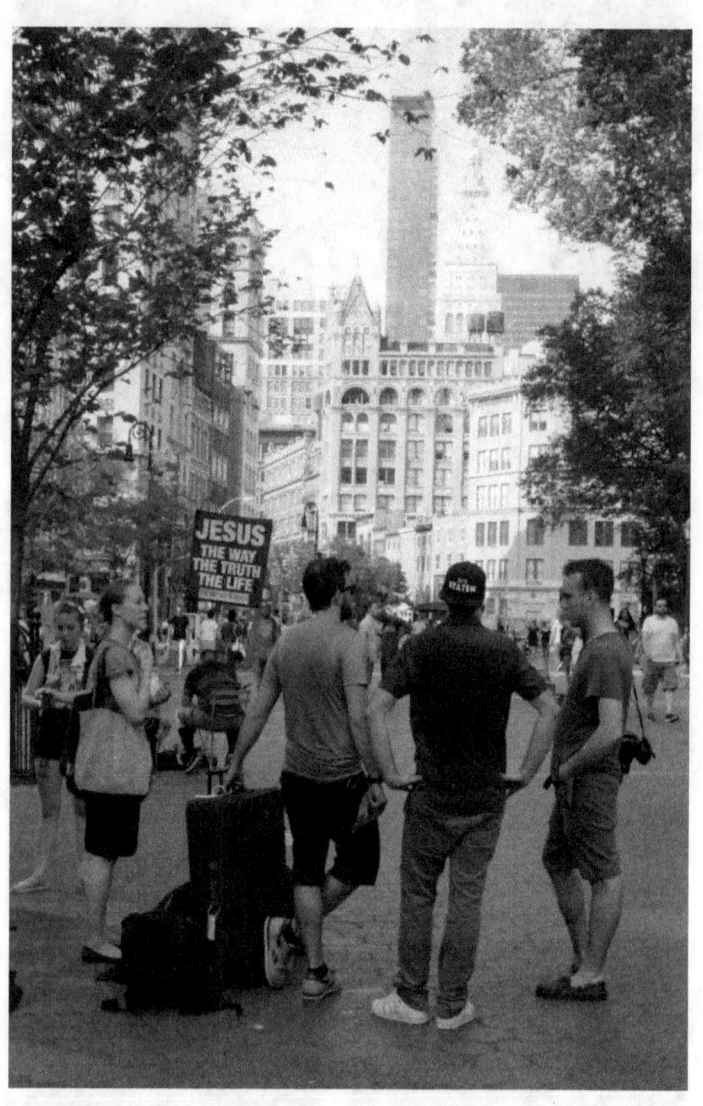

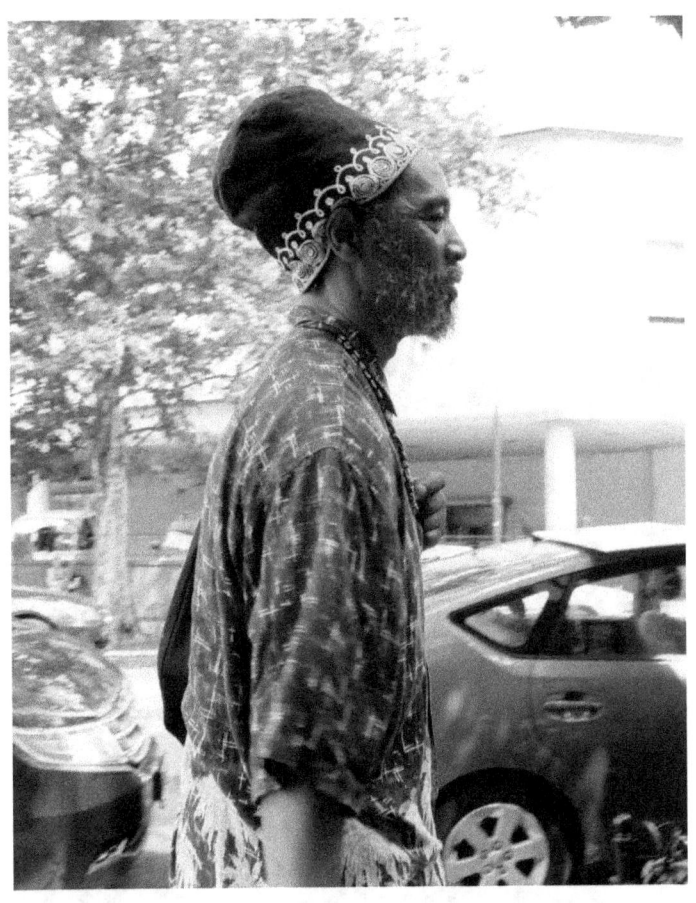

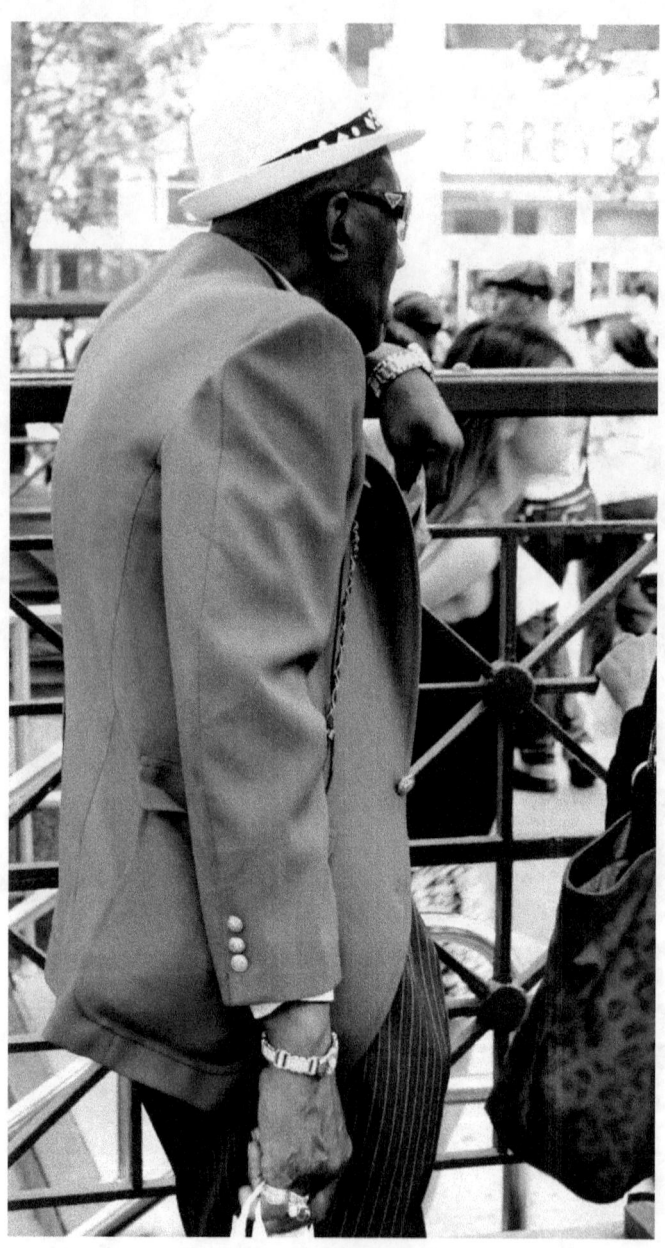

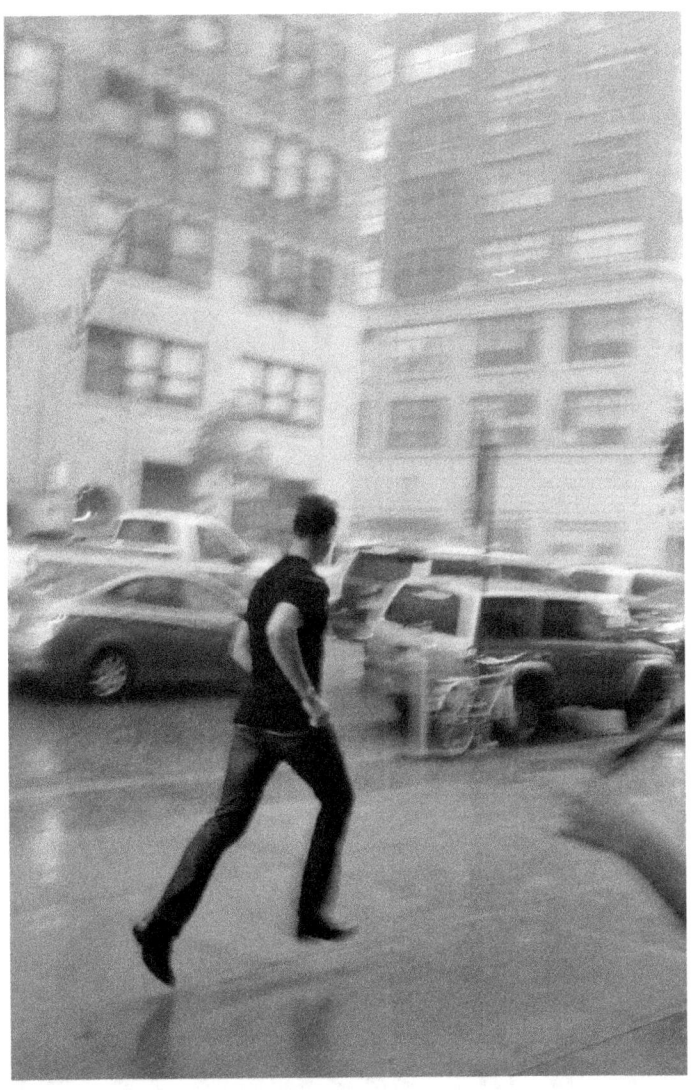

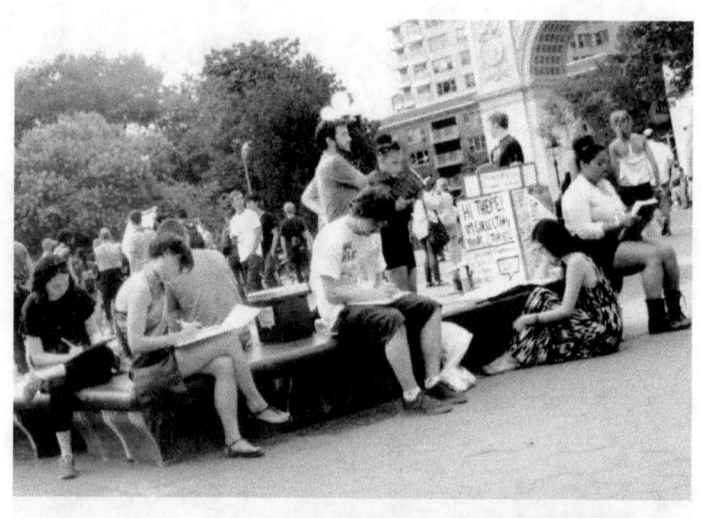

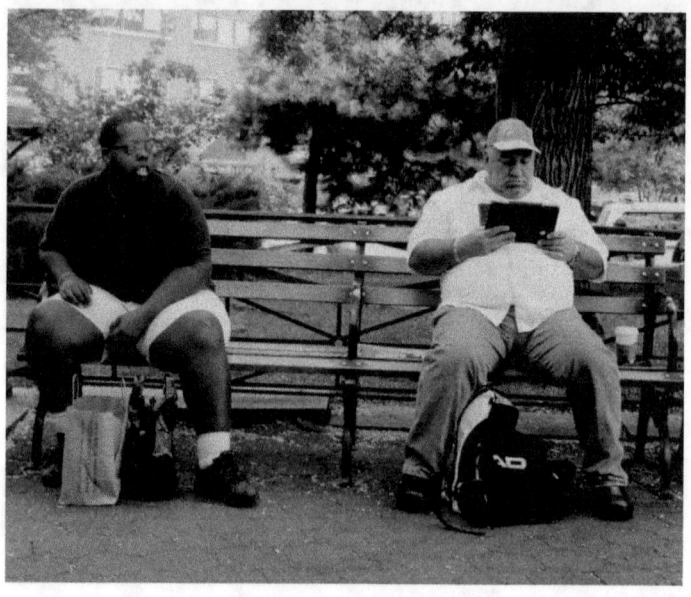

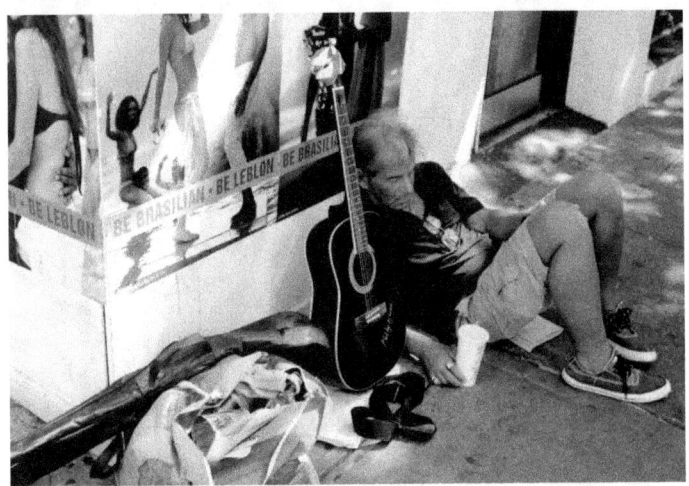

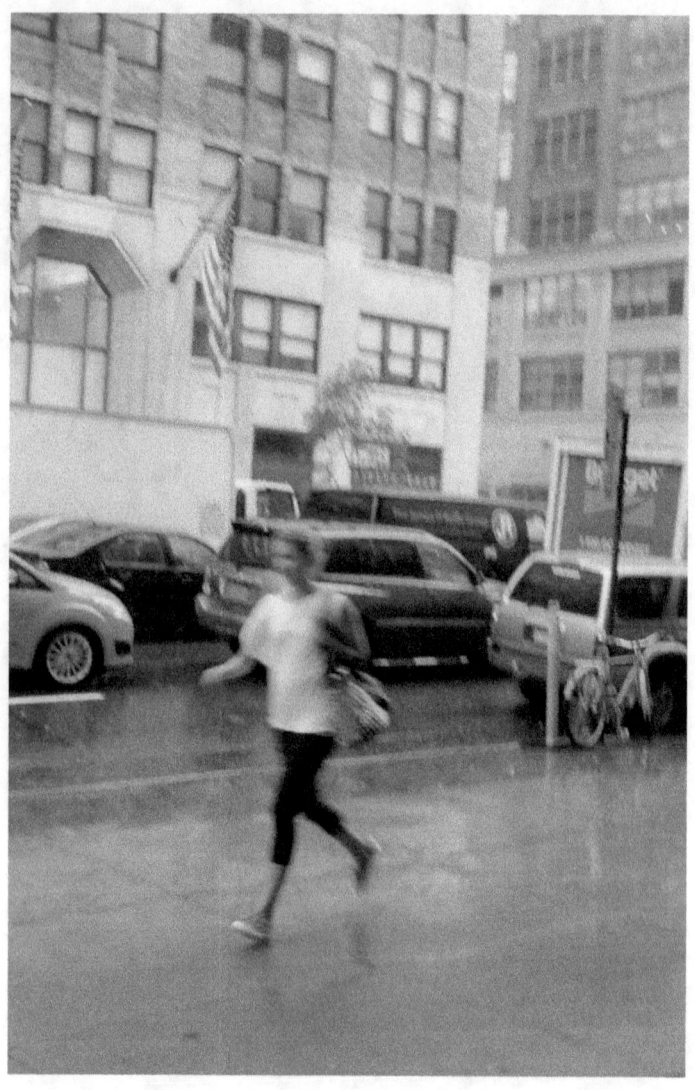

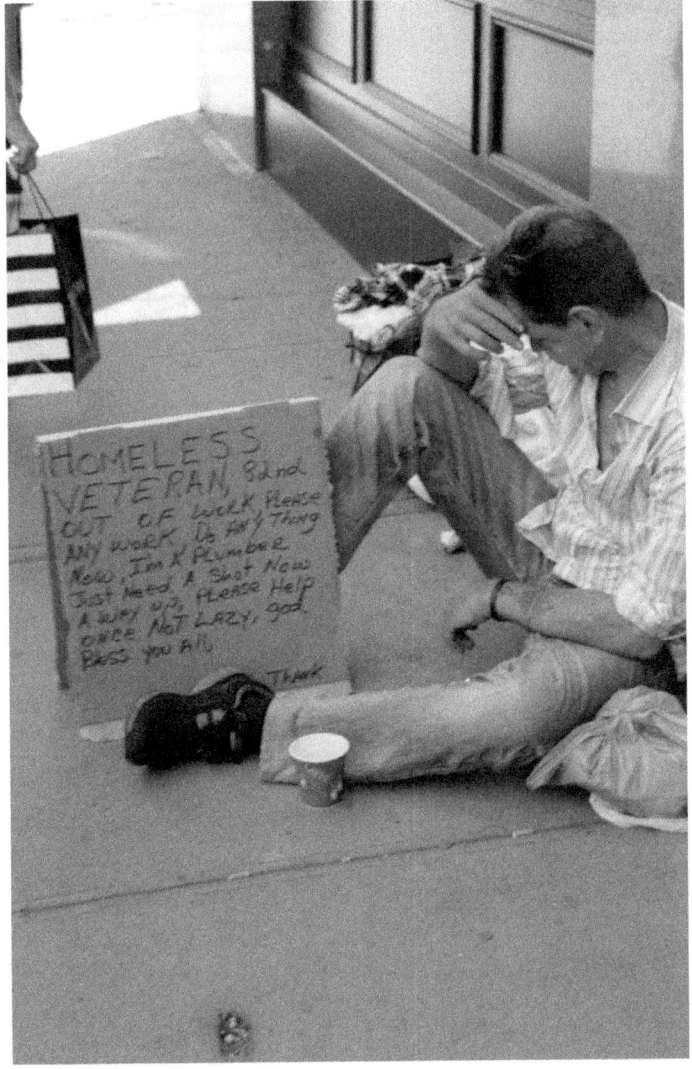

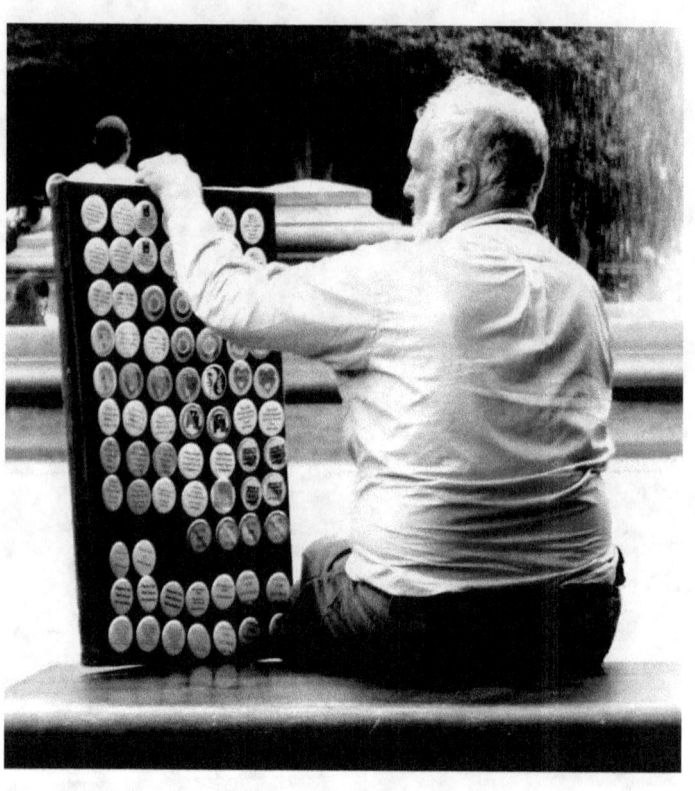

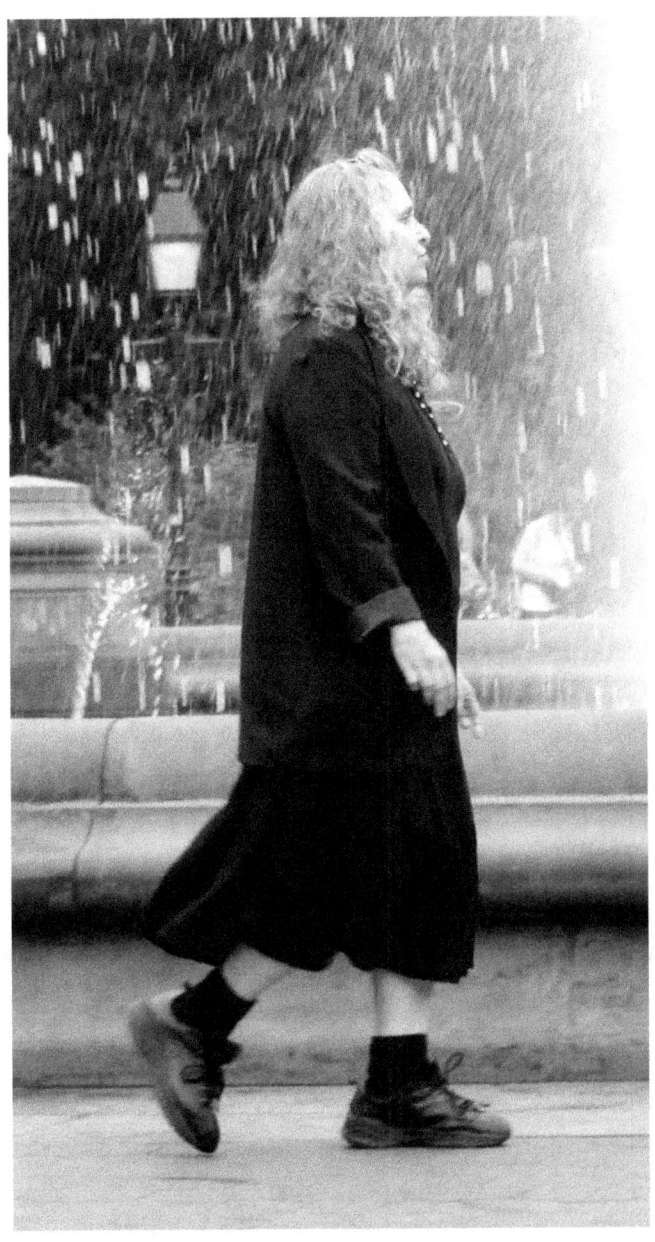

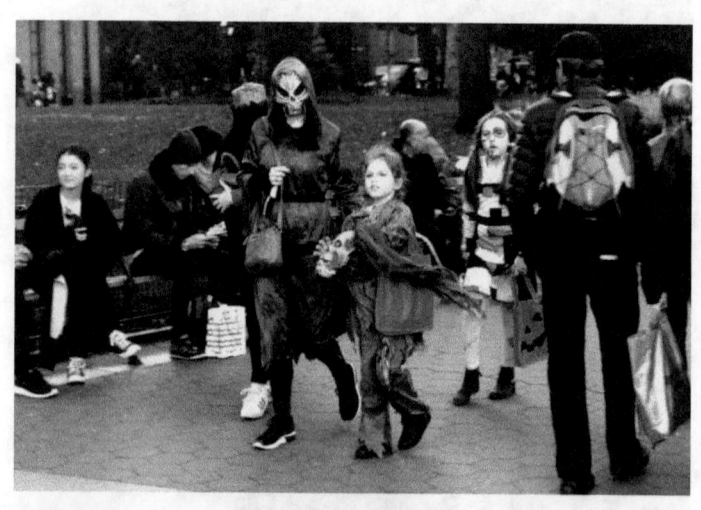

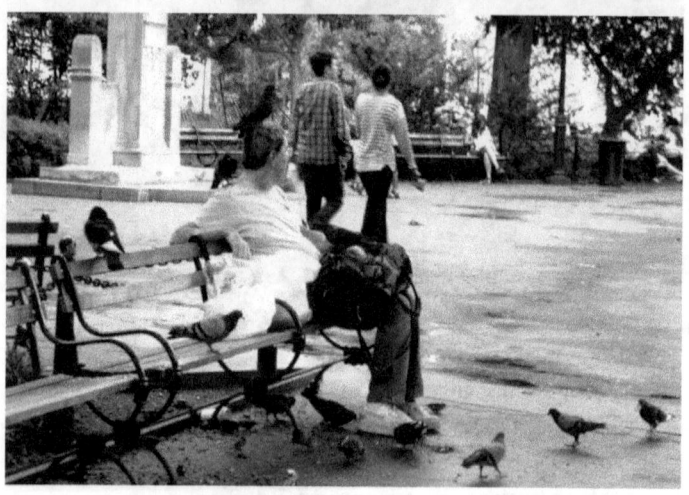

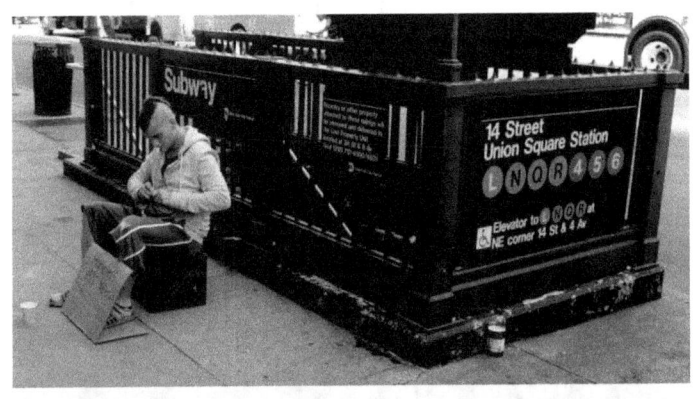

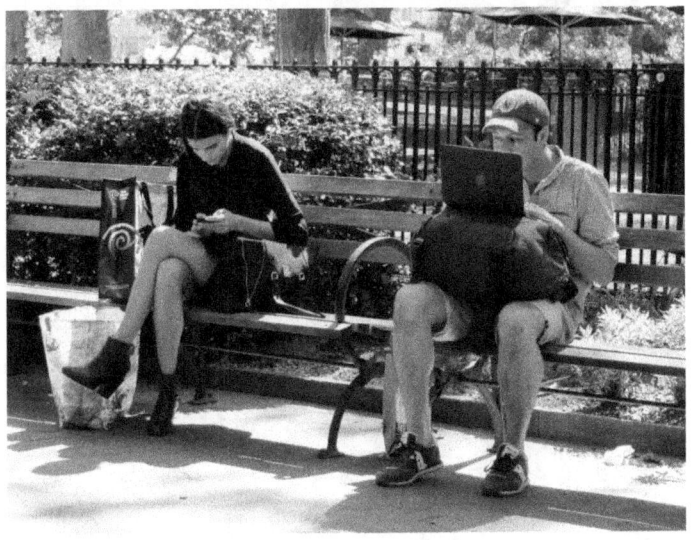

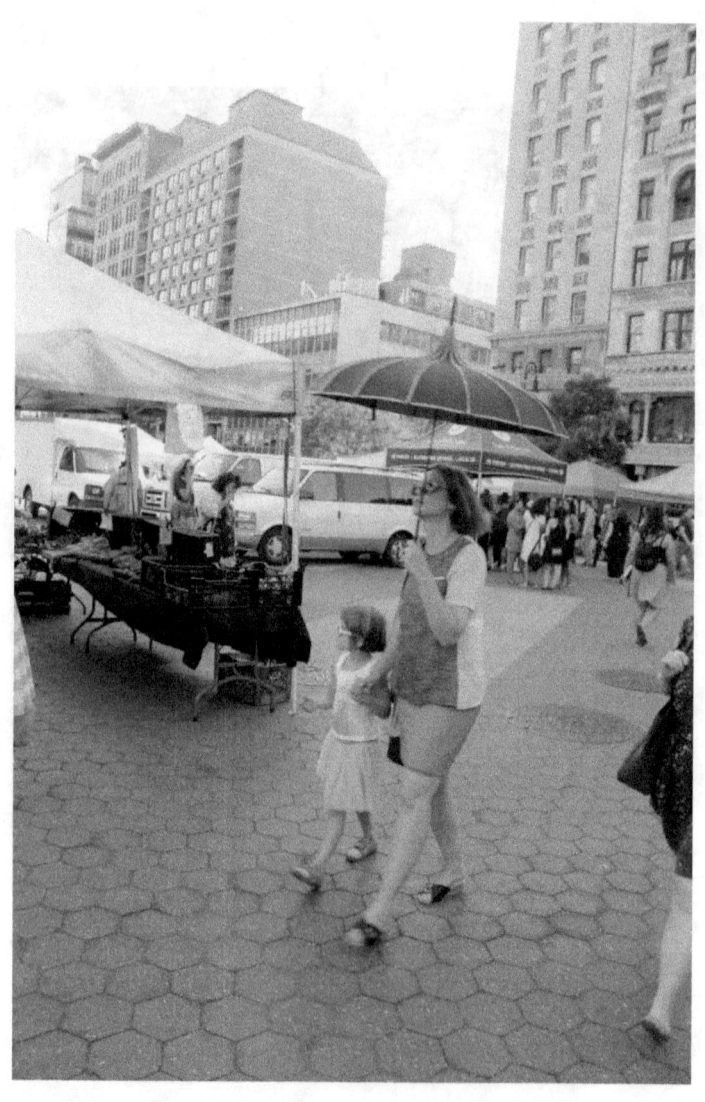

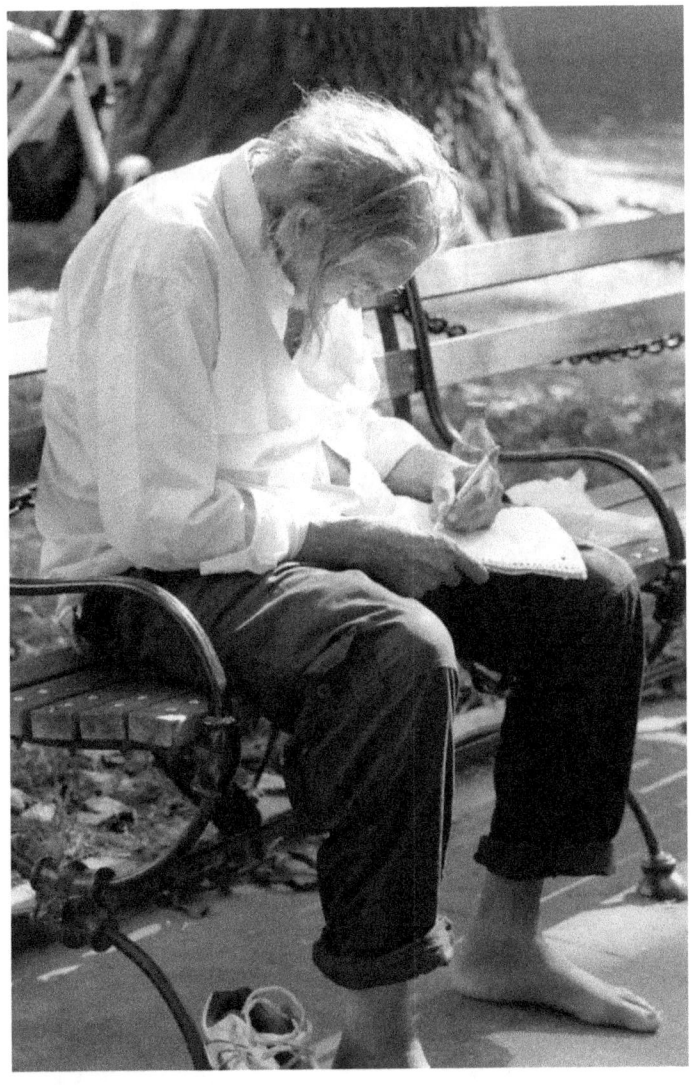

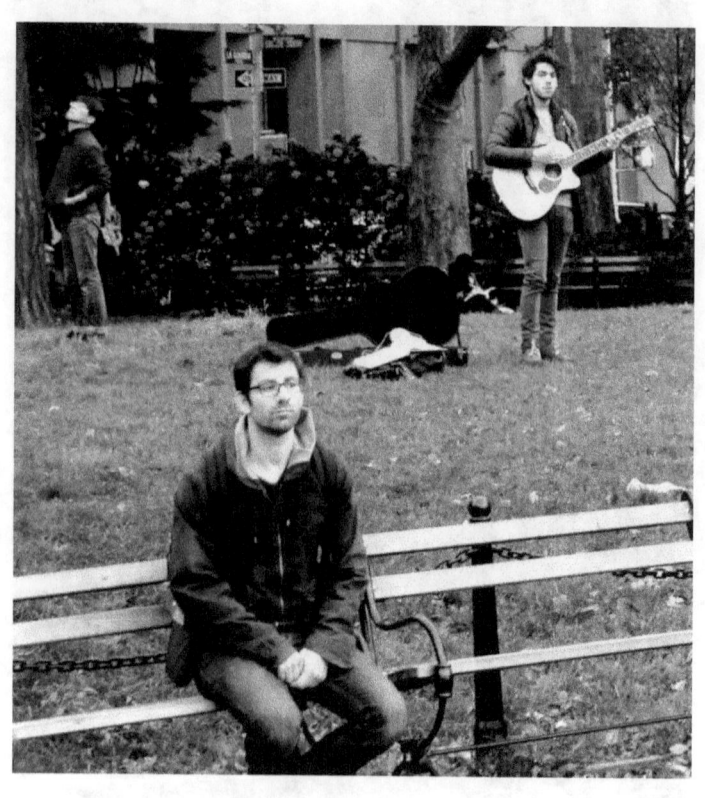

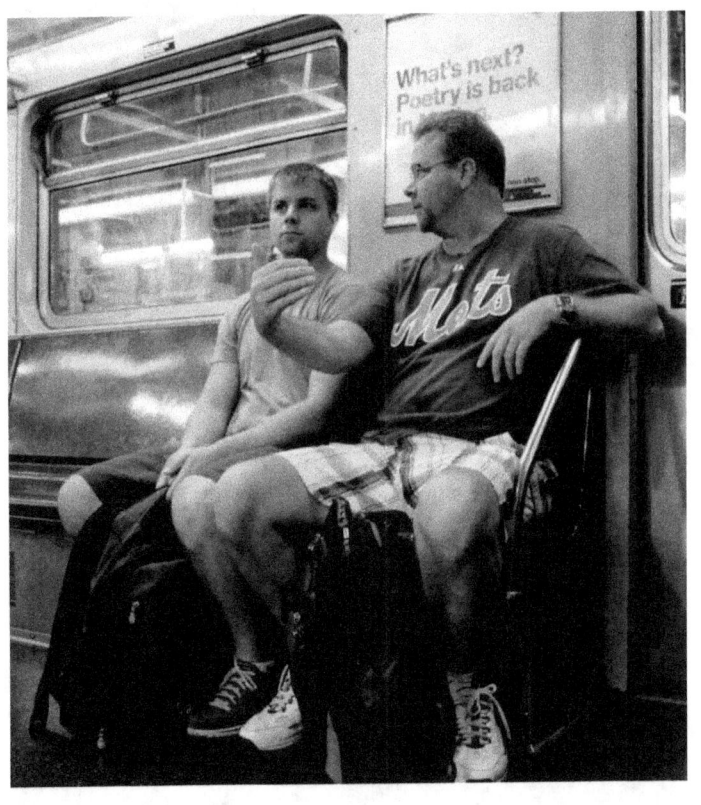

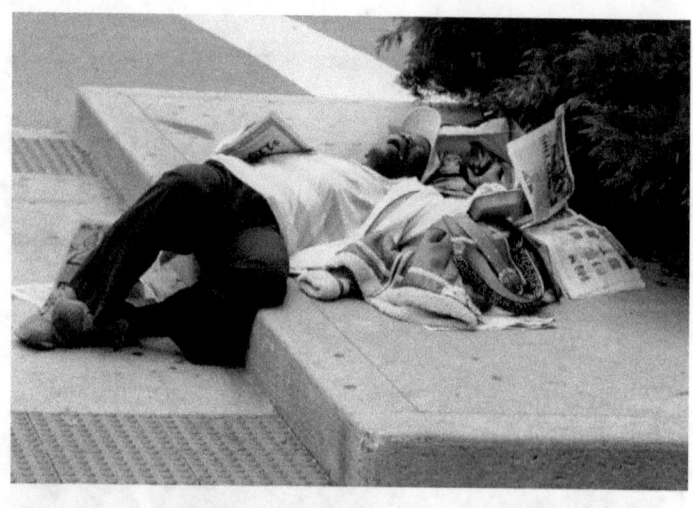

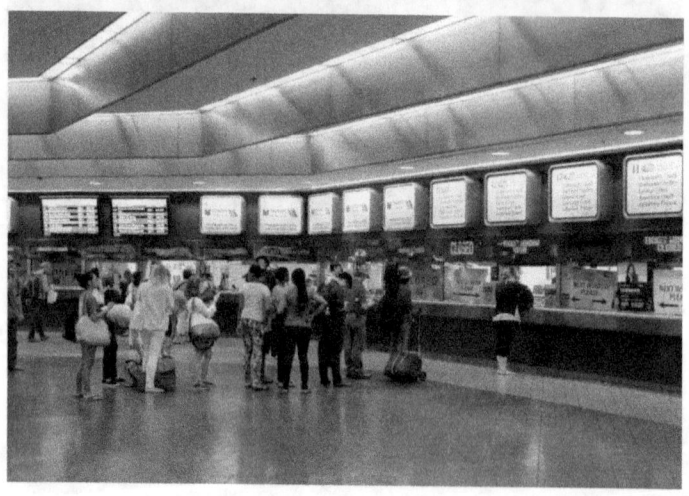

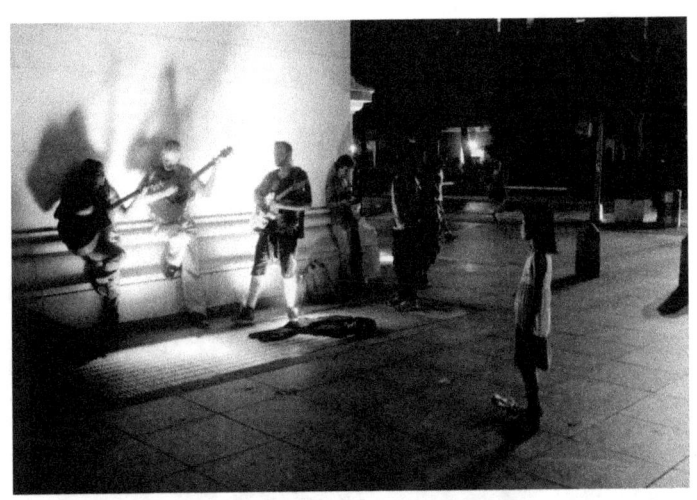

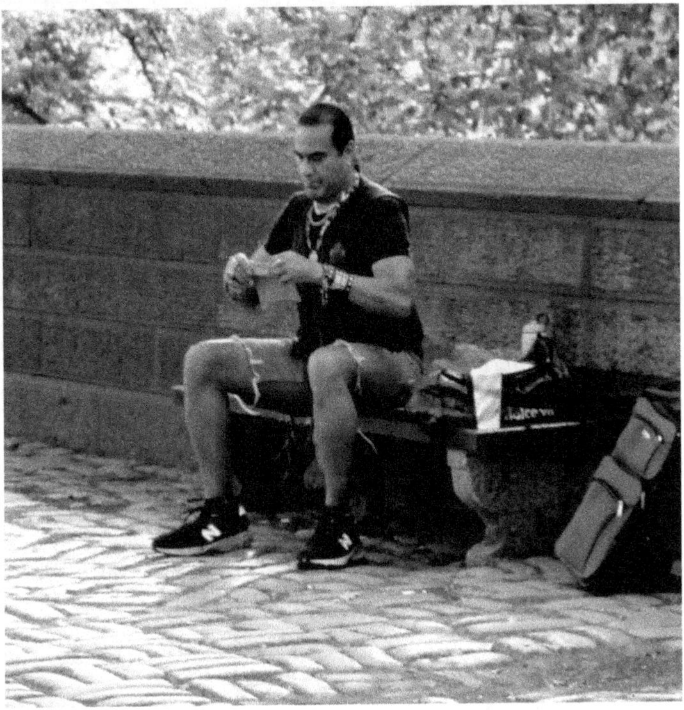

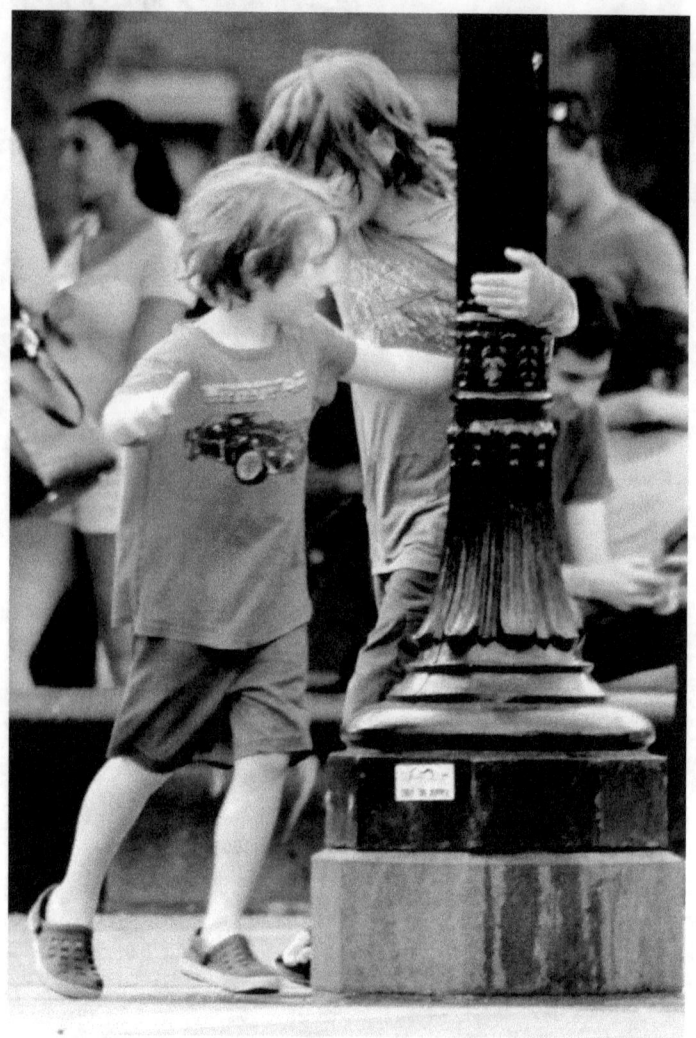

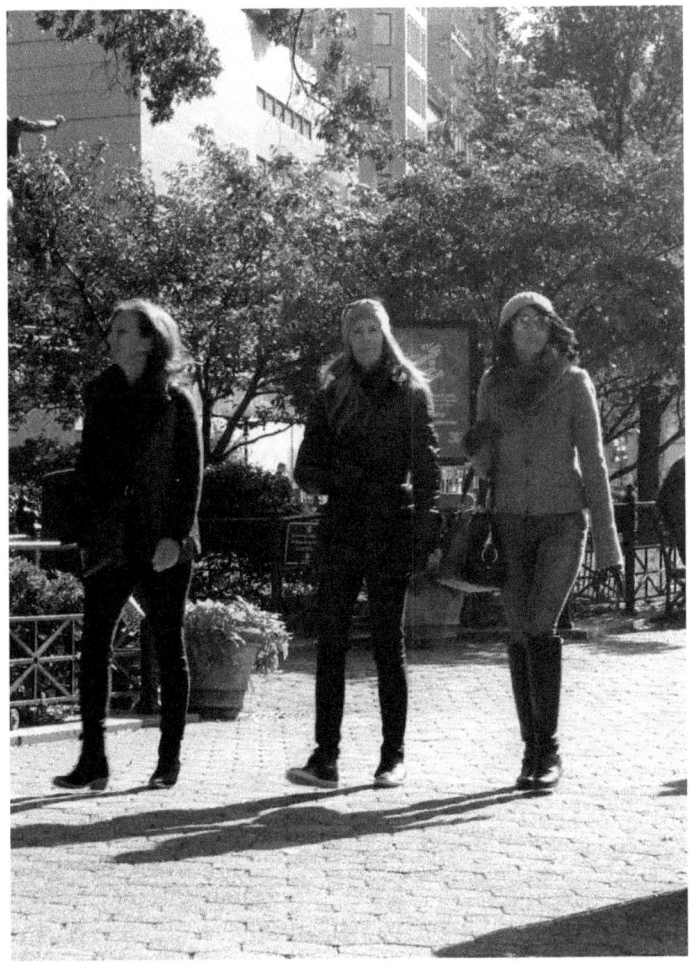

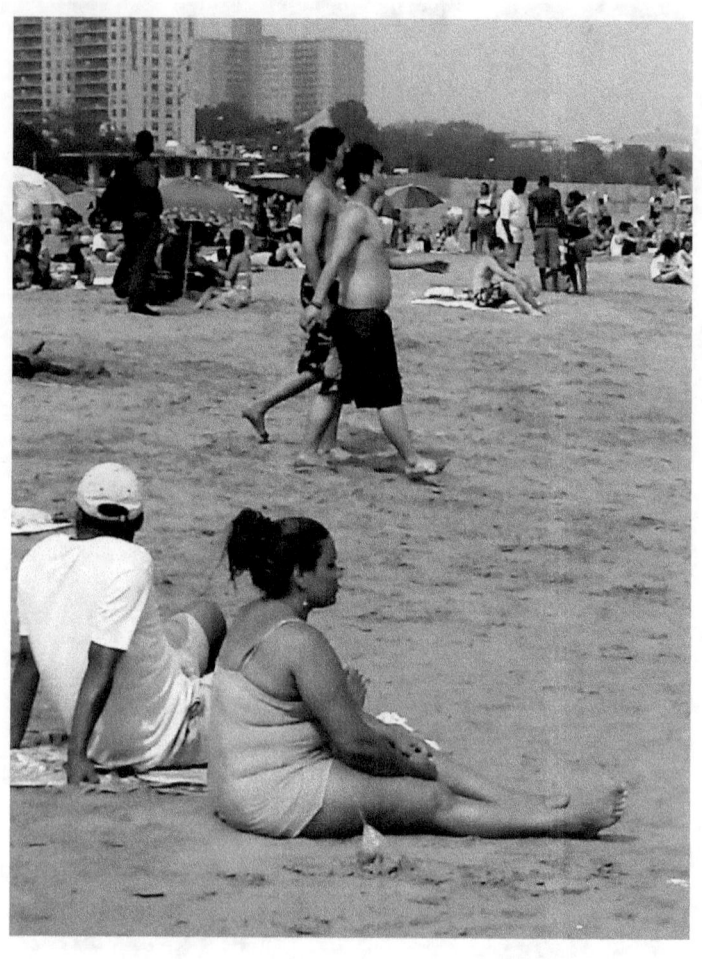

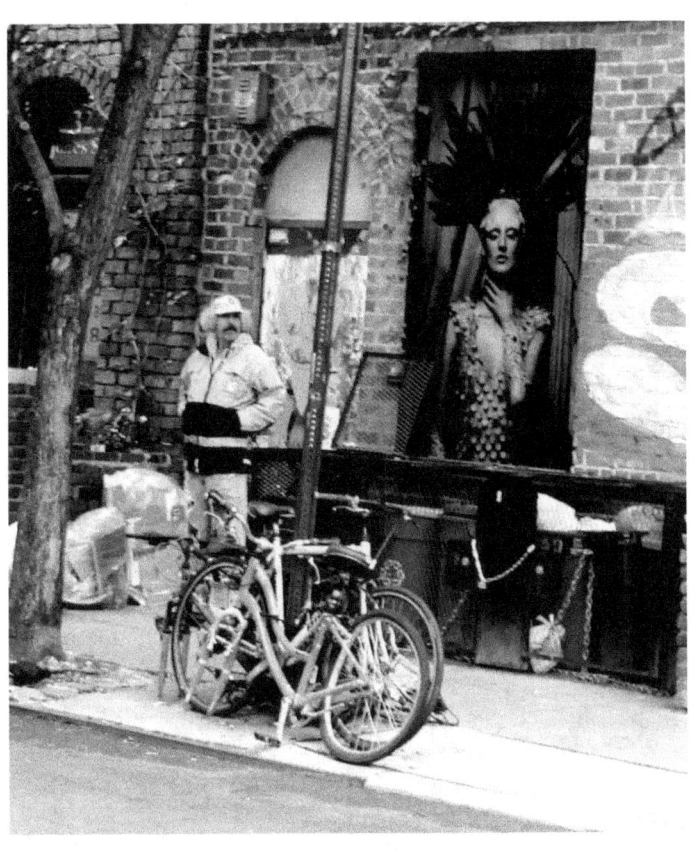

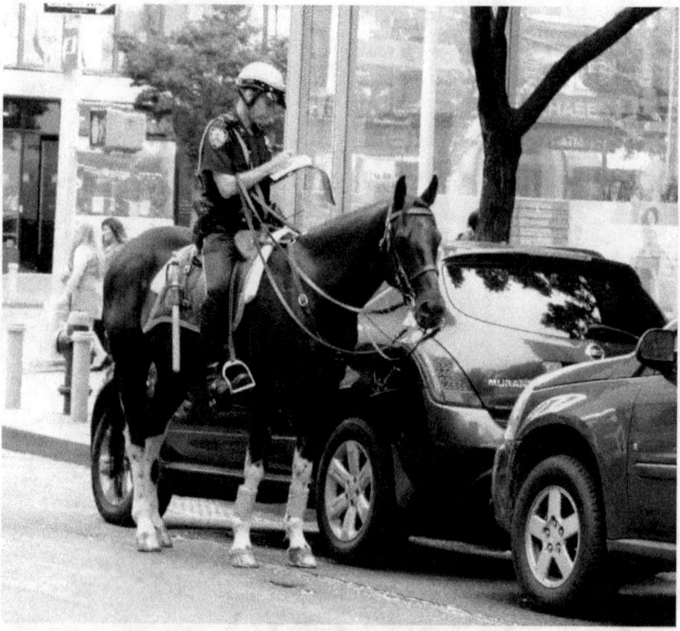

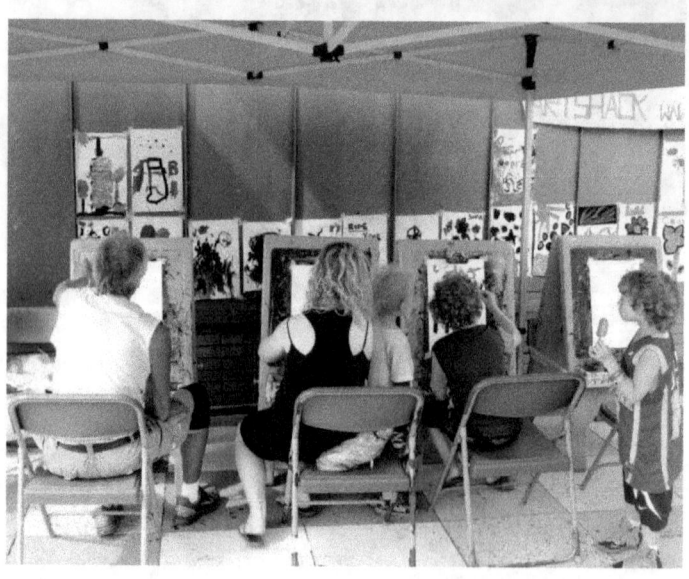

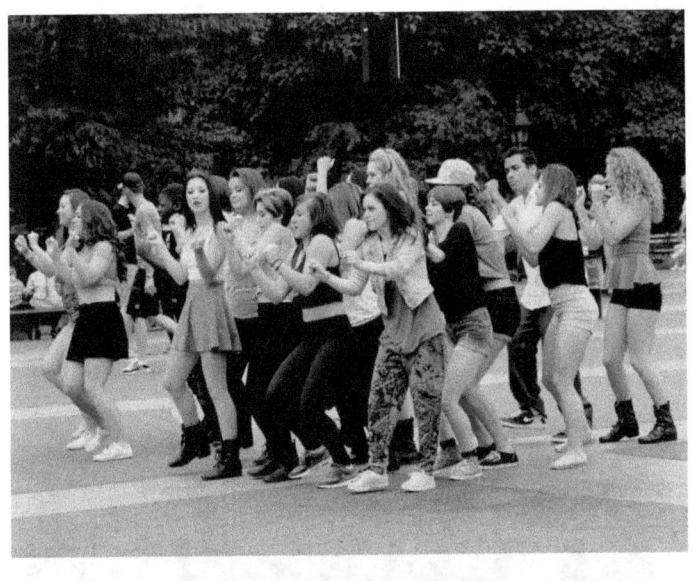

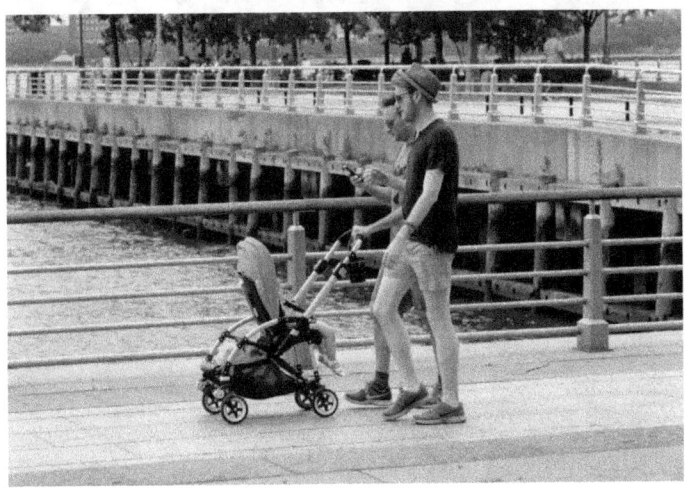

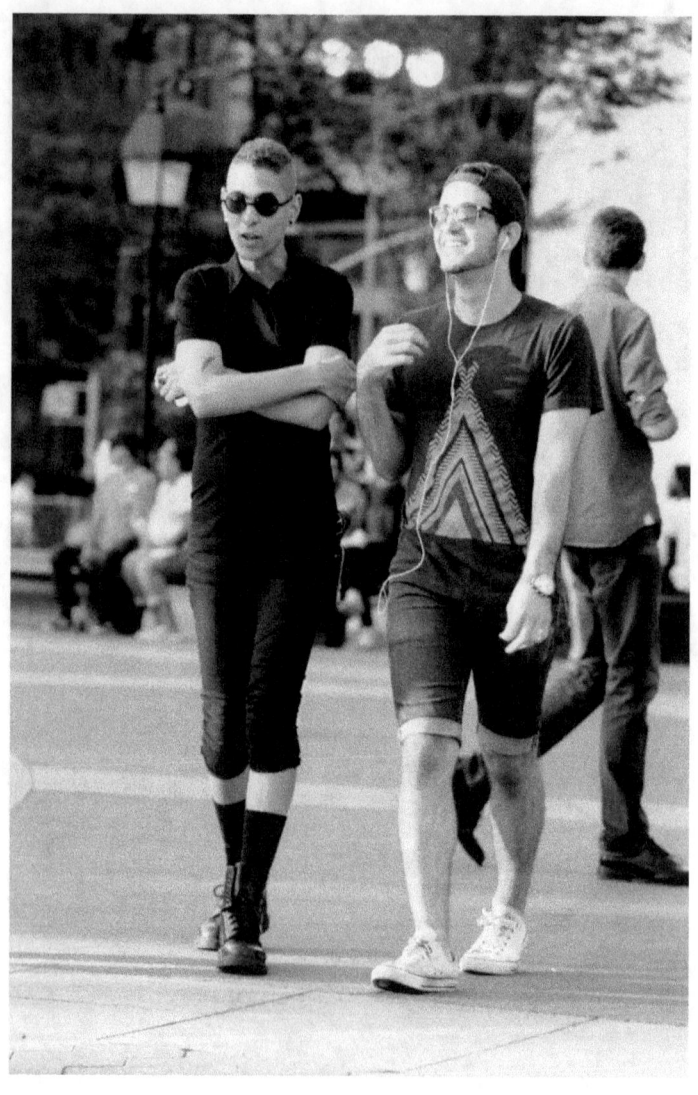

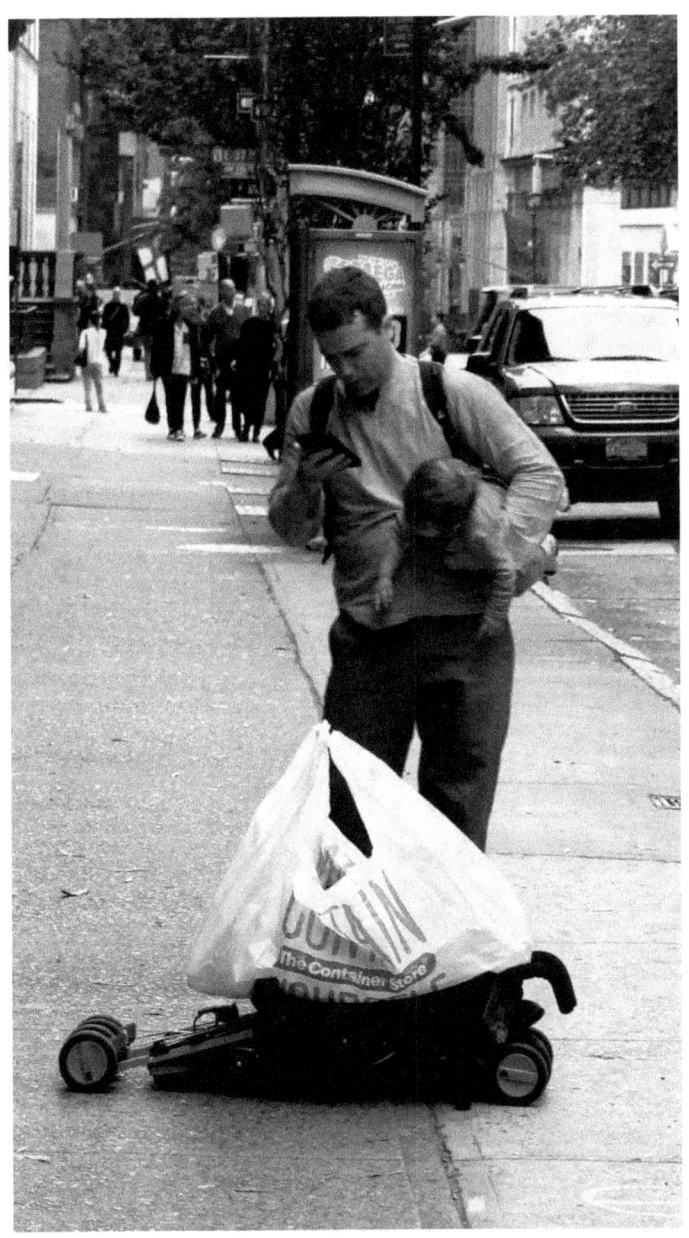

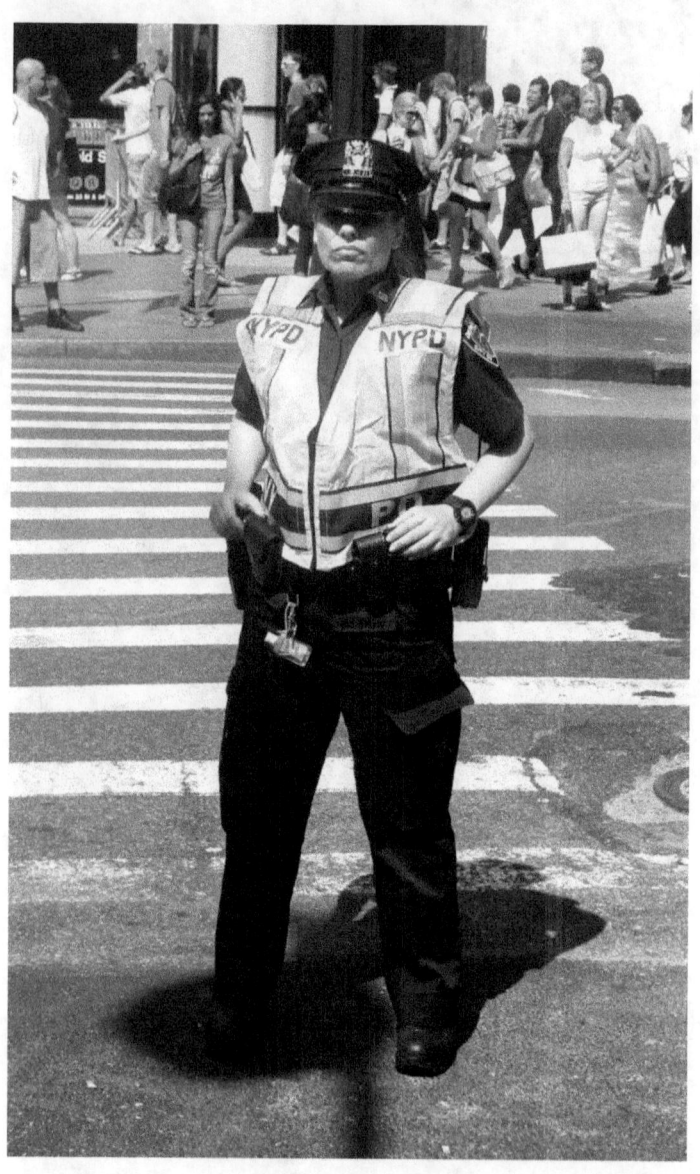

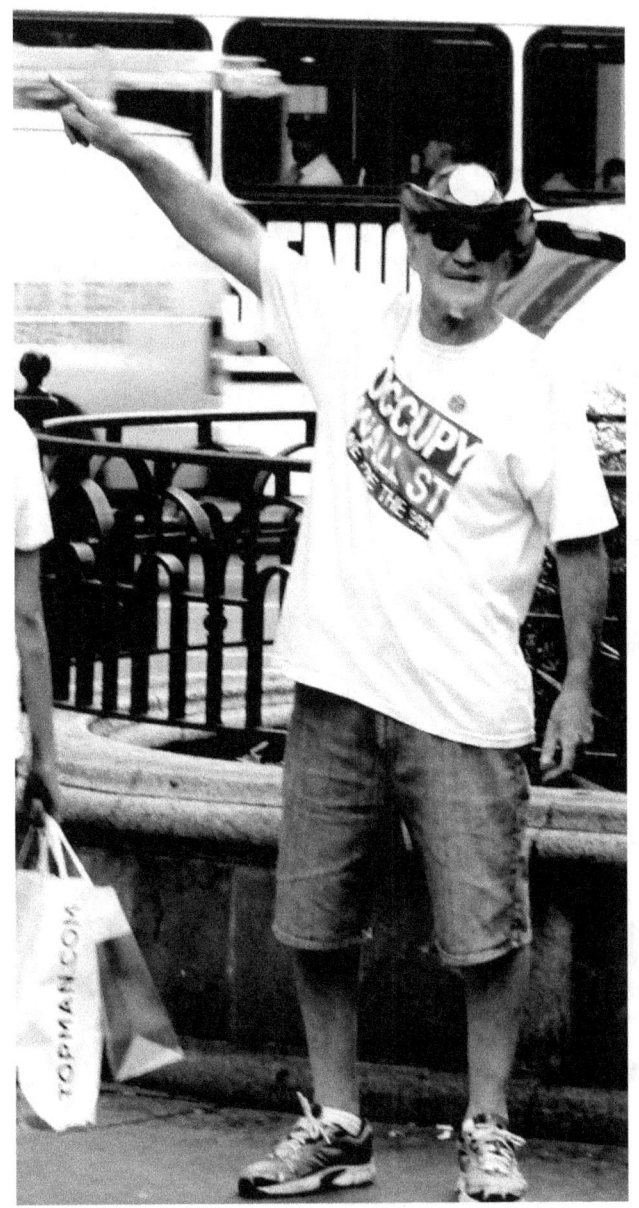

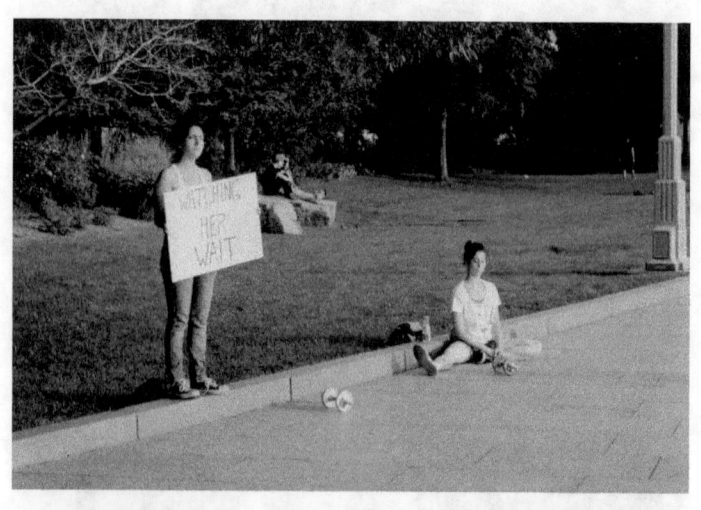

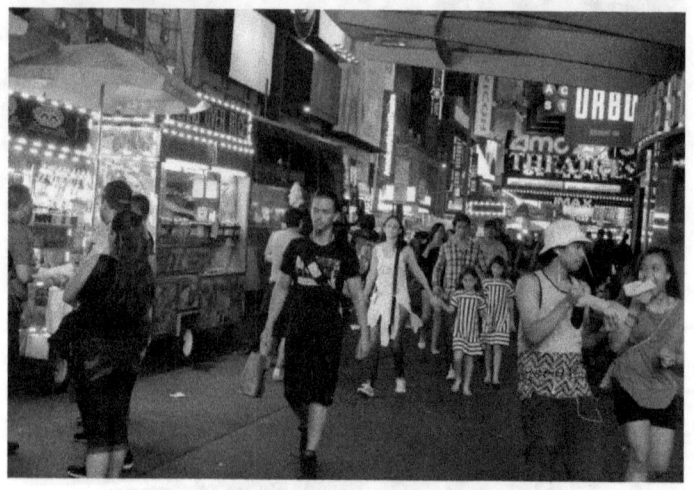

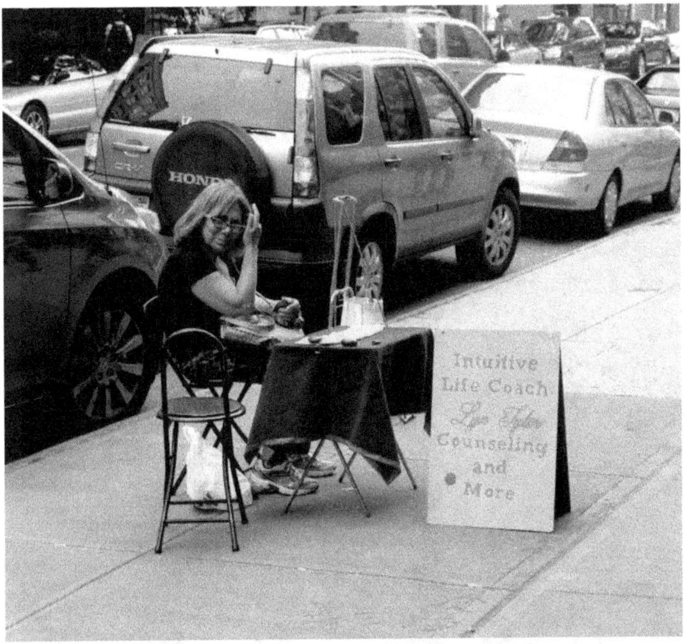

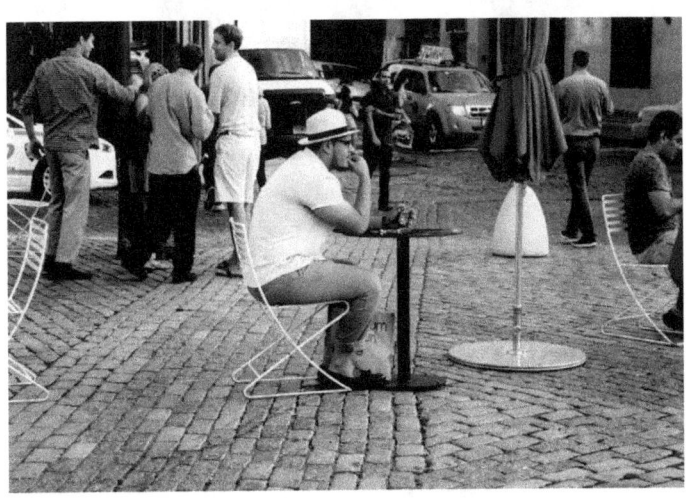

Intuitive
Life Coach
Lyn Tyler
Counseling
and
More

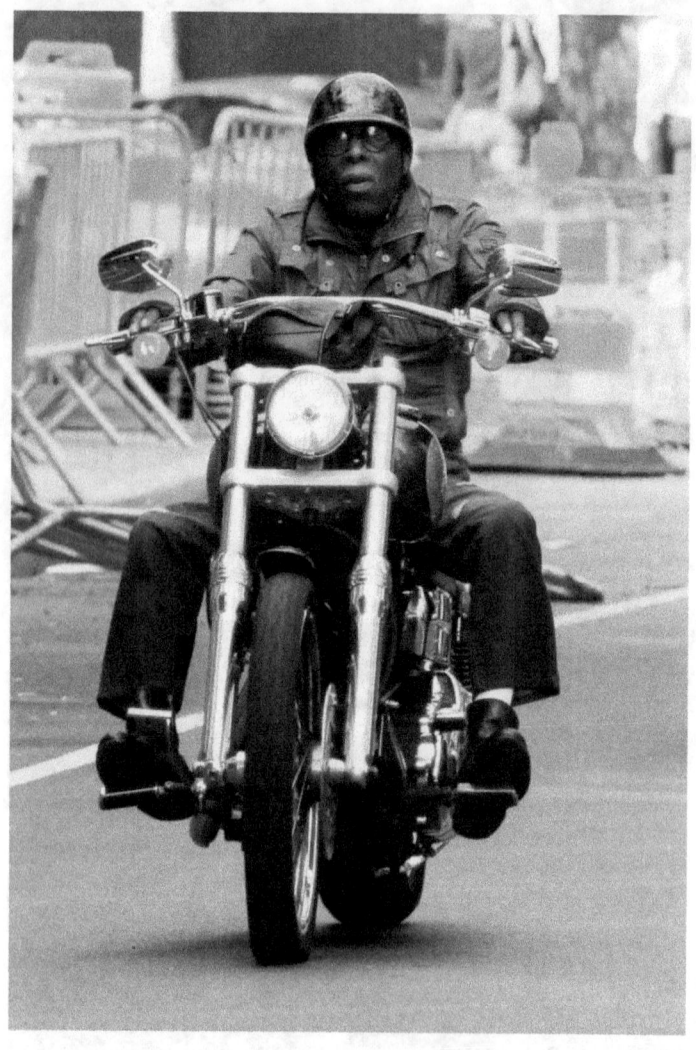

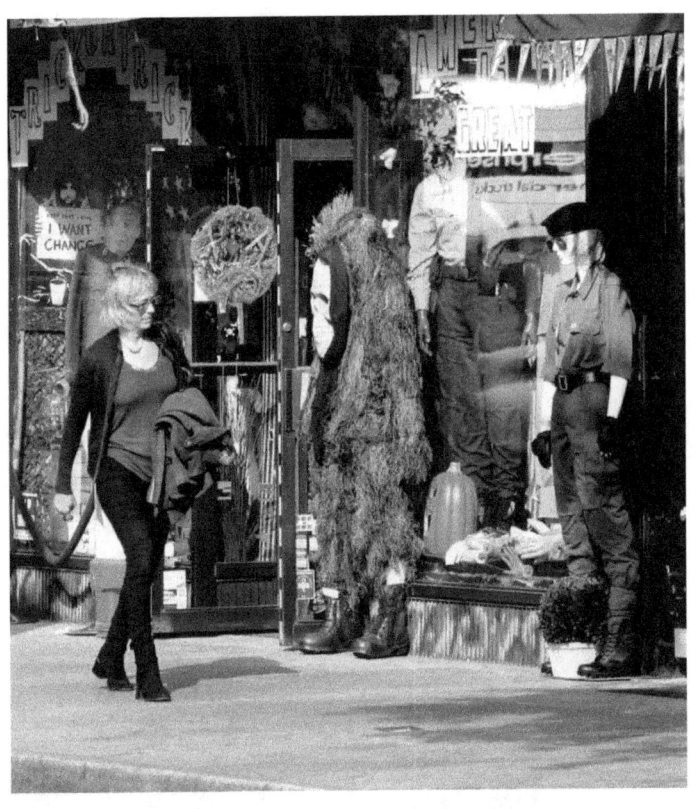

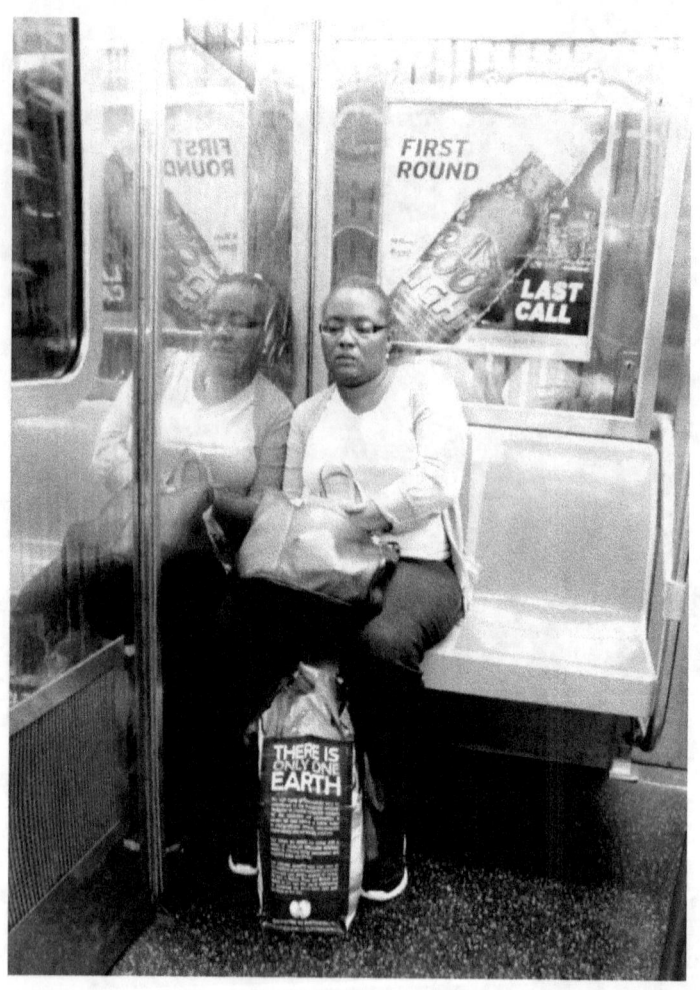

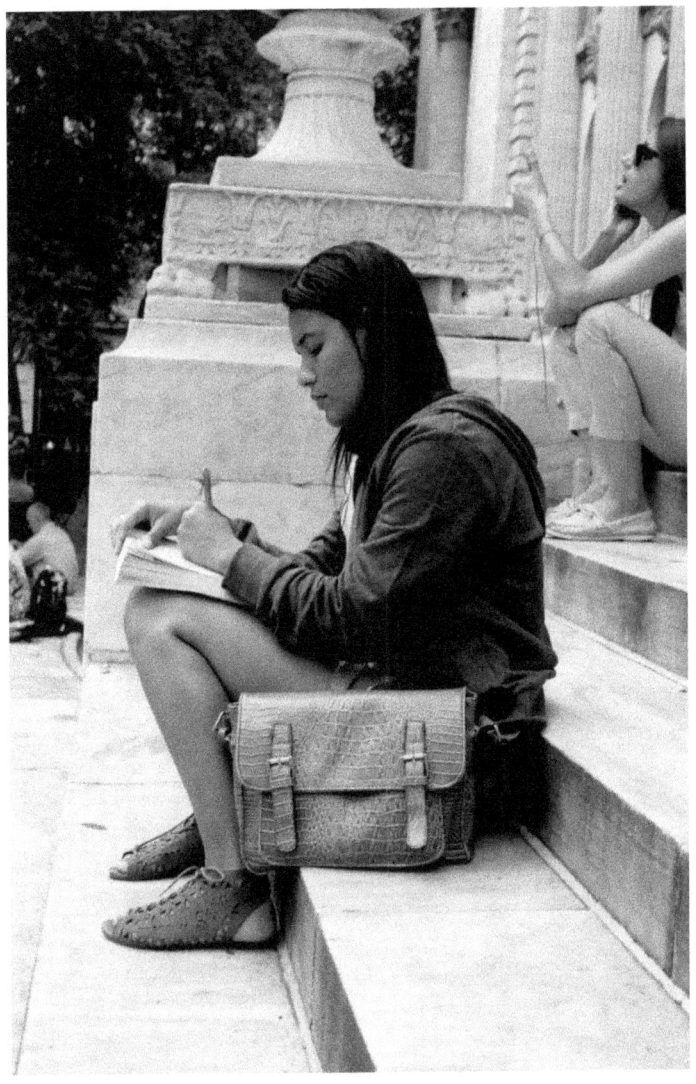

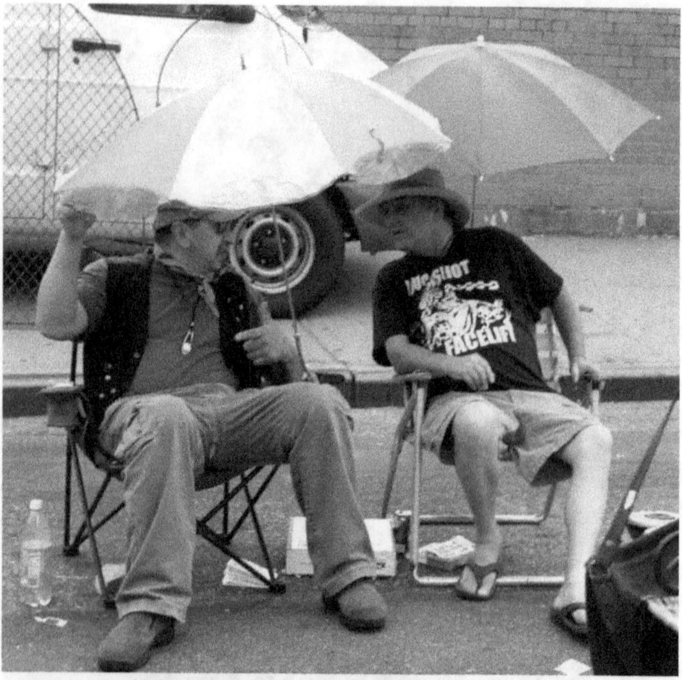

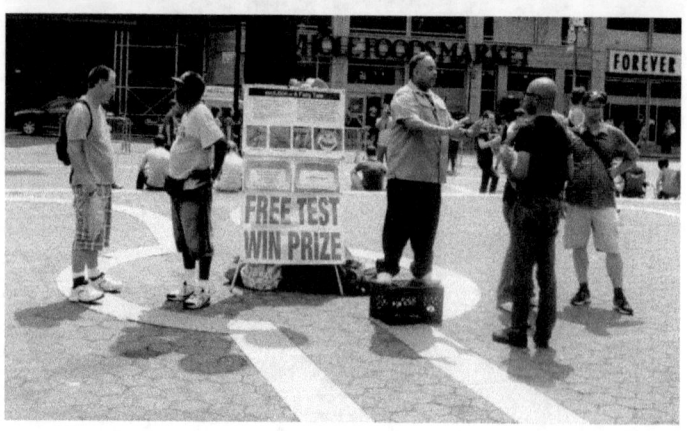

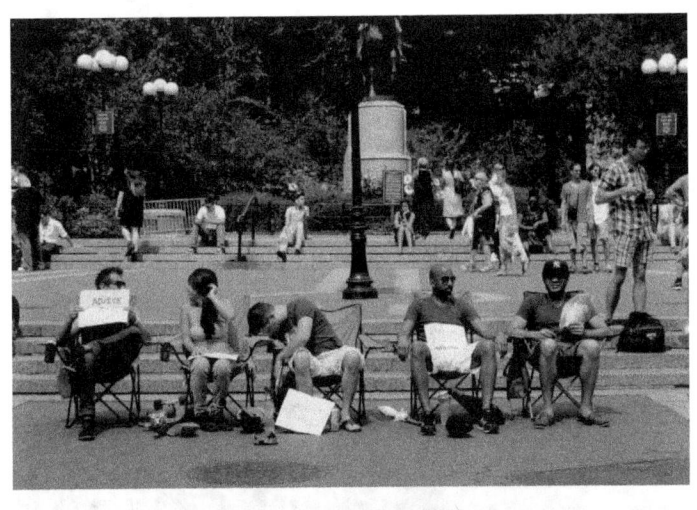

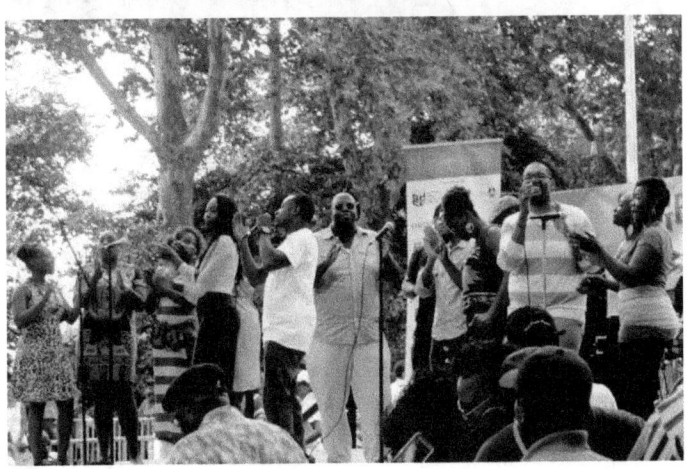

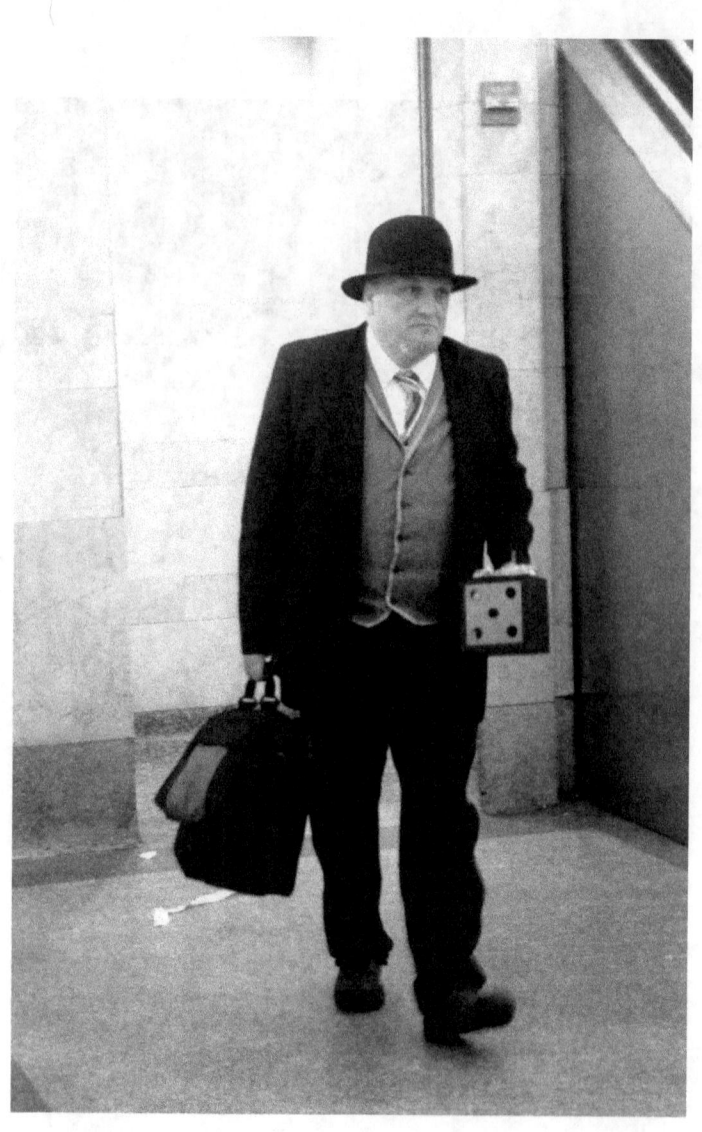

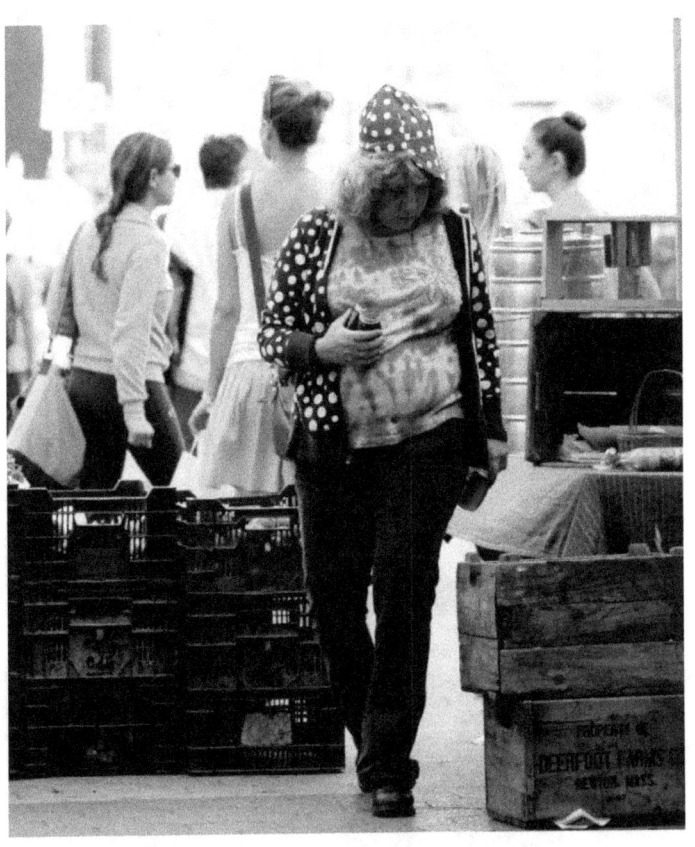

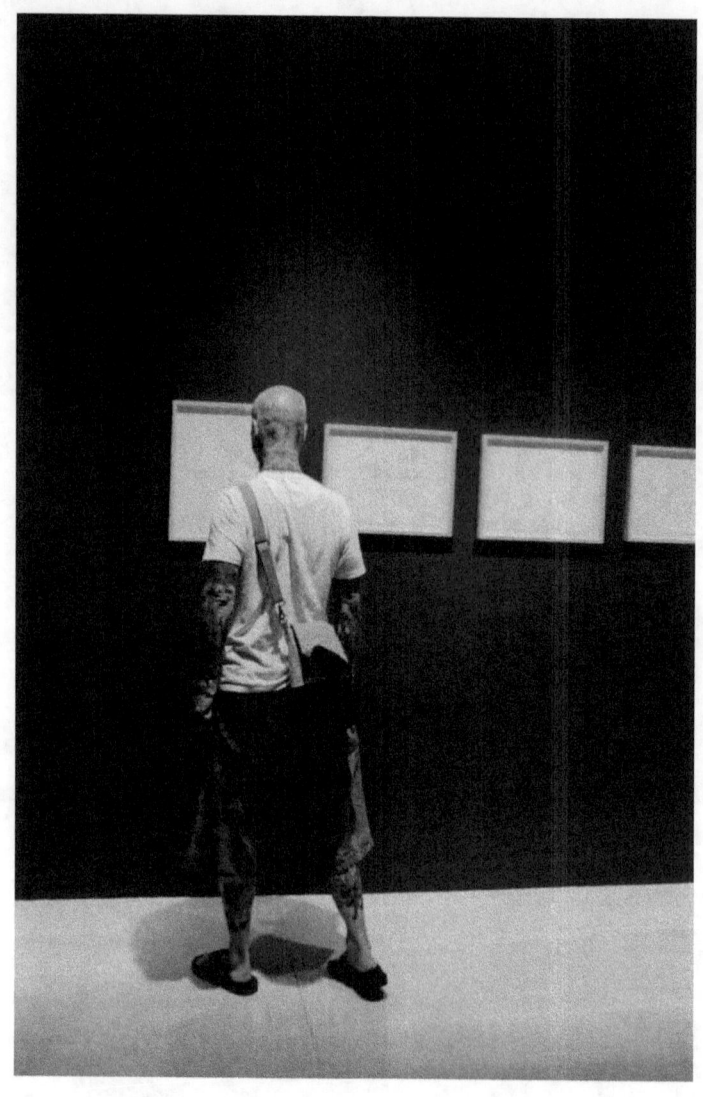

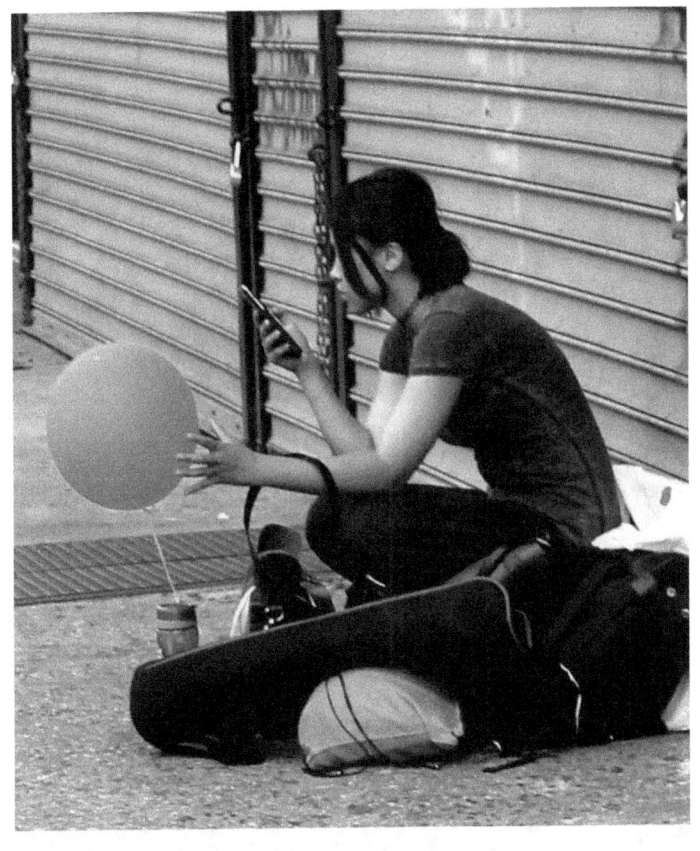

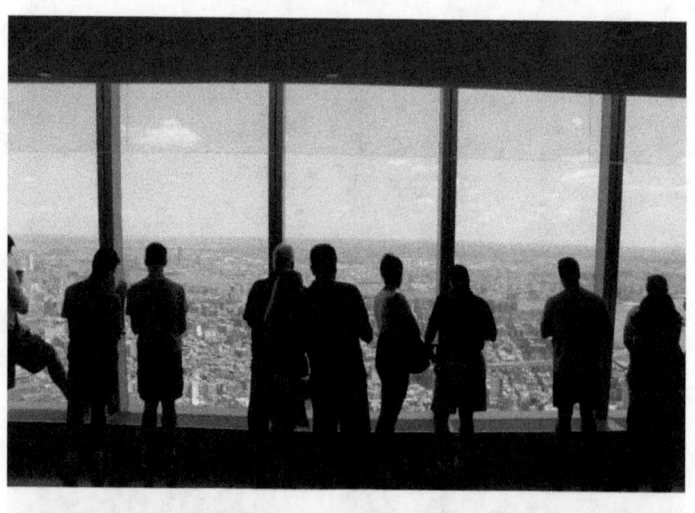

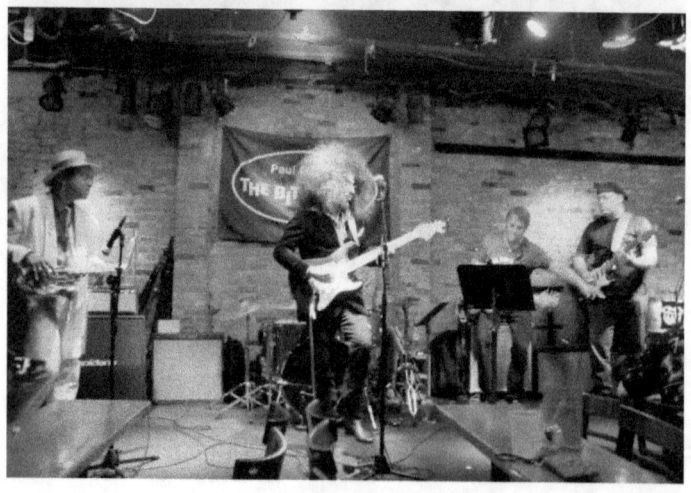

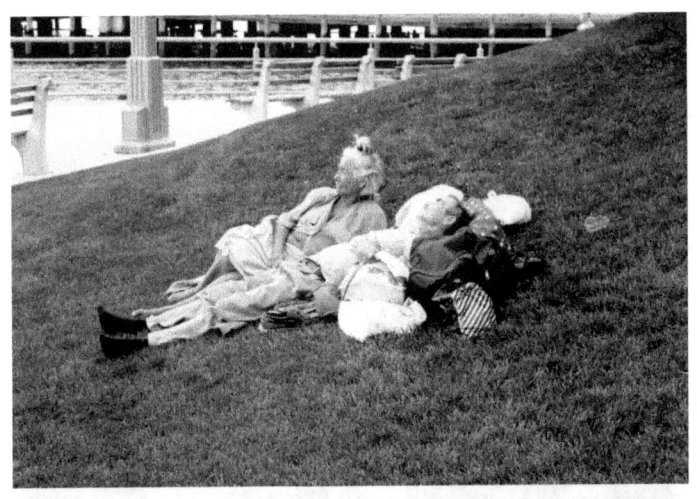

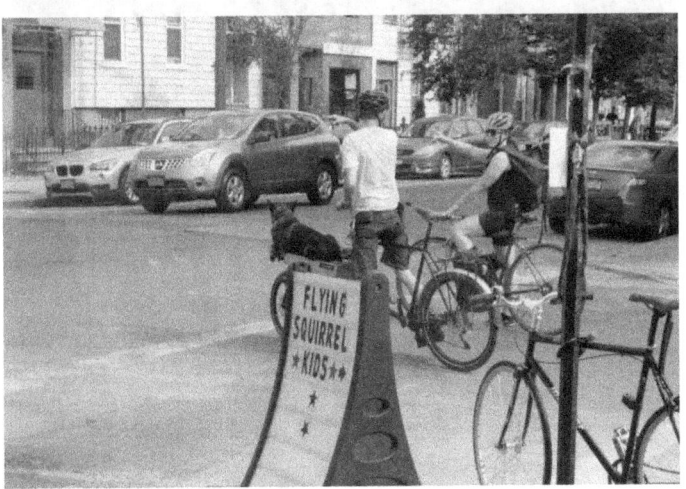

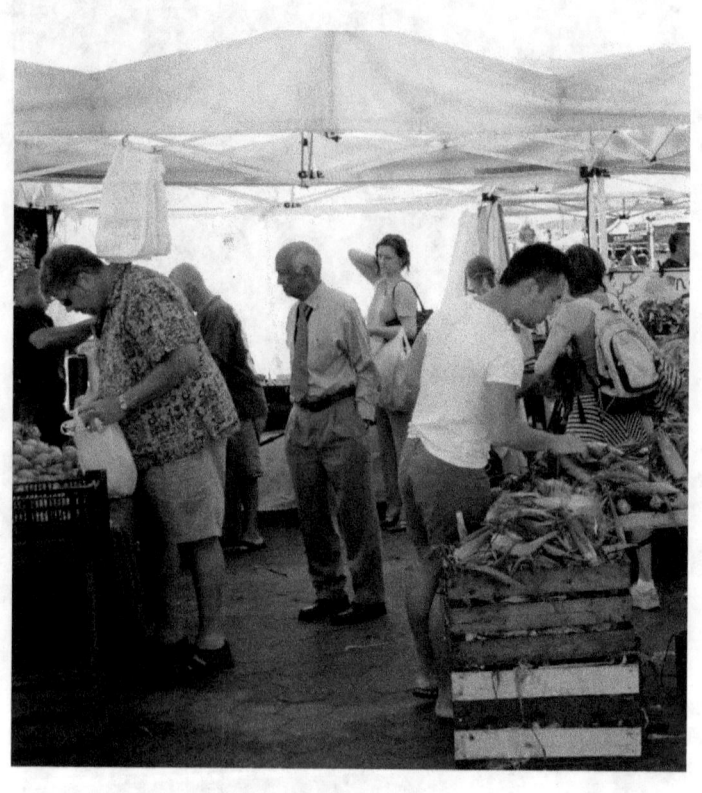

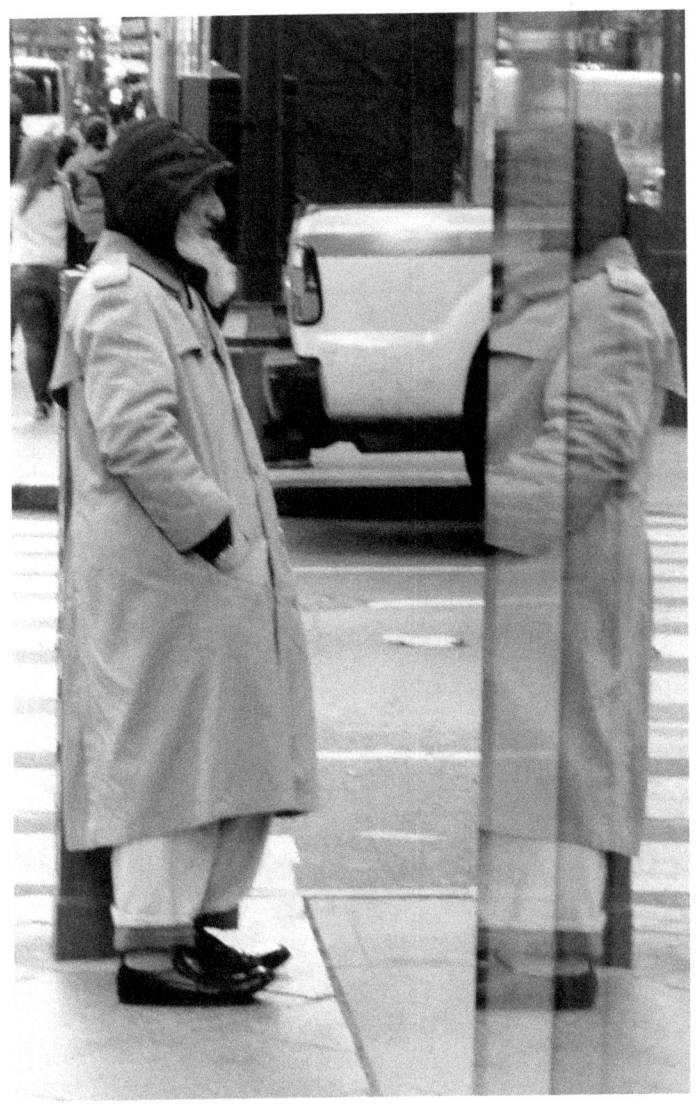

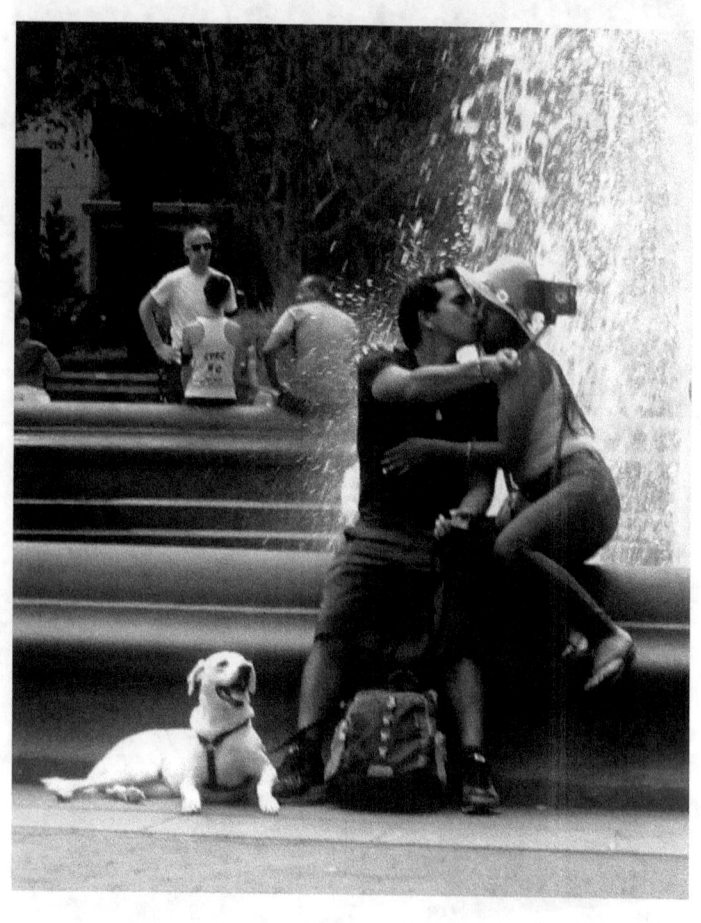

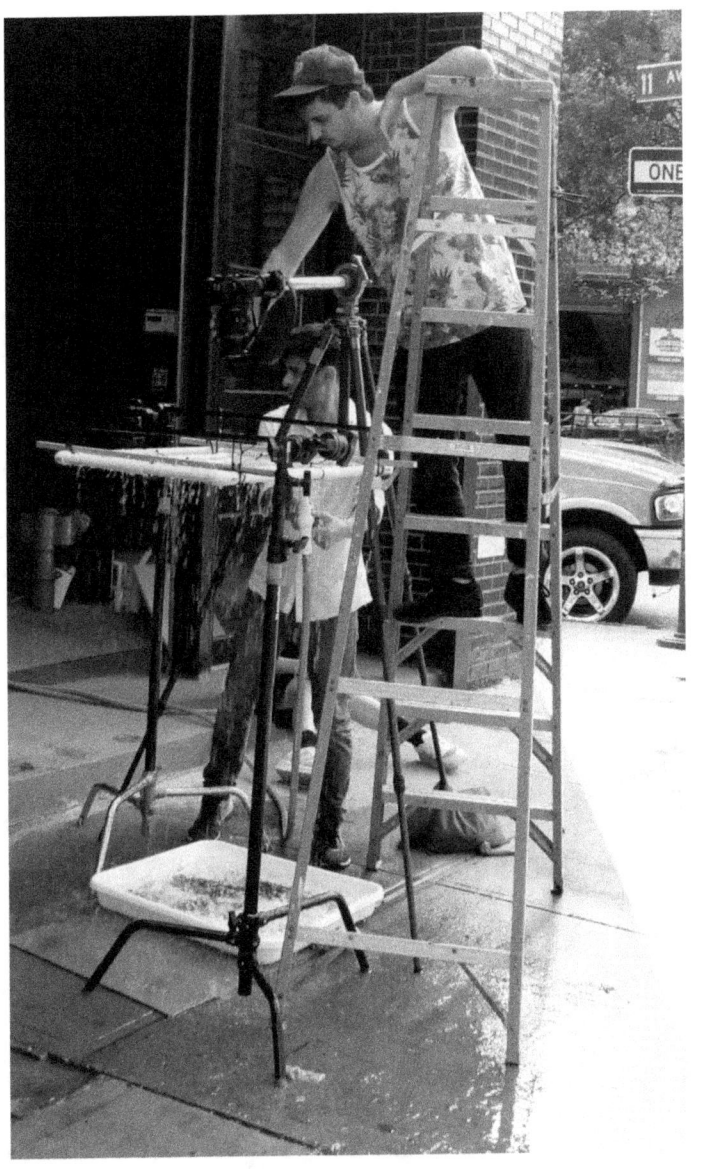

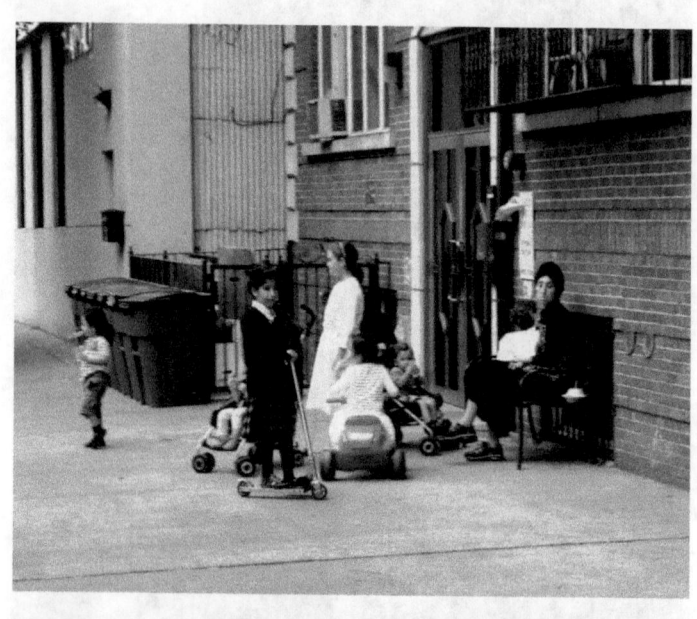

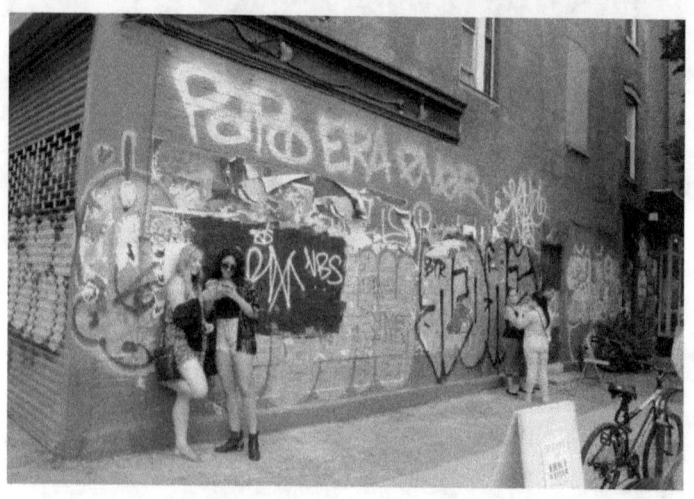

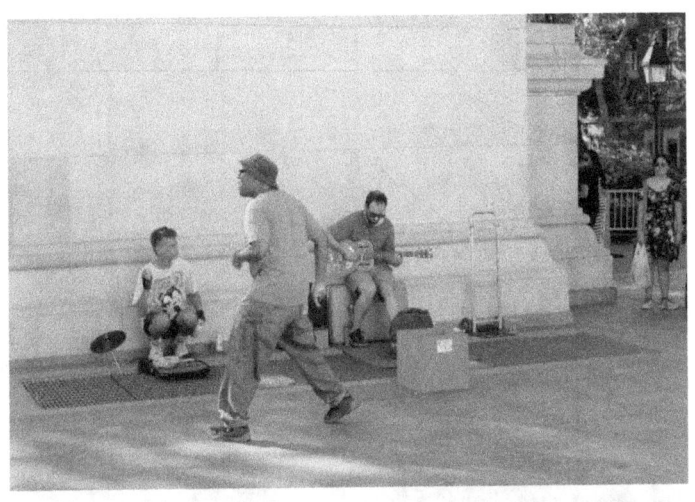

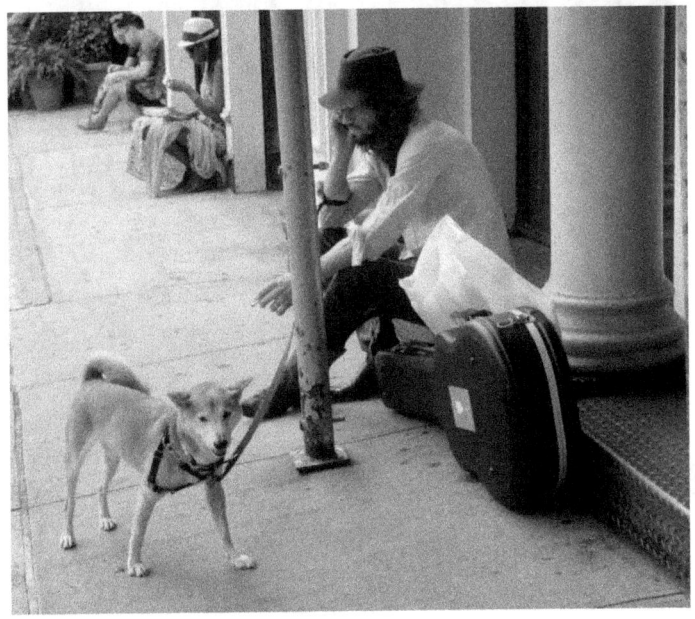

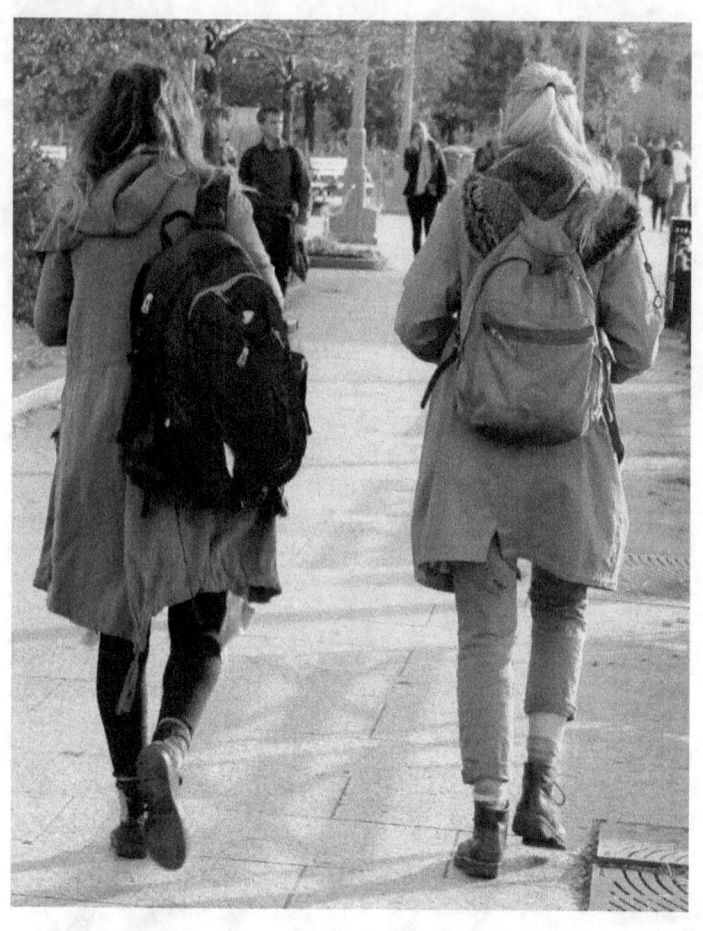

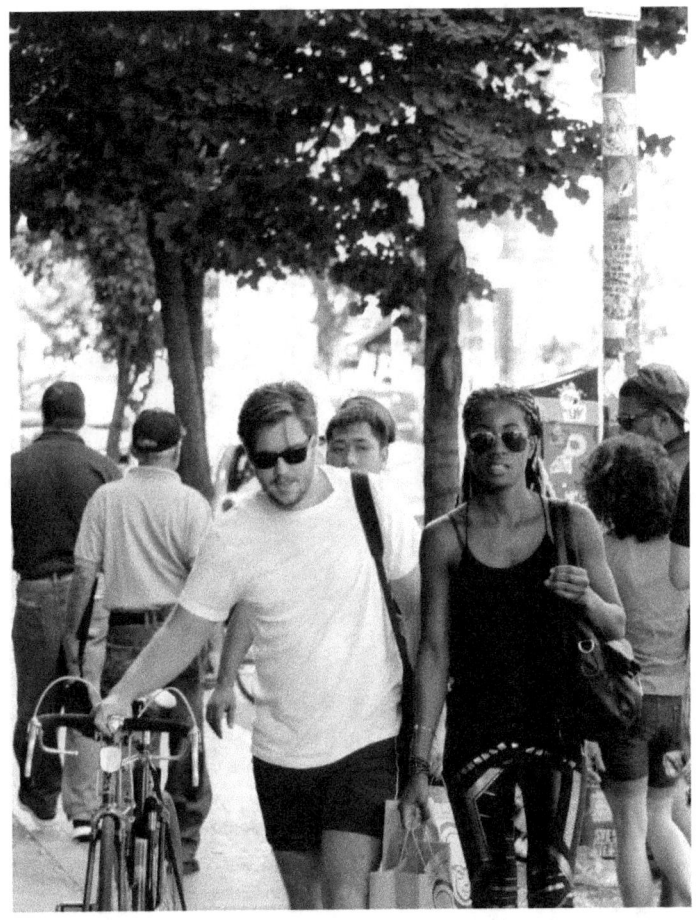

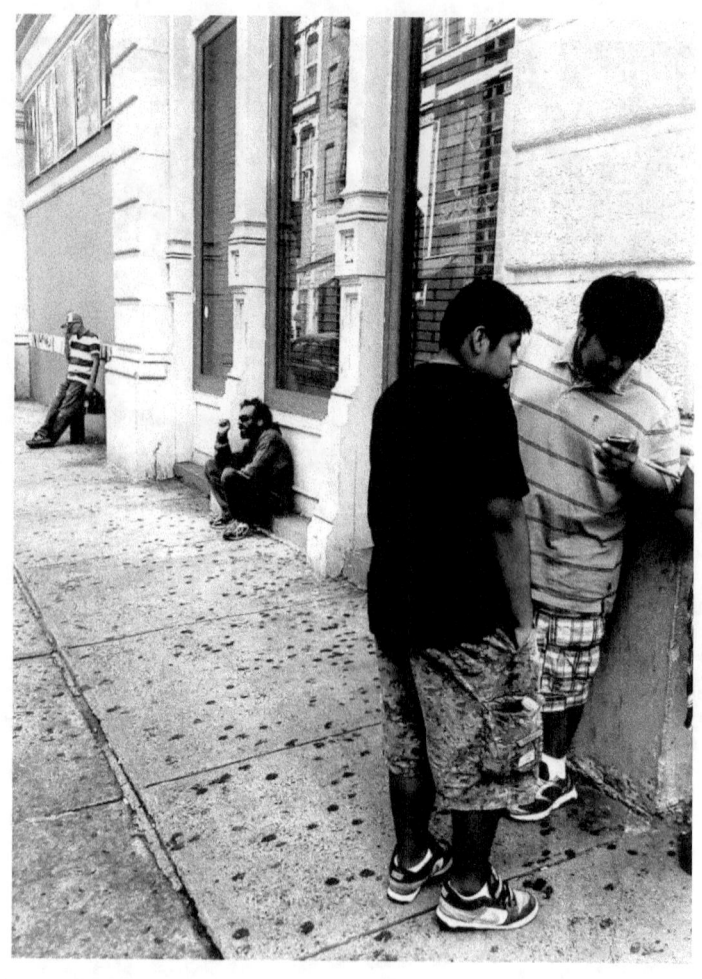

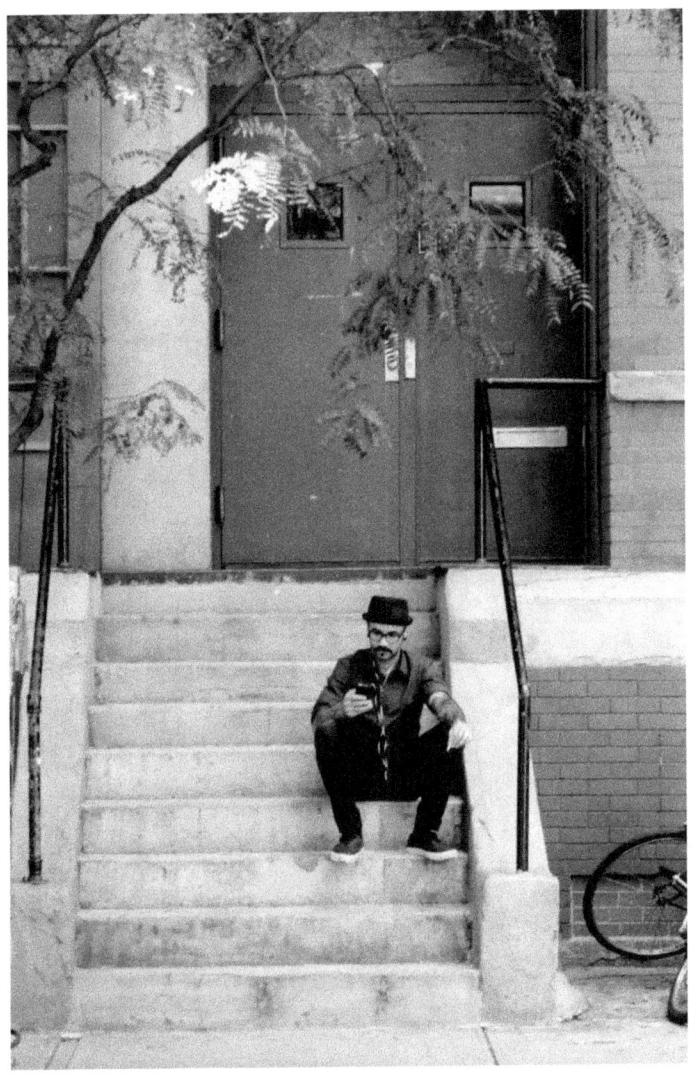

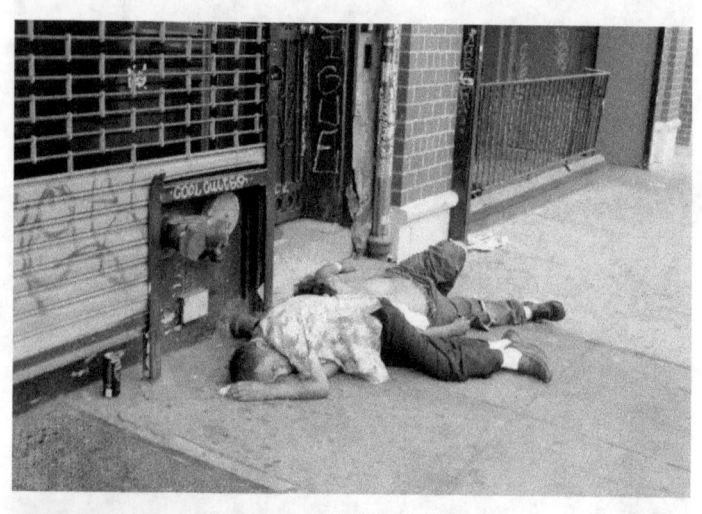

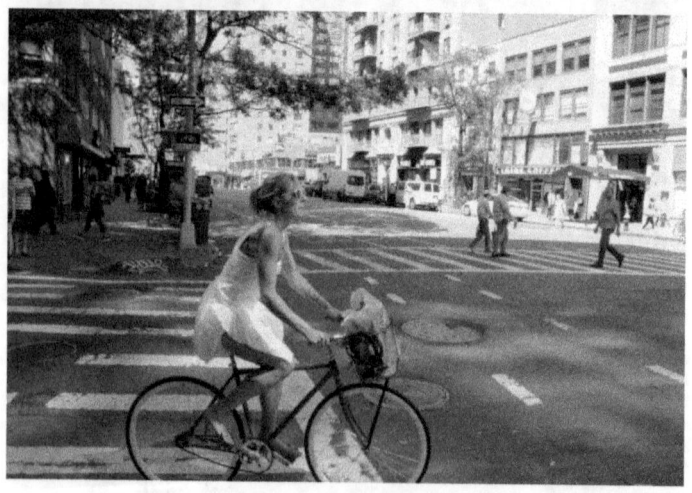

154

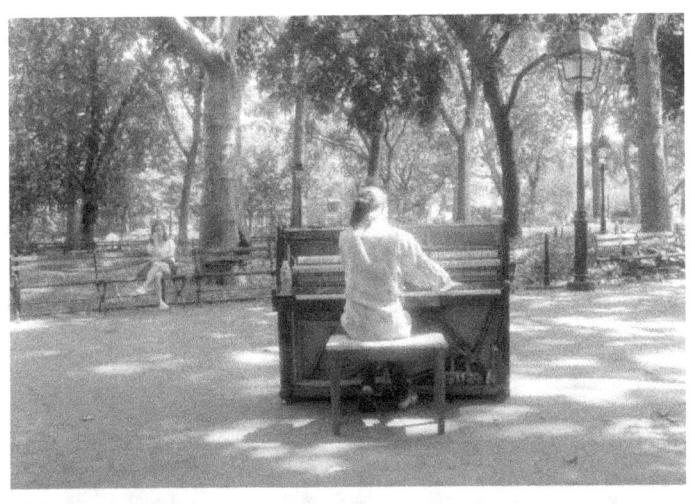

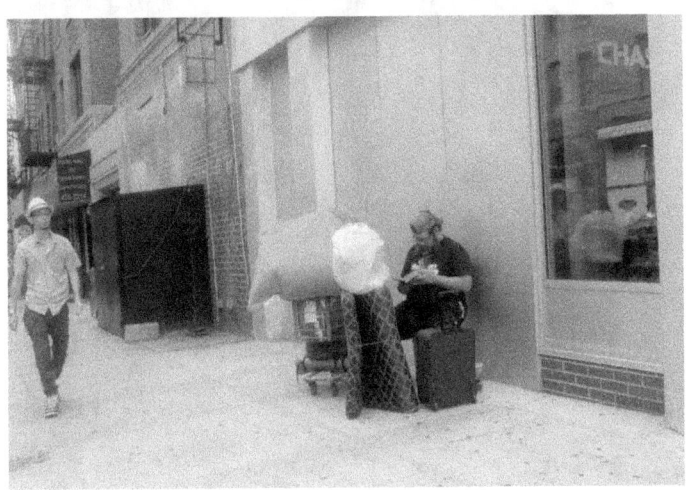

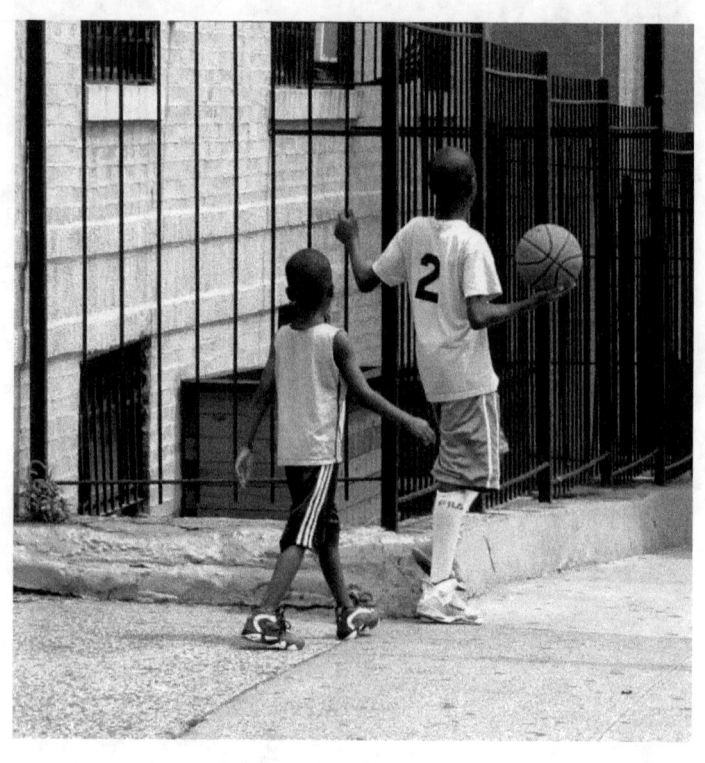

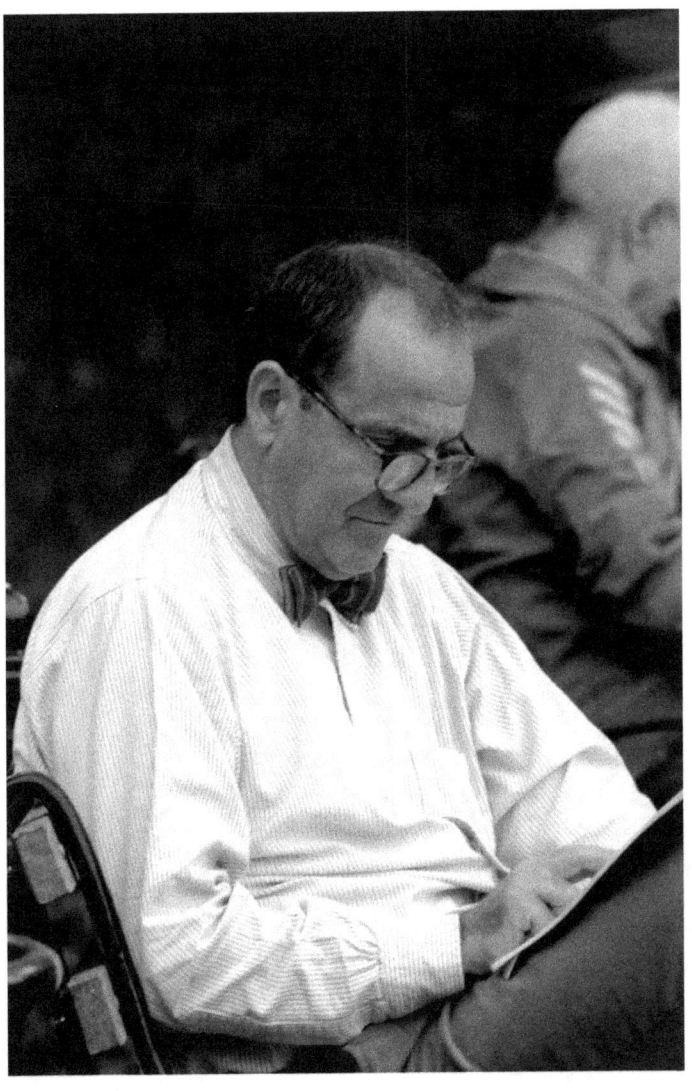

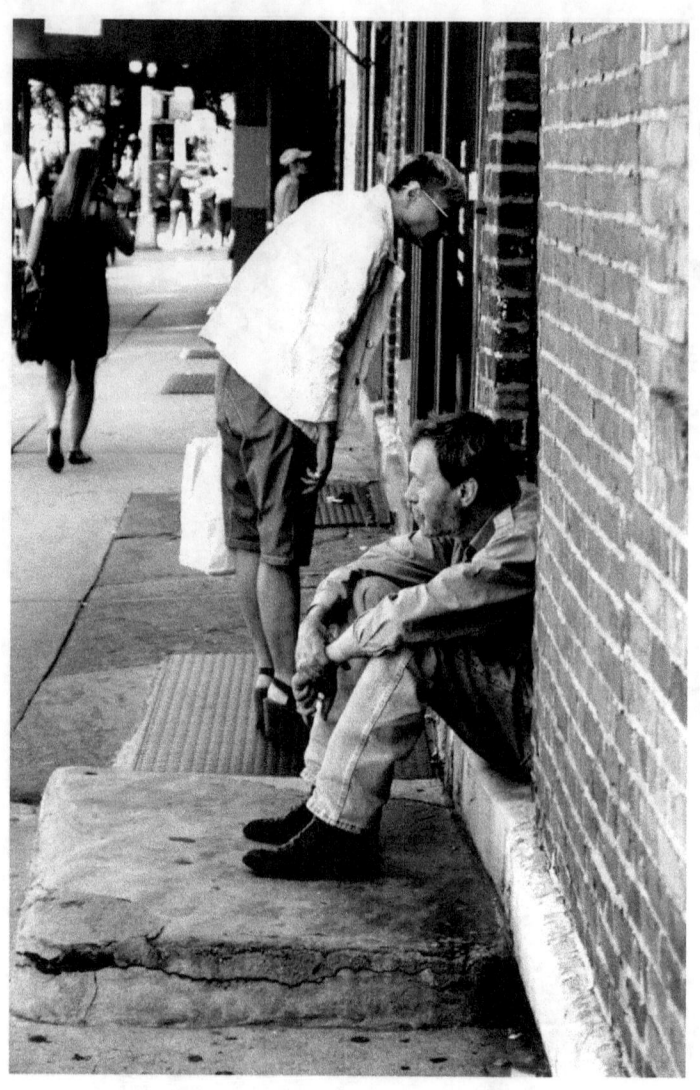

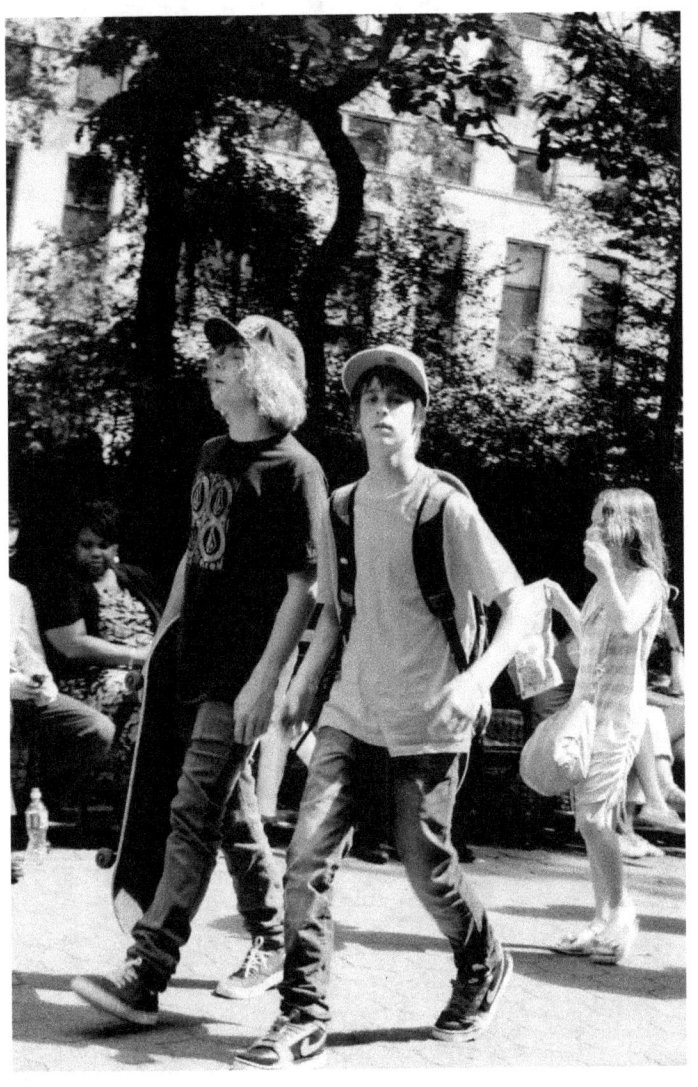

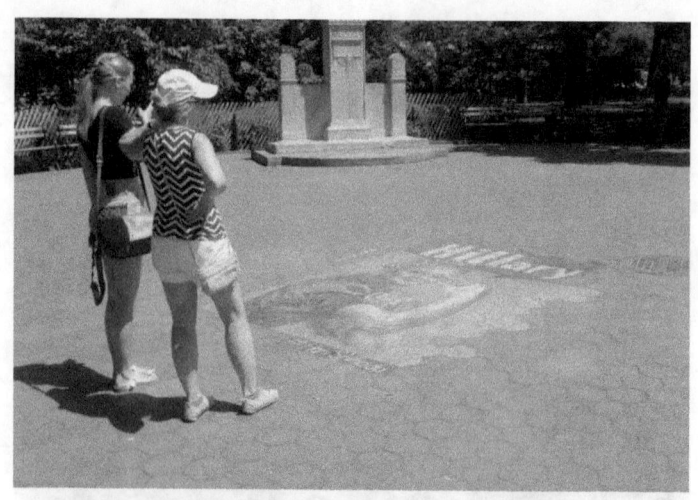

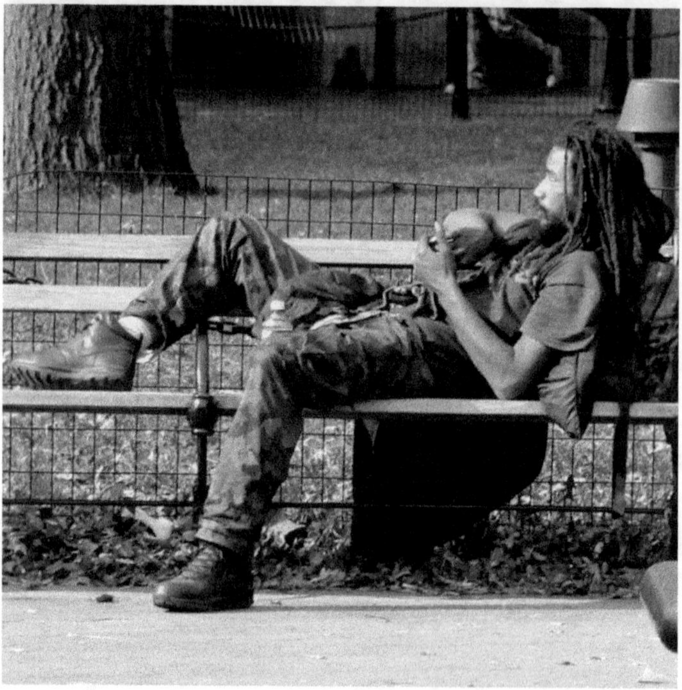

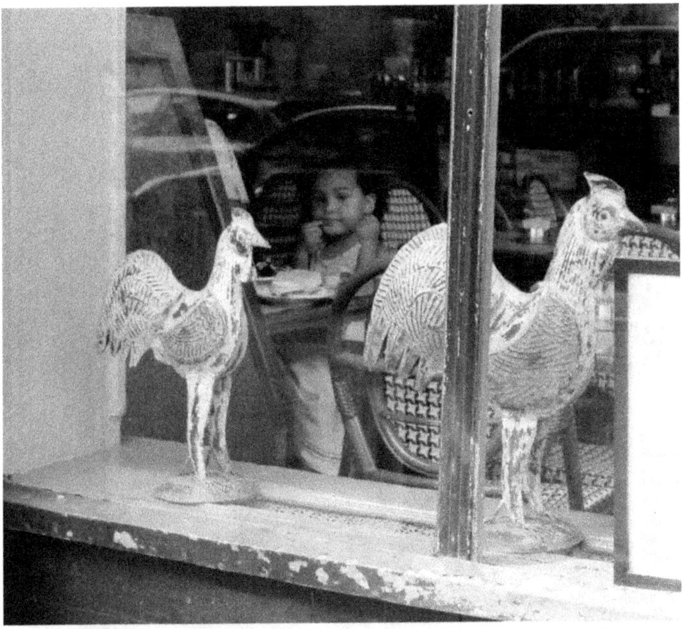

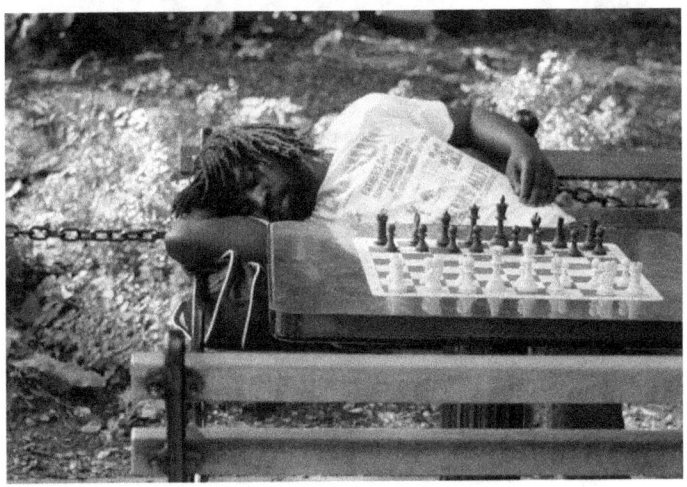

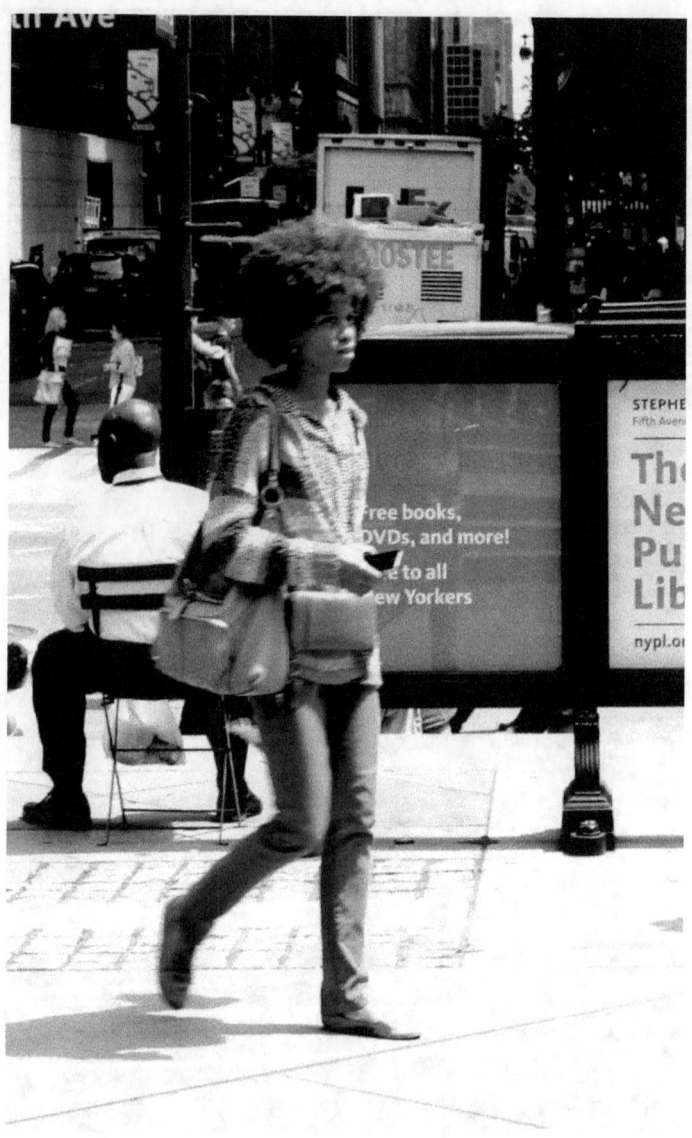

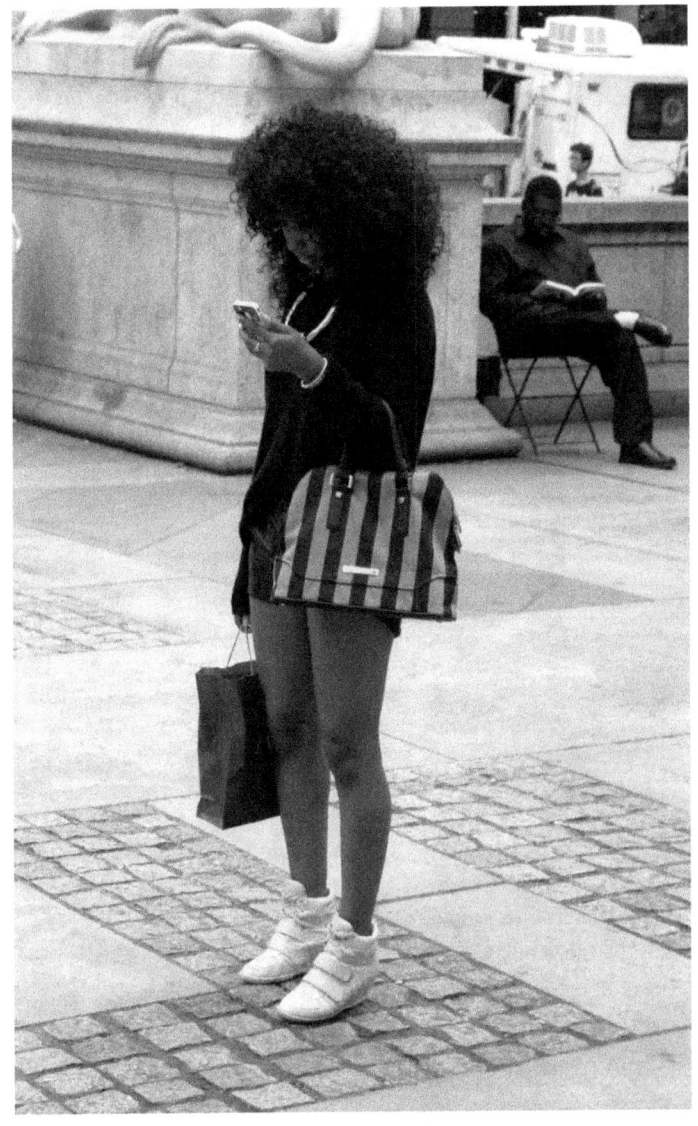

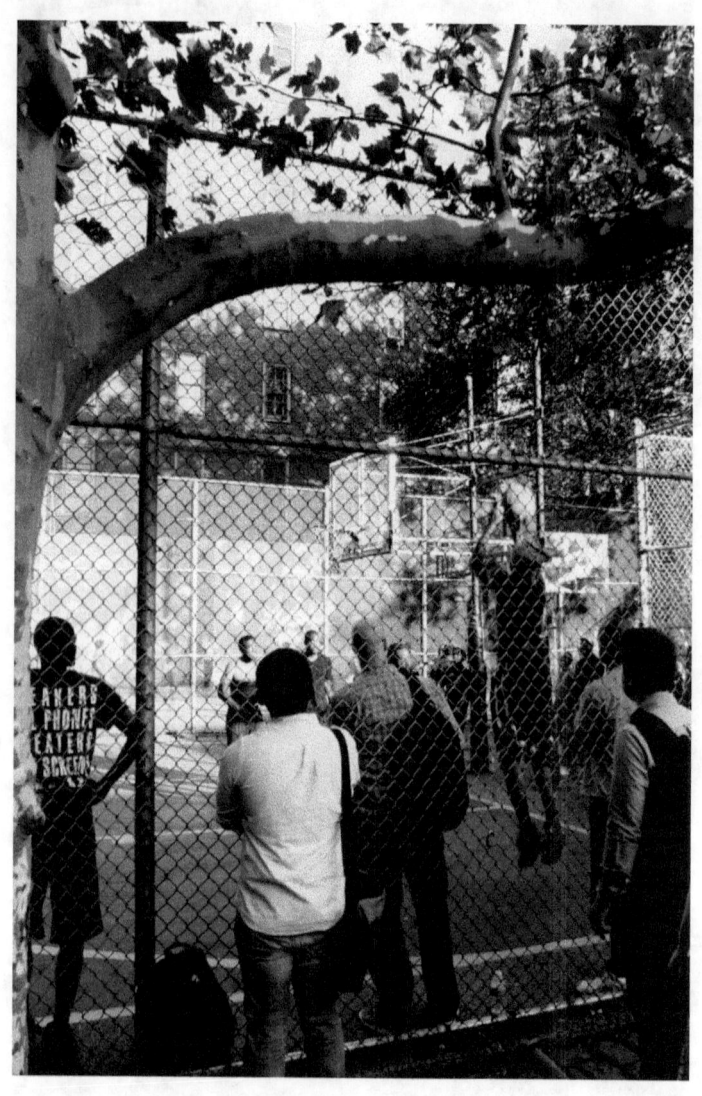

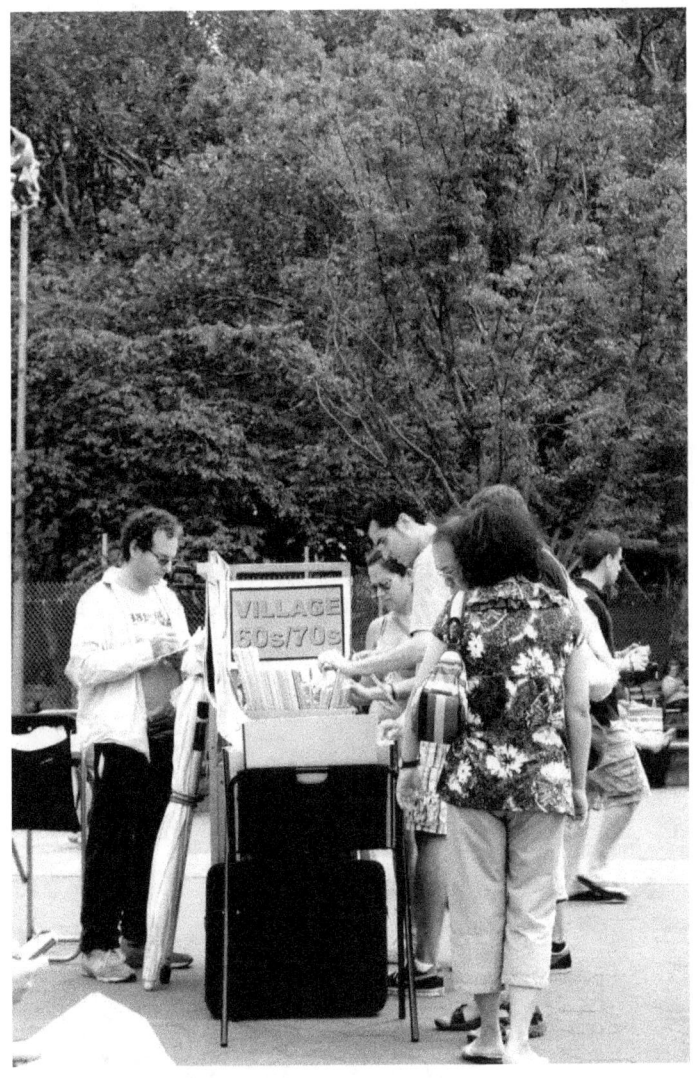

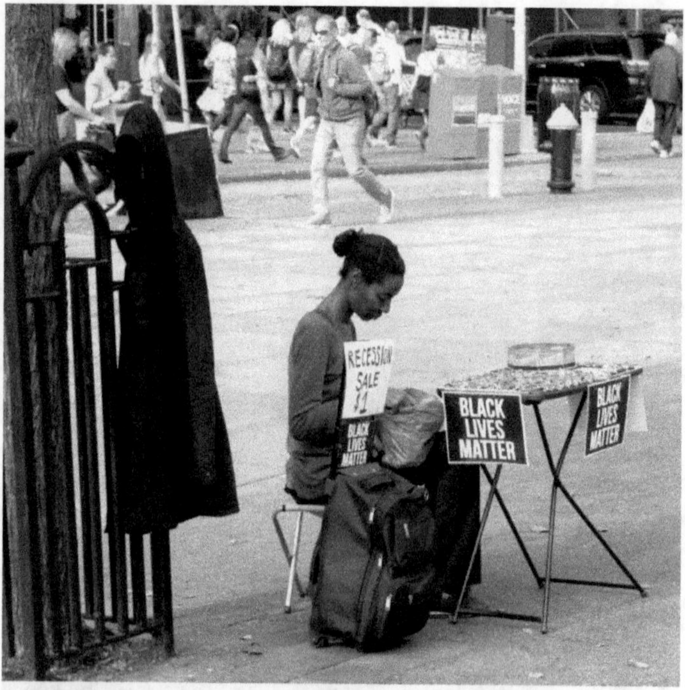

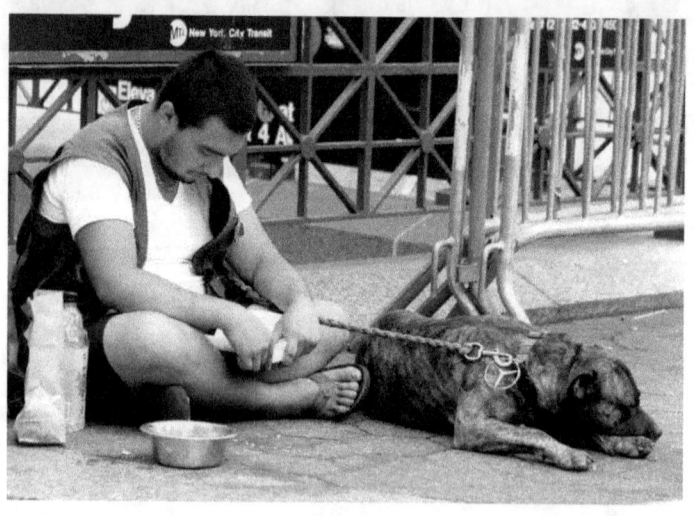

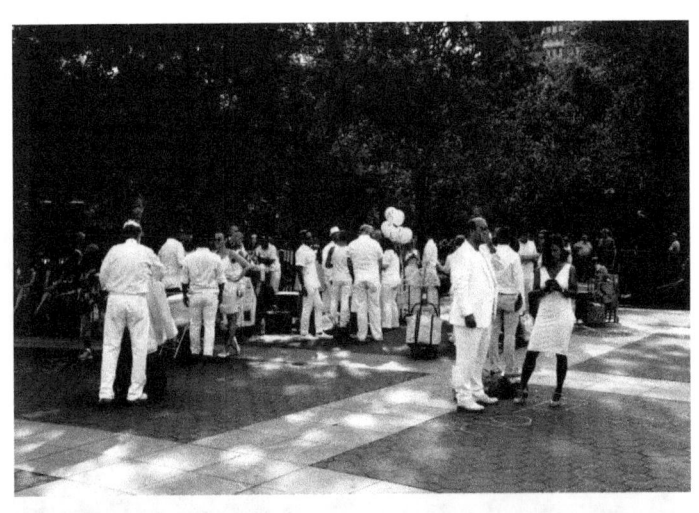

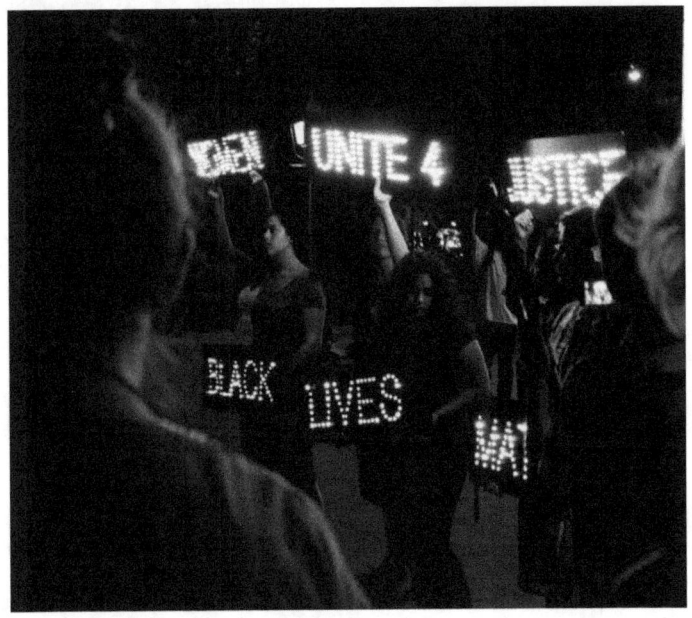

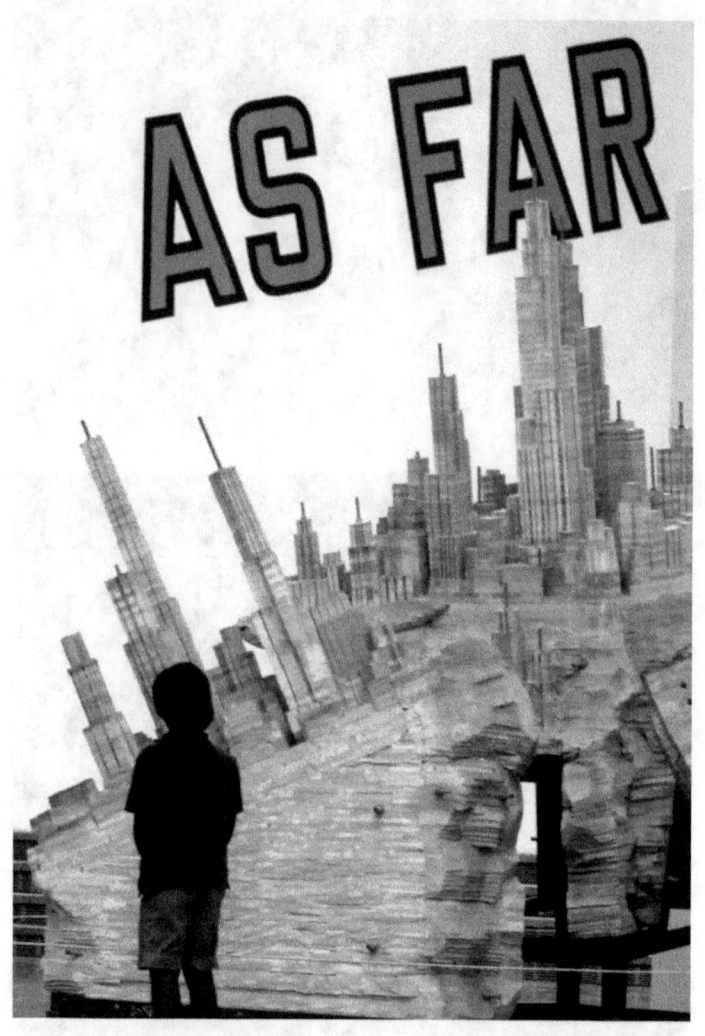

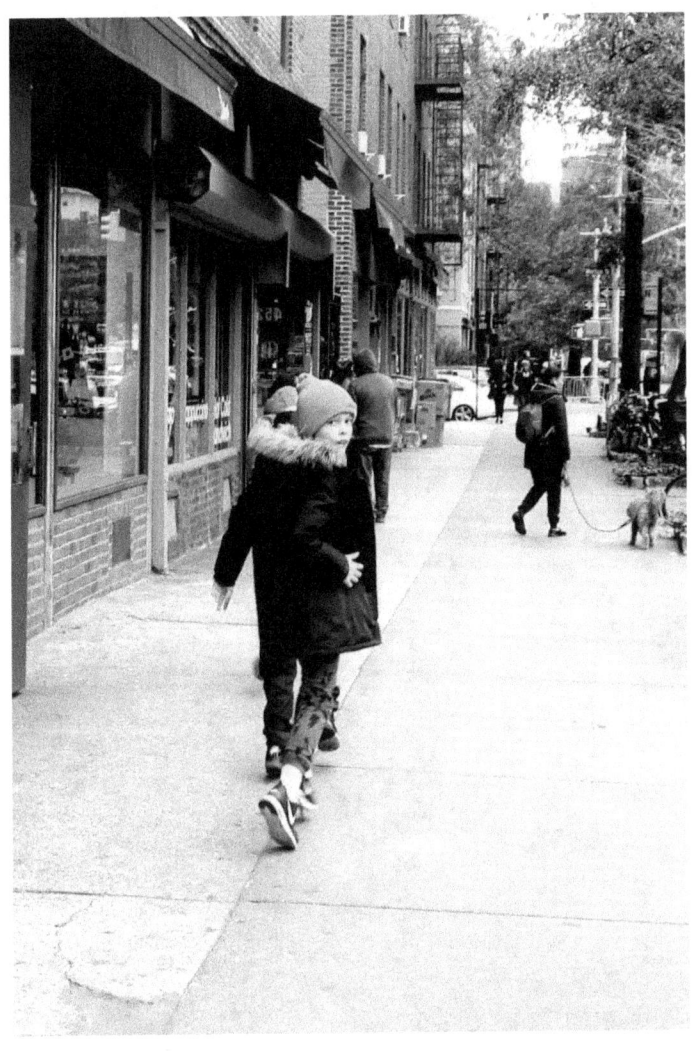

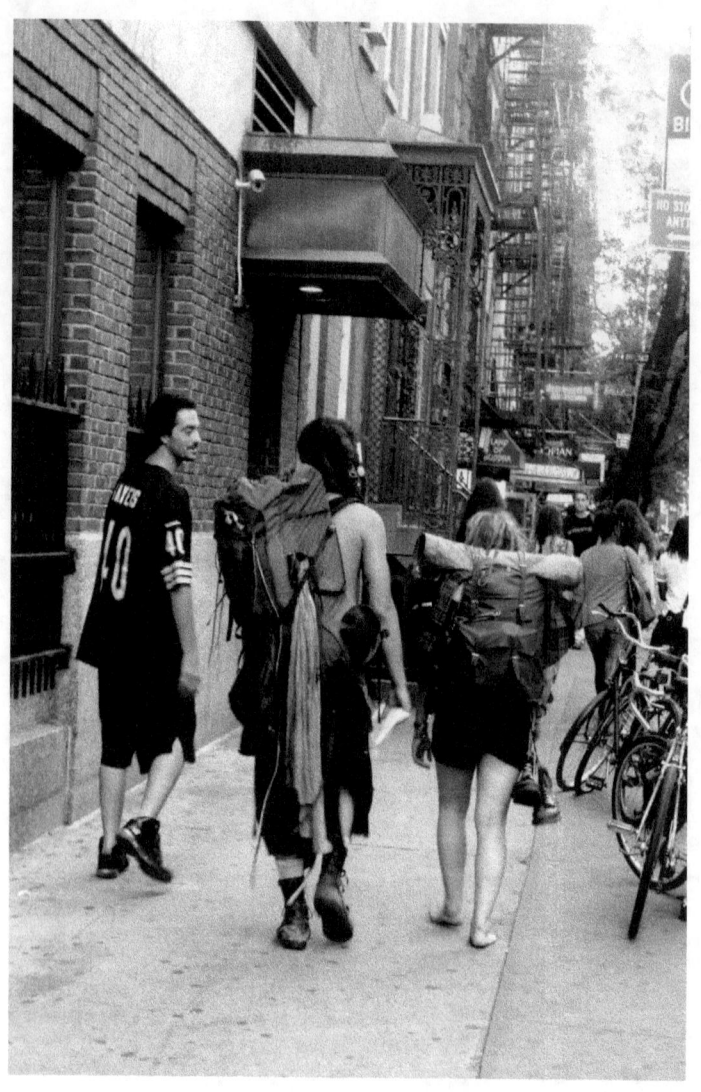

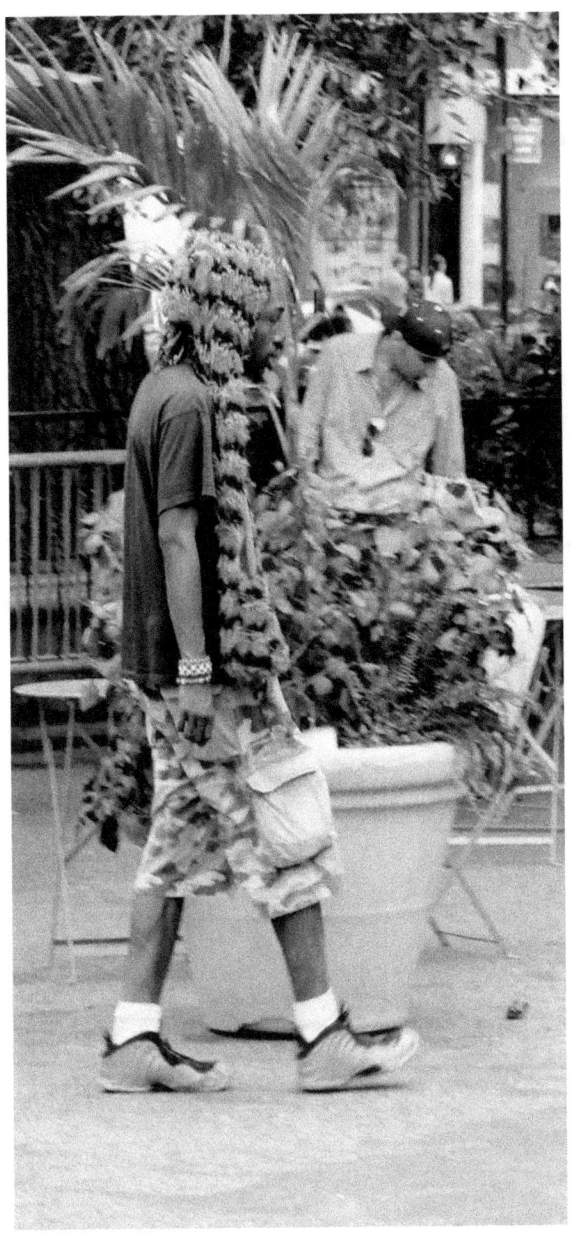

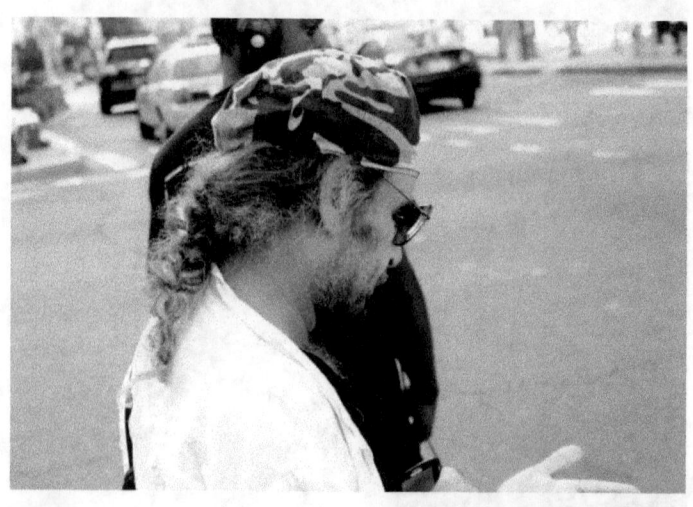

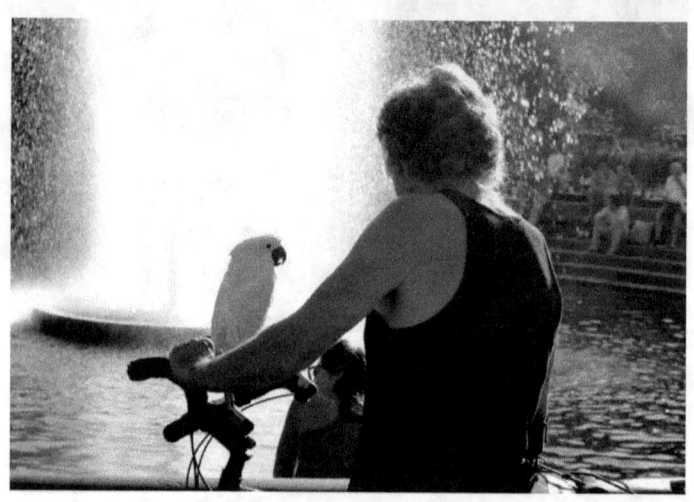

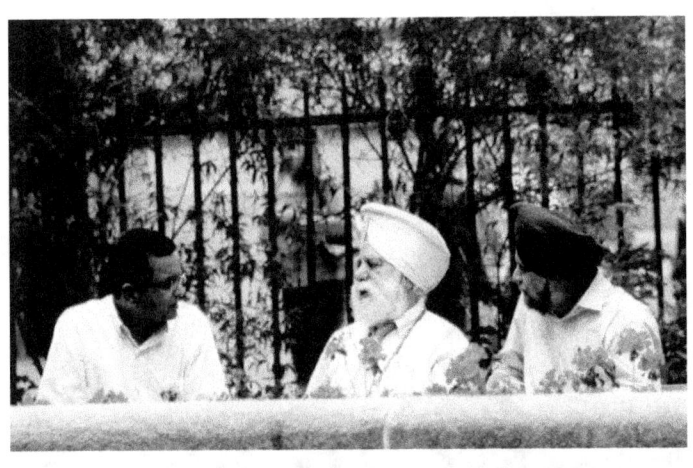

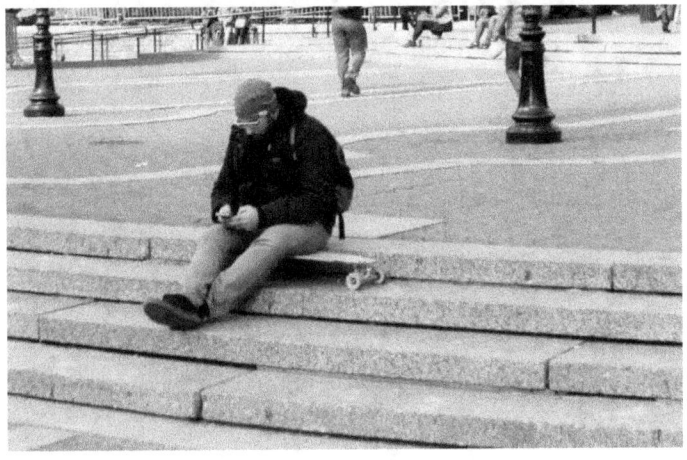

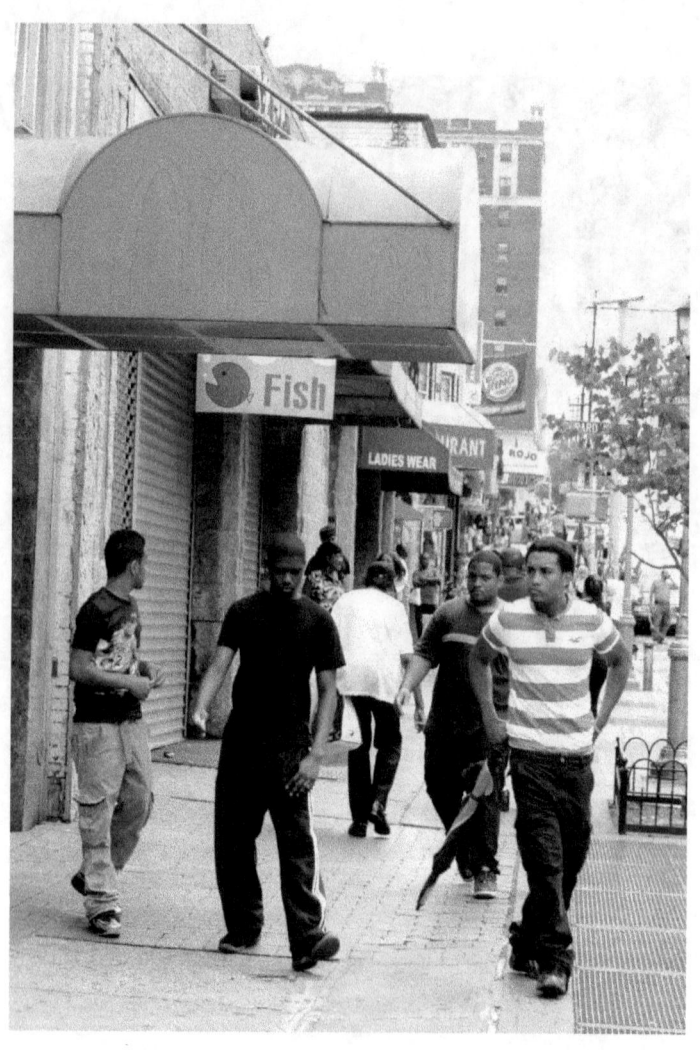

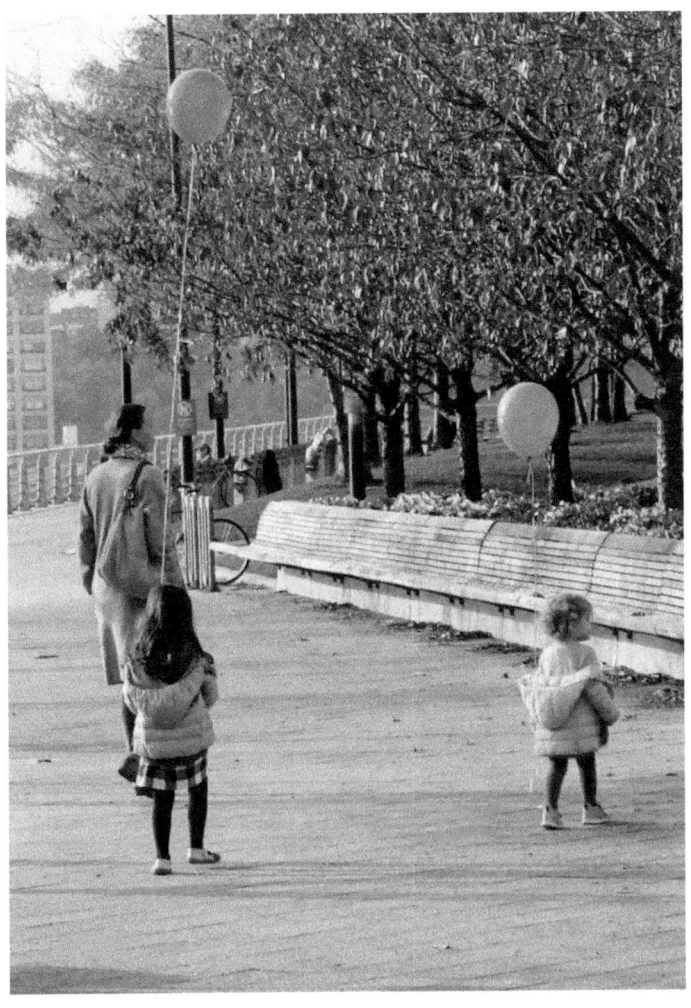

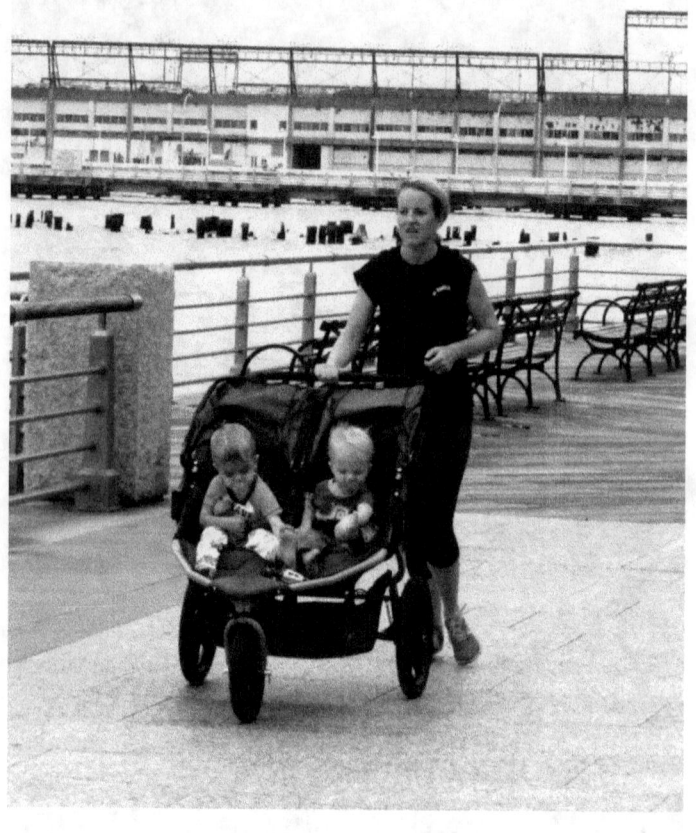

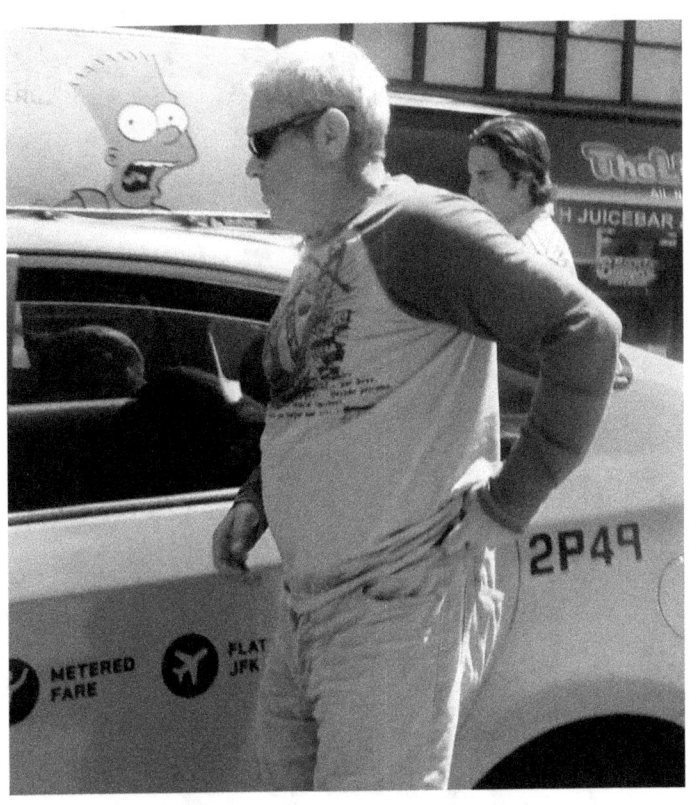

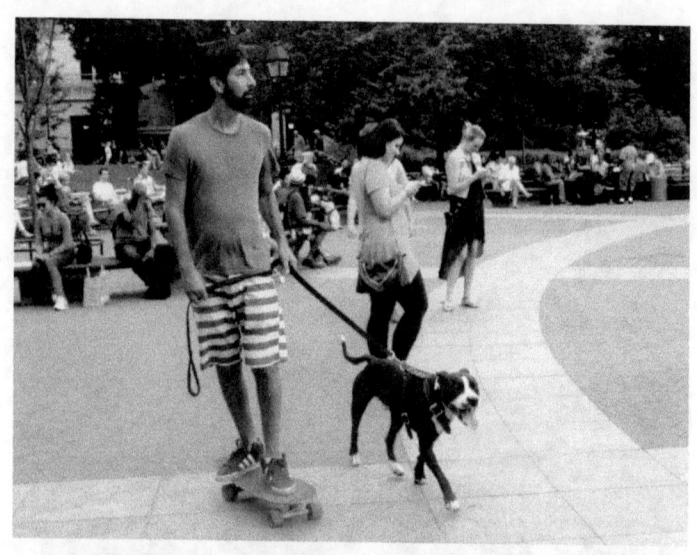

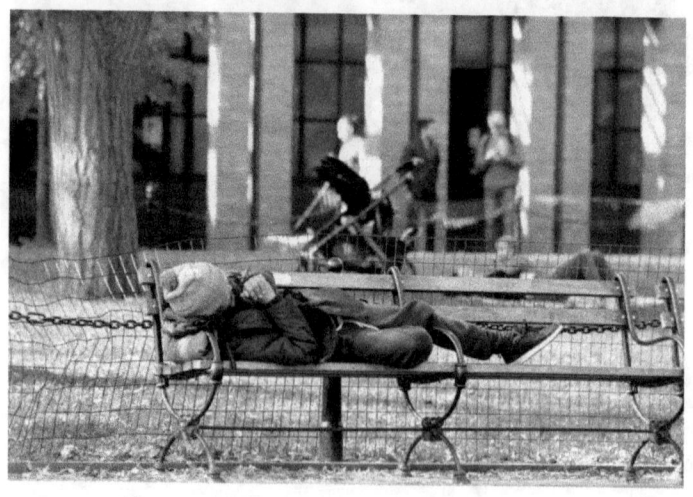

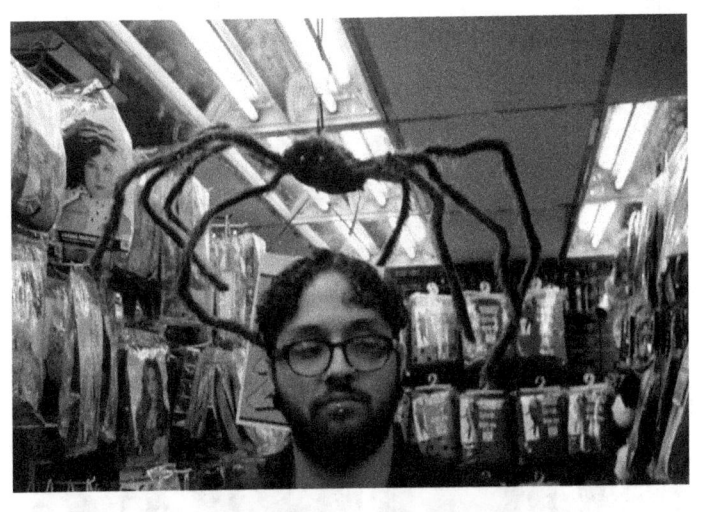

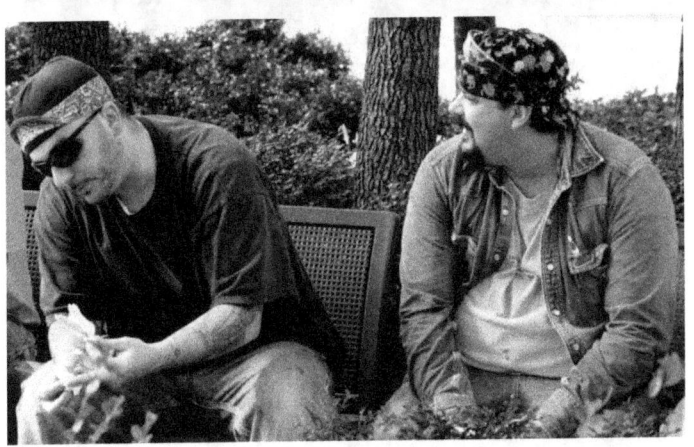

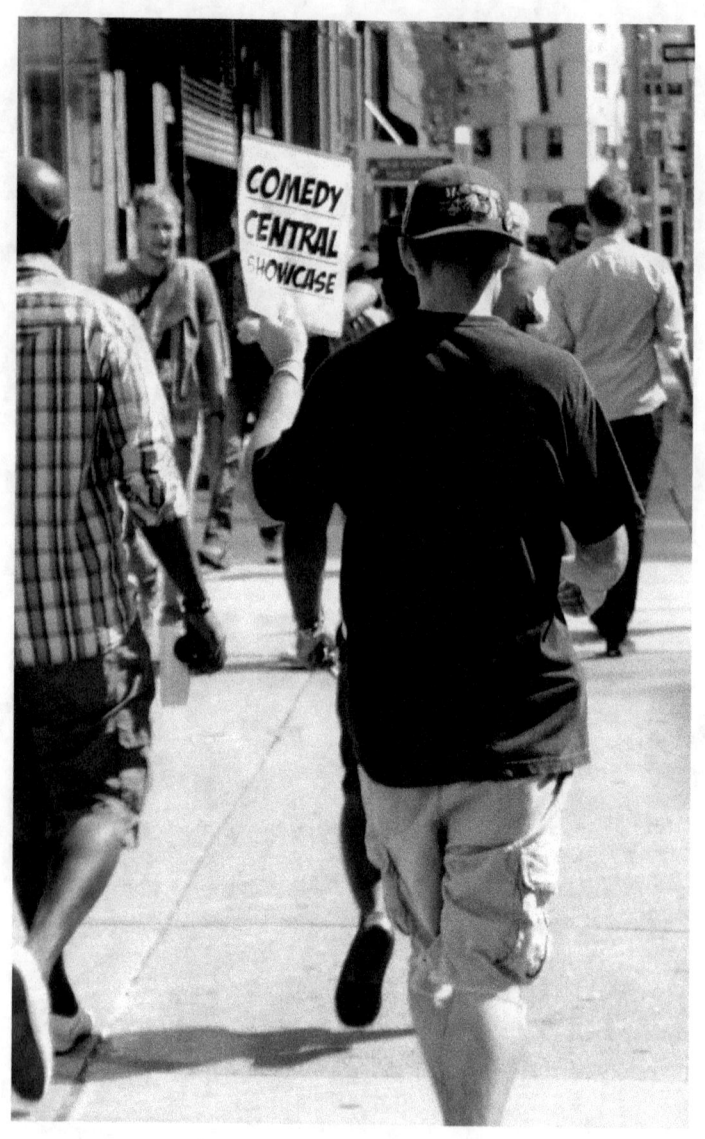

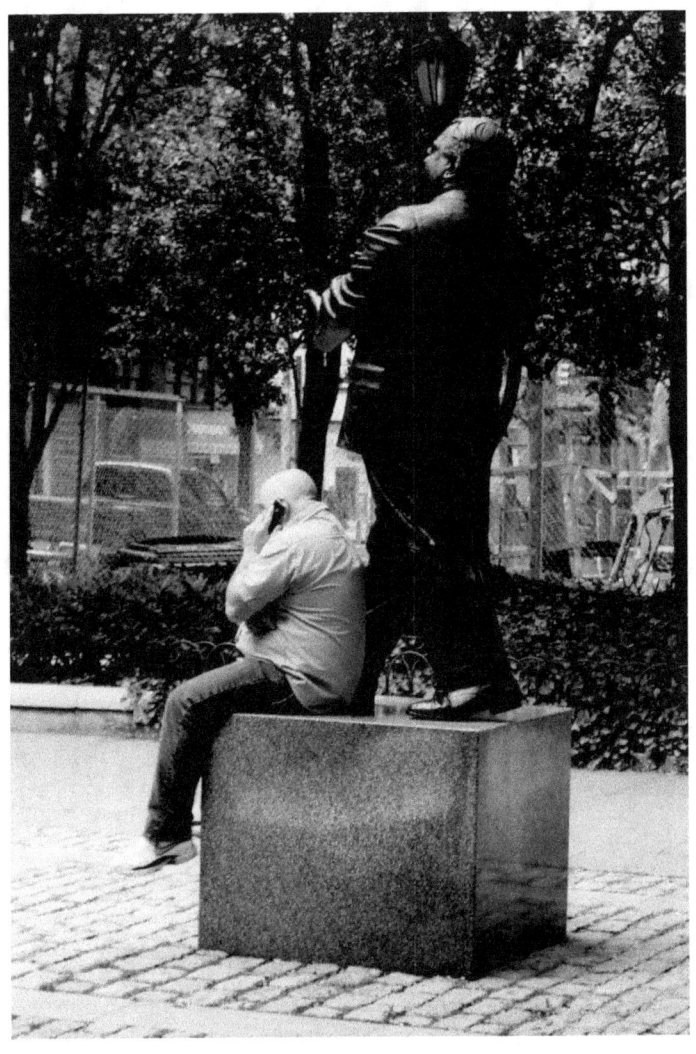

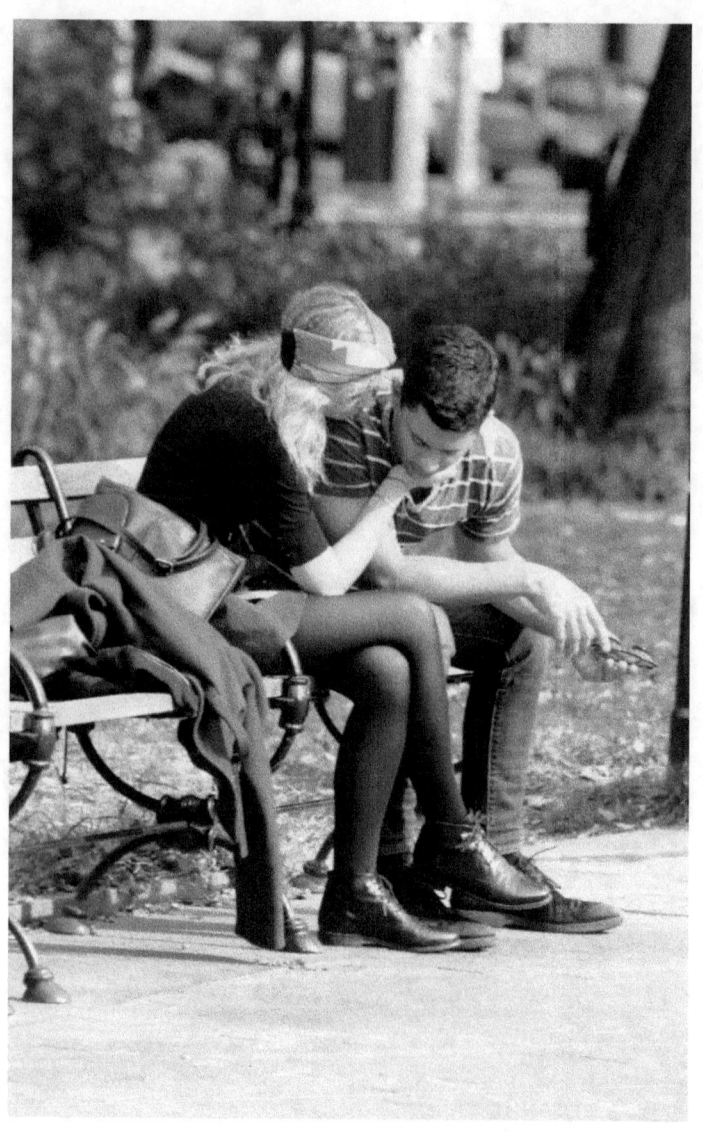

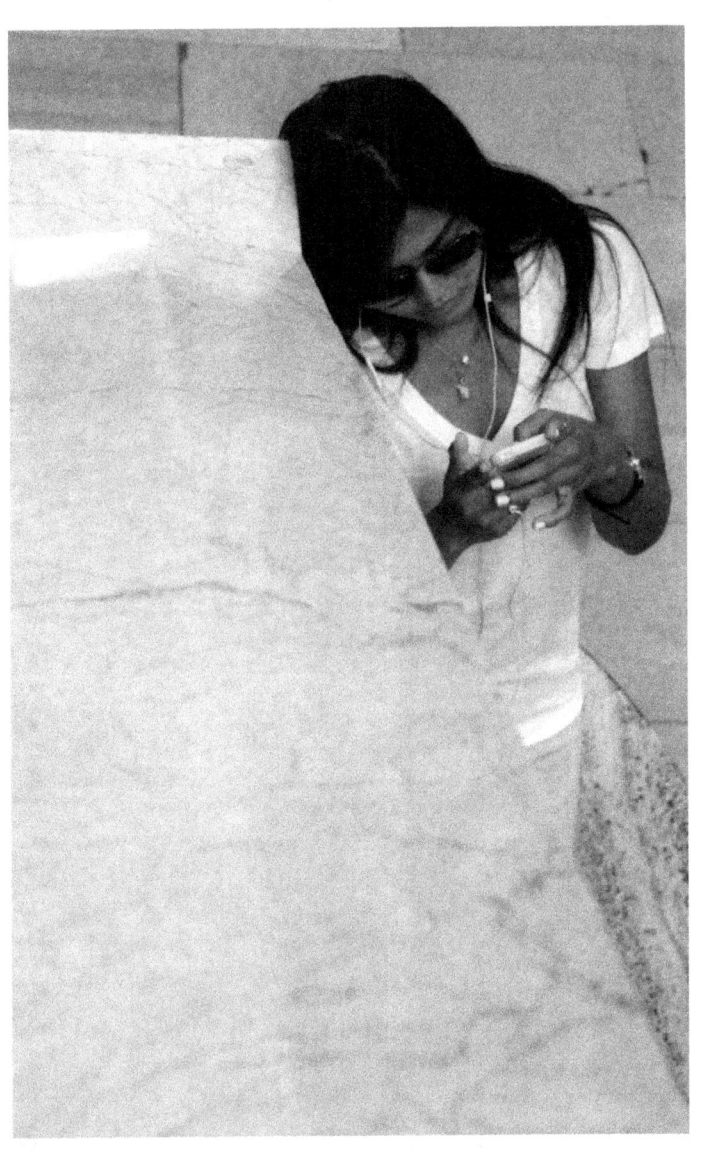

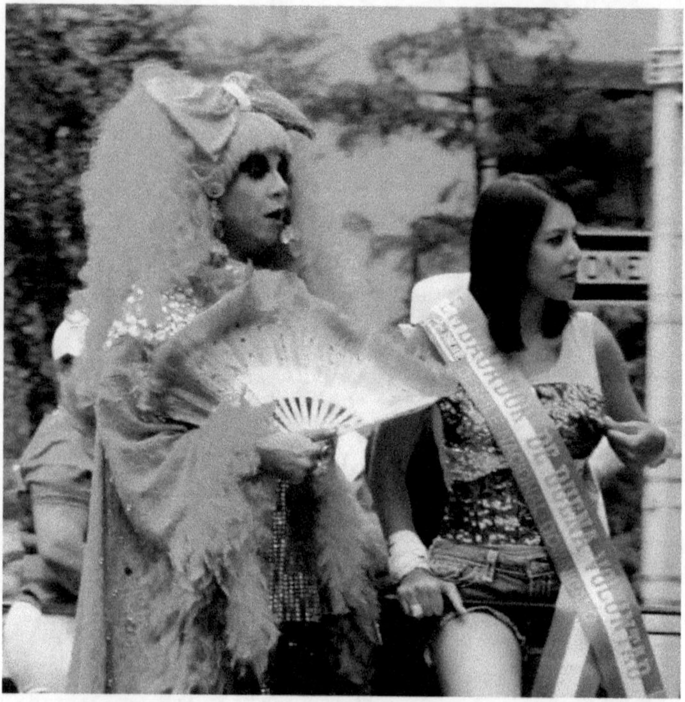

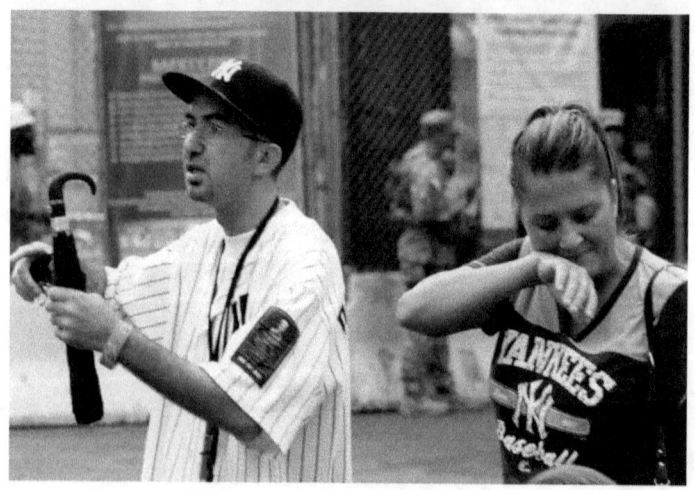

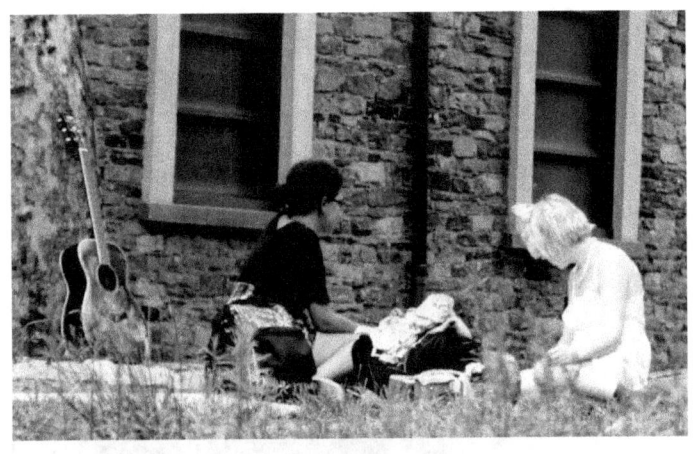

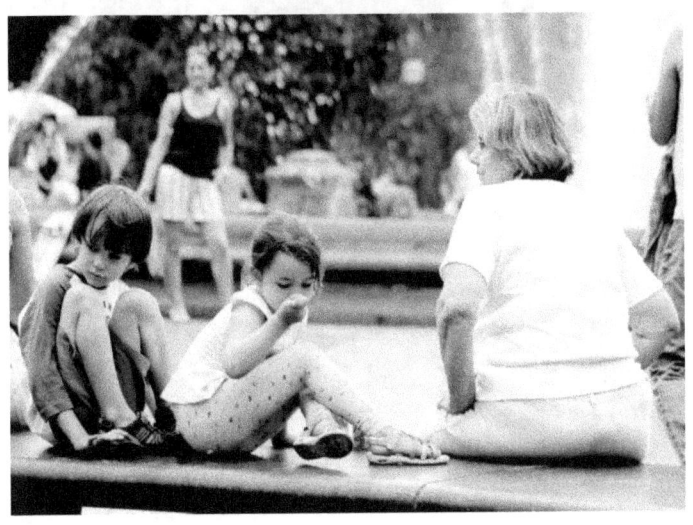

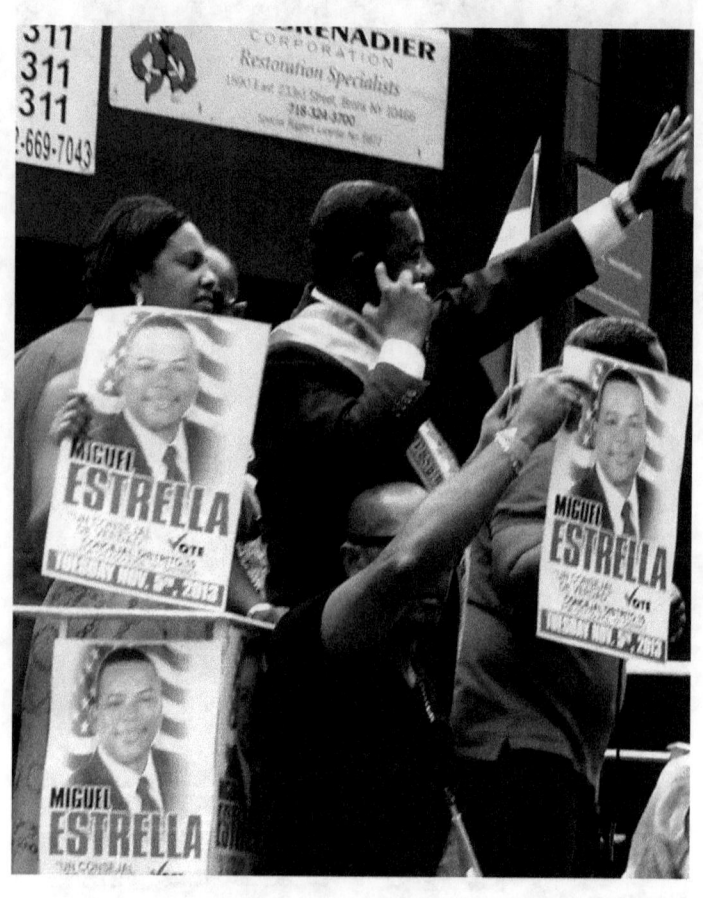

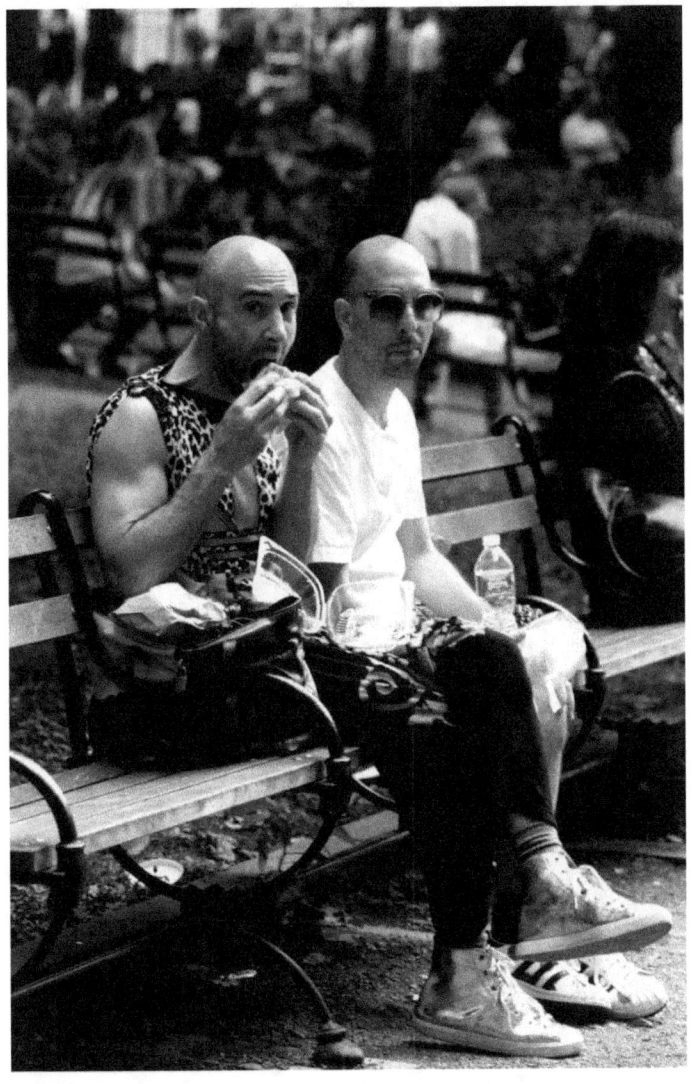

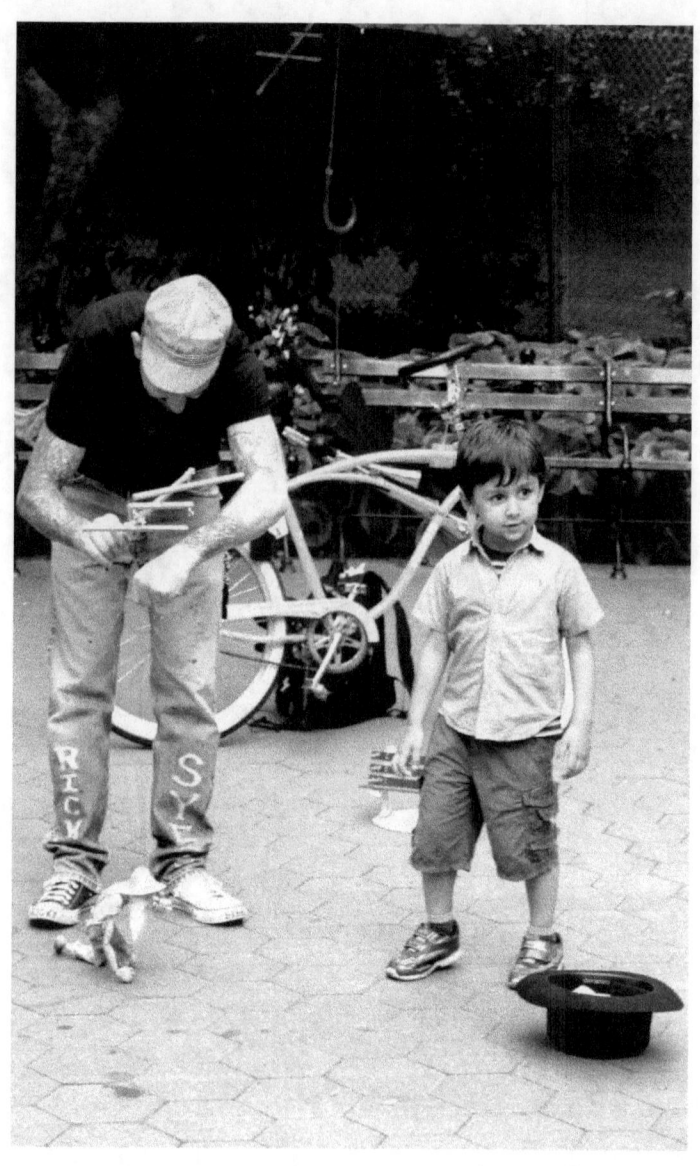

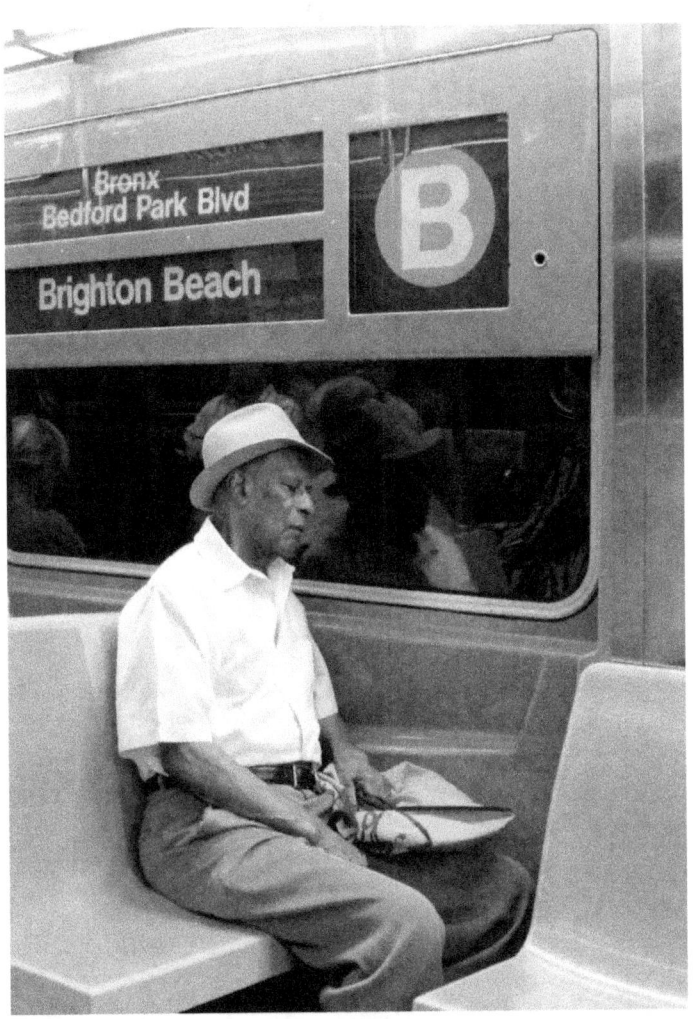

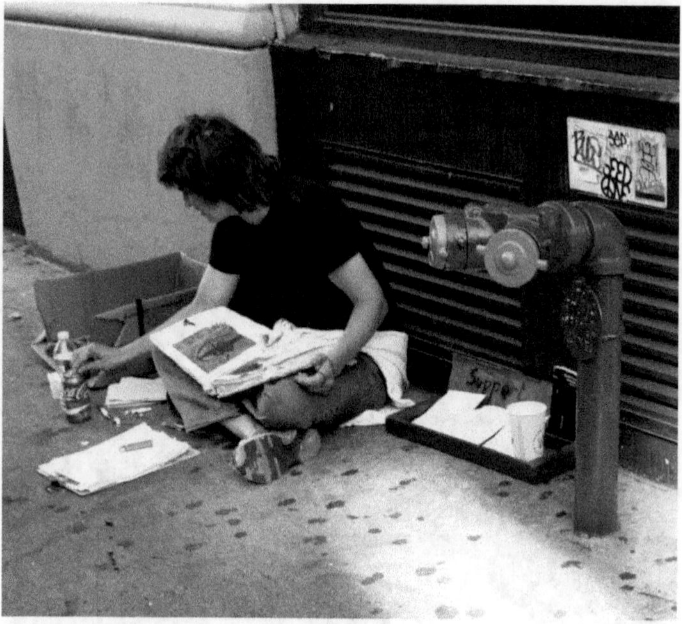

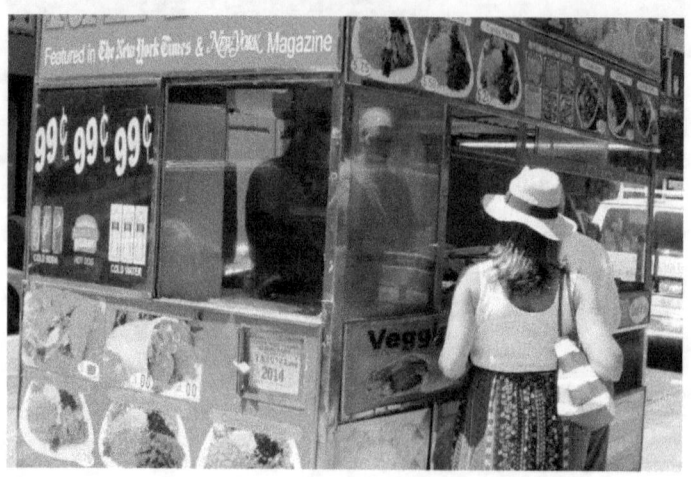

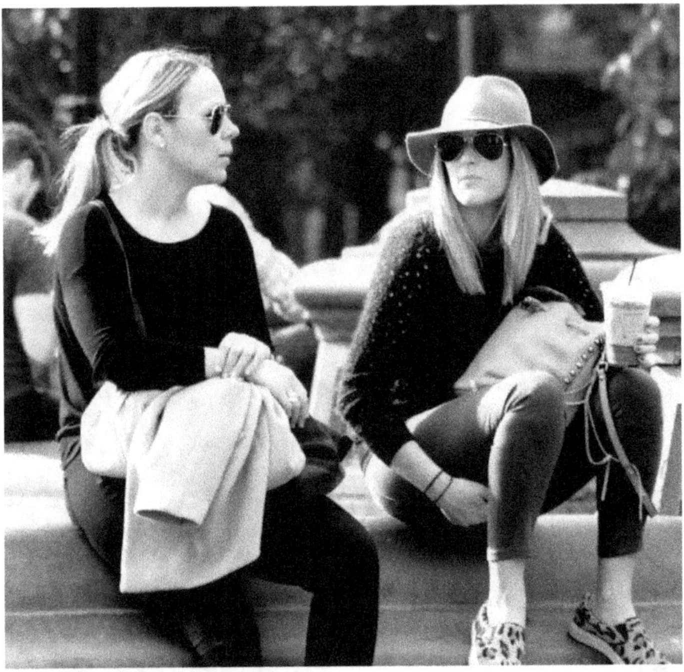

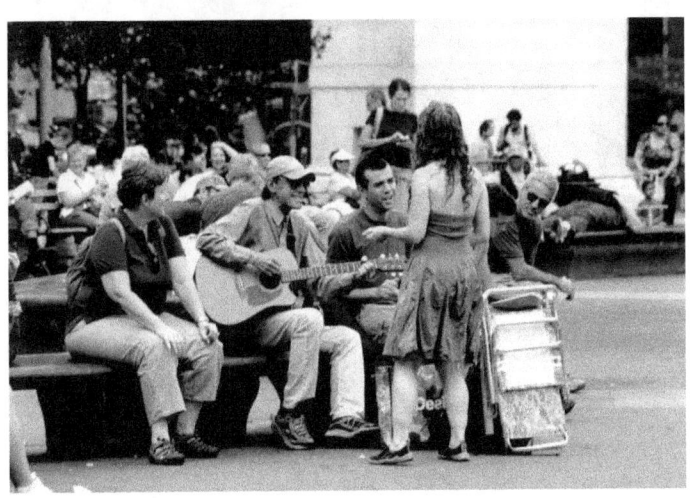

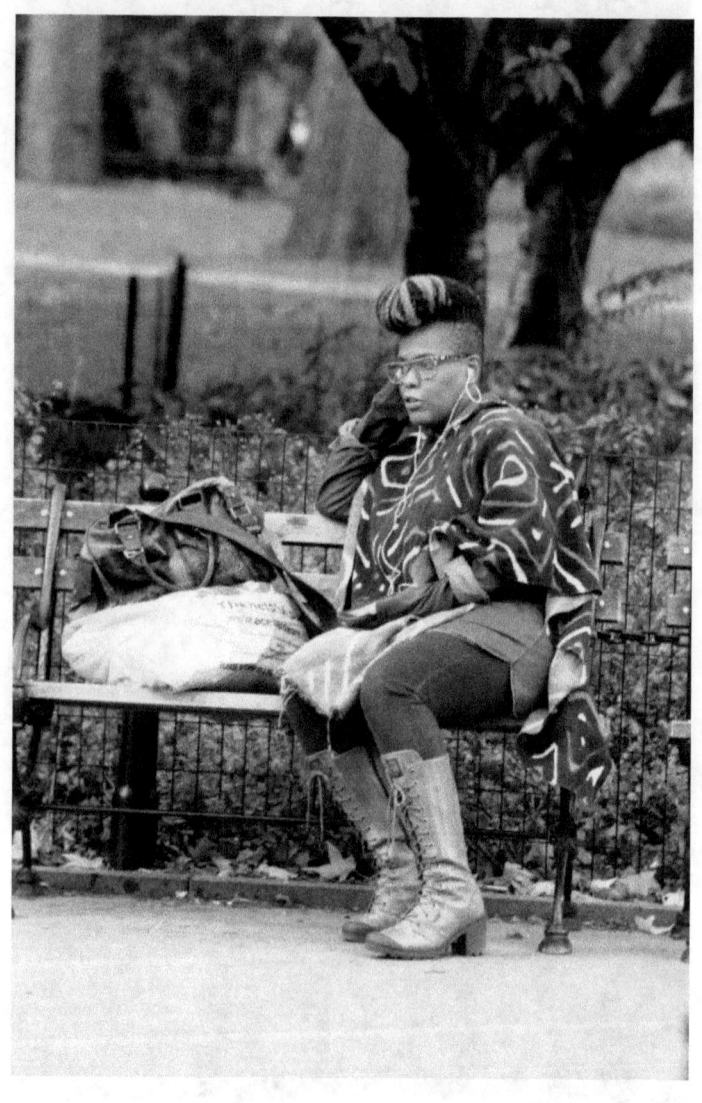

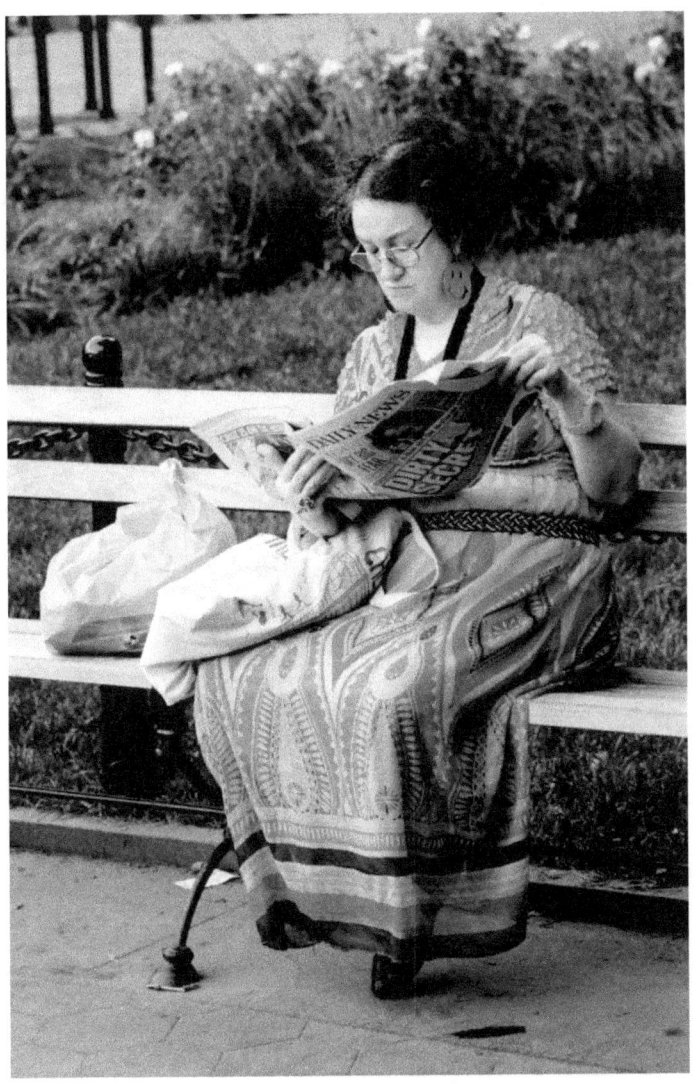

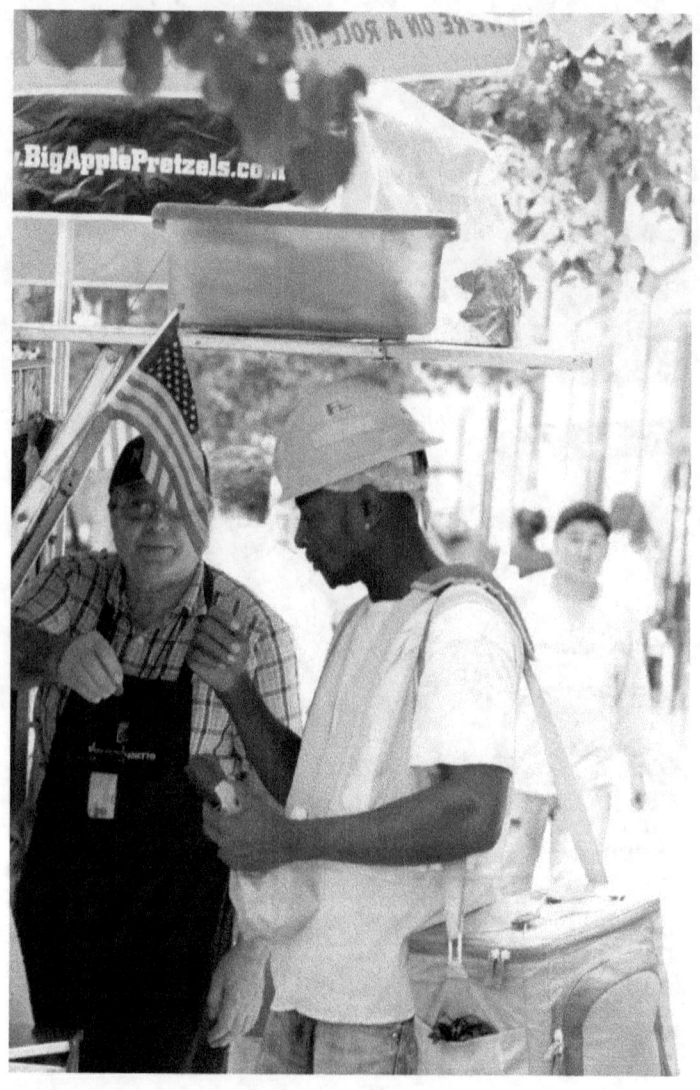

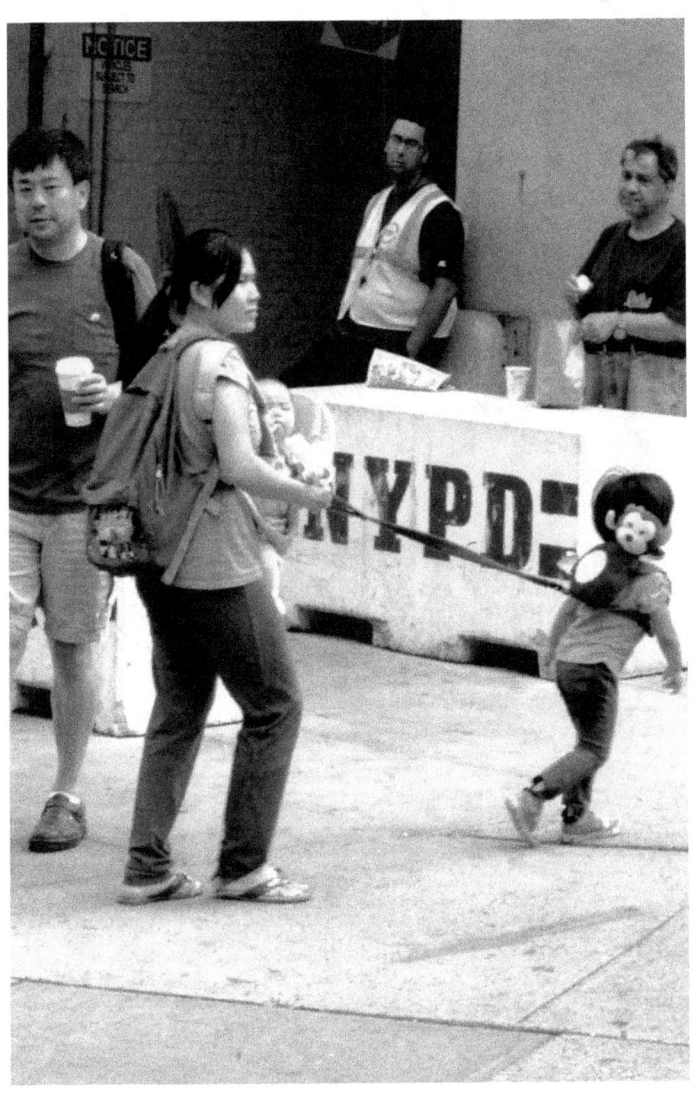

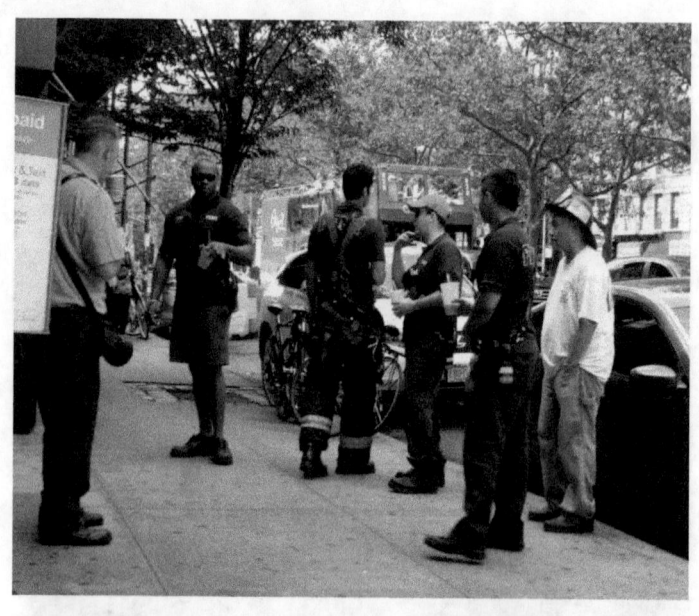

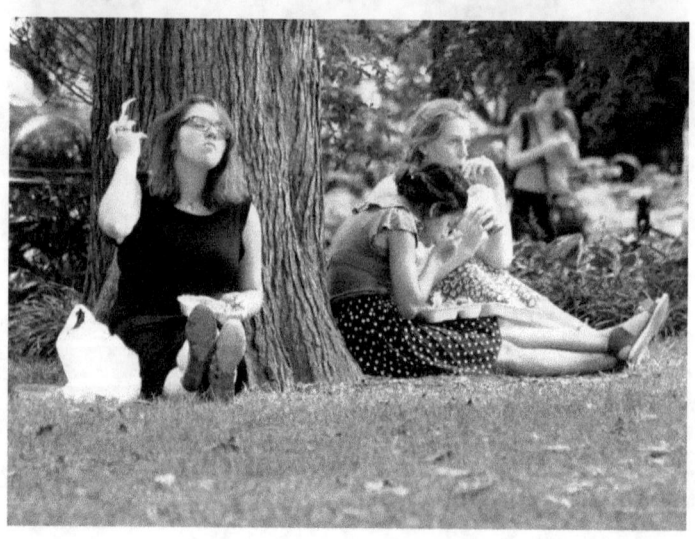

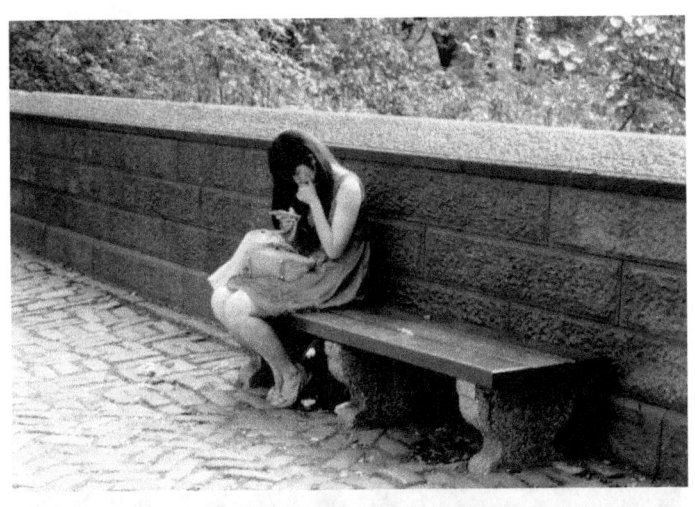

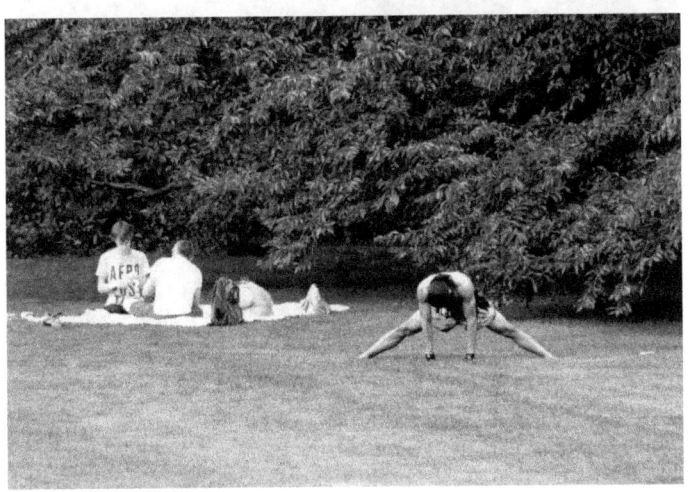

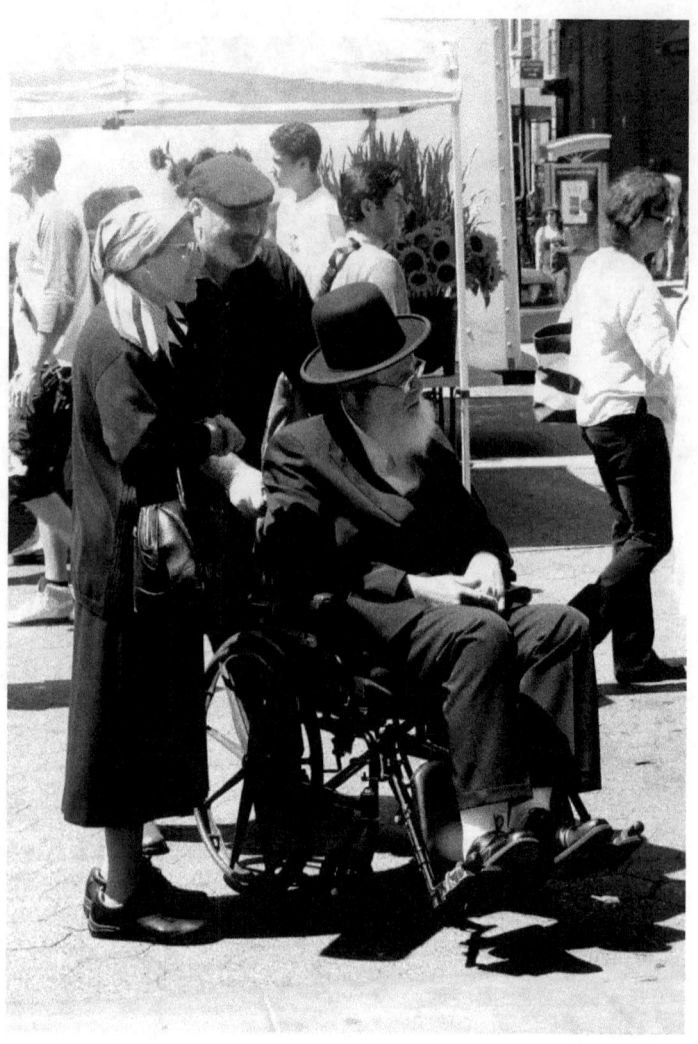

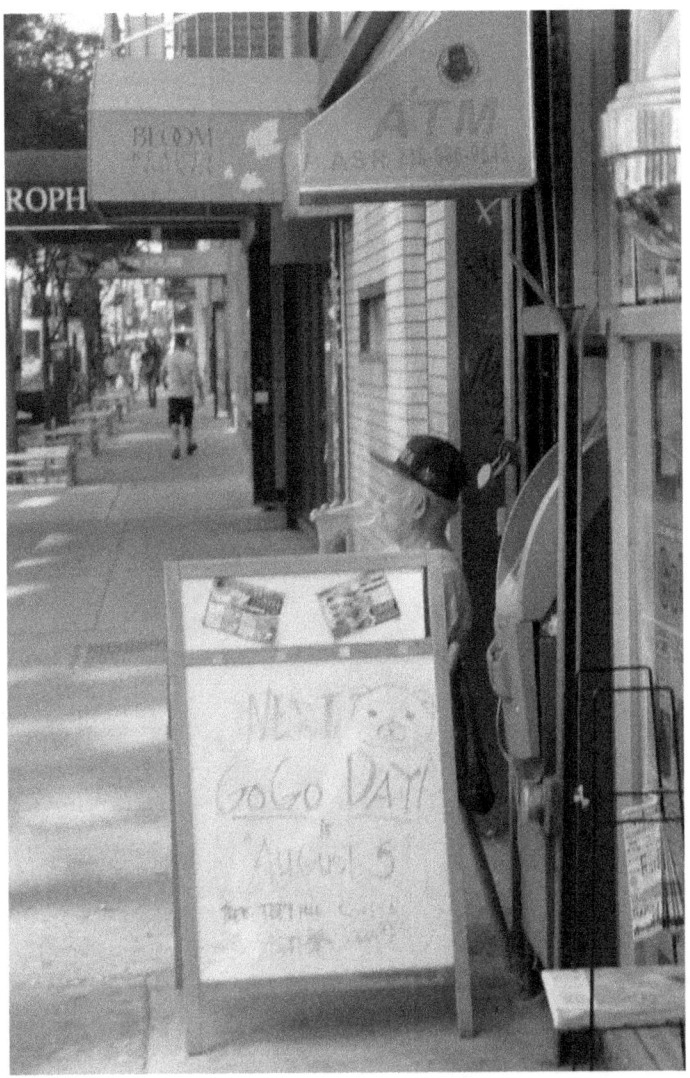

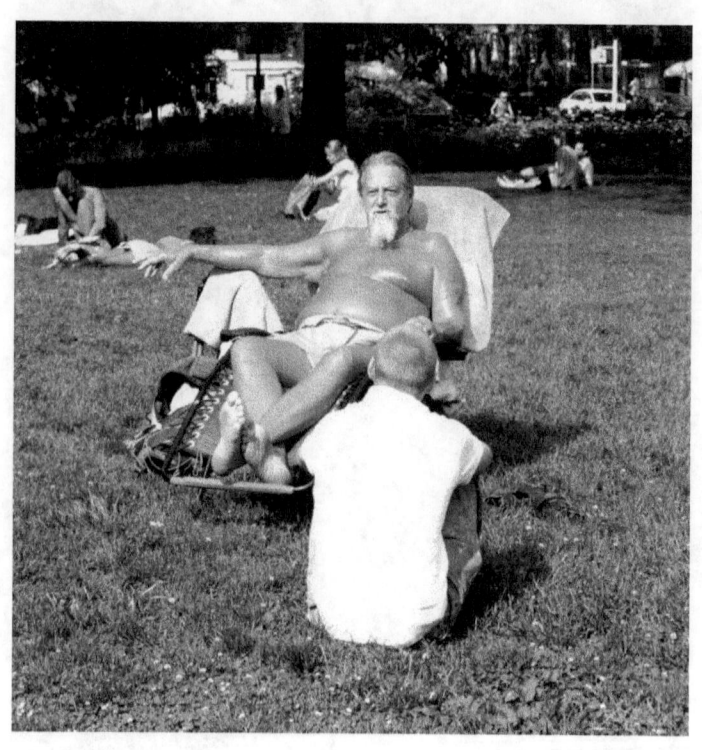

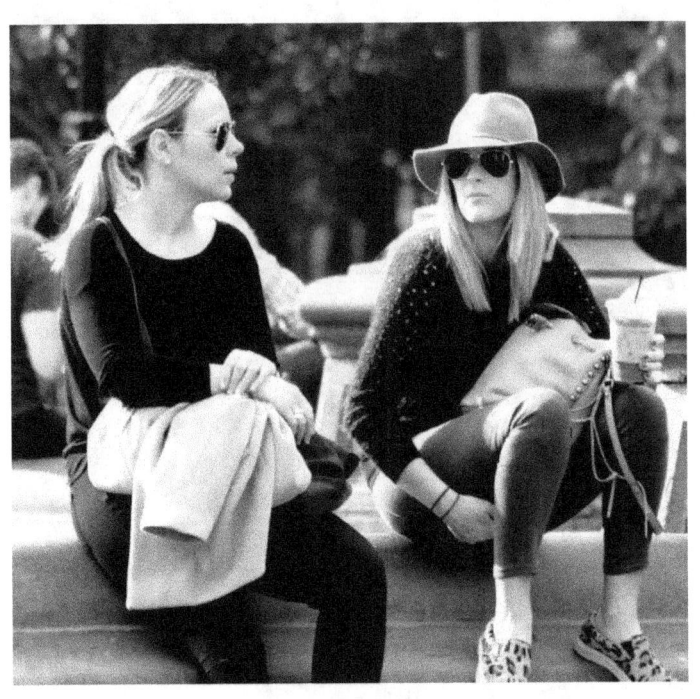

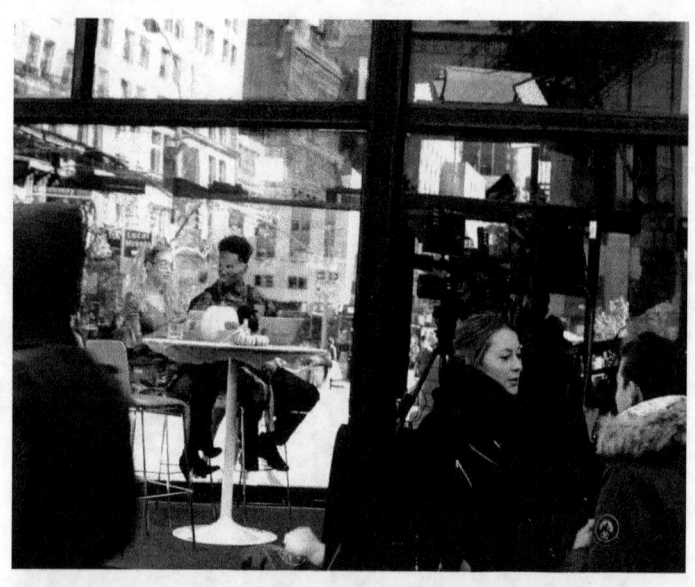

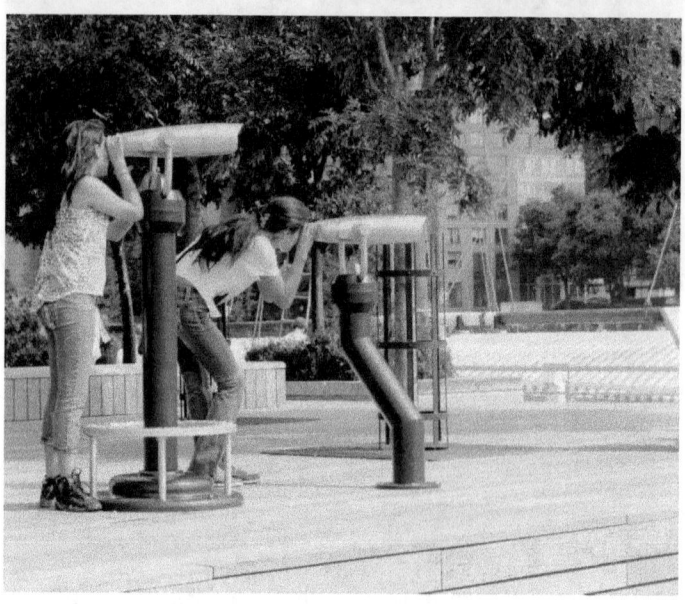

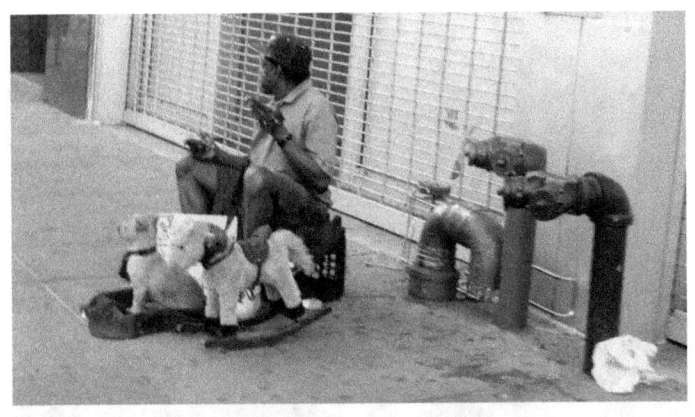

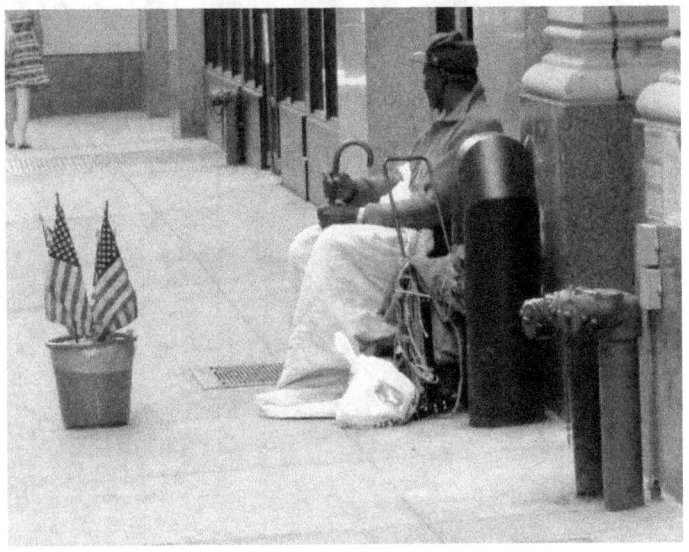

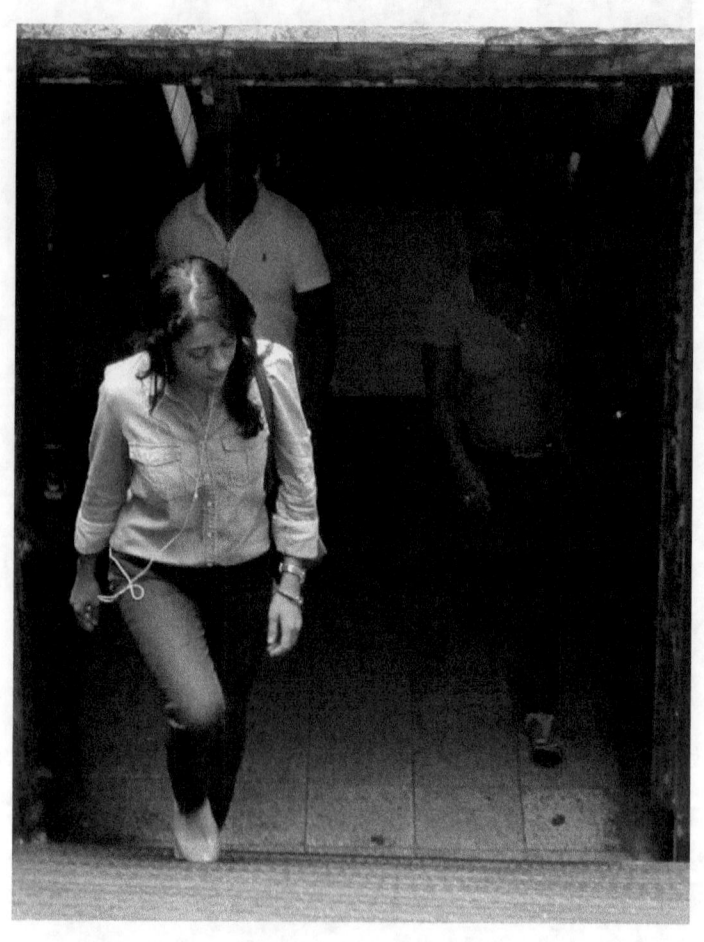

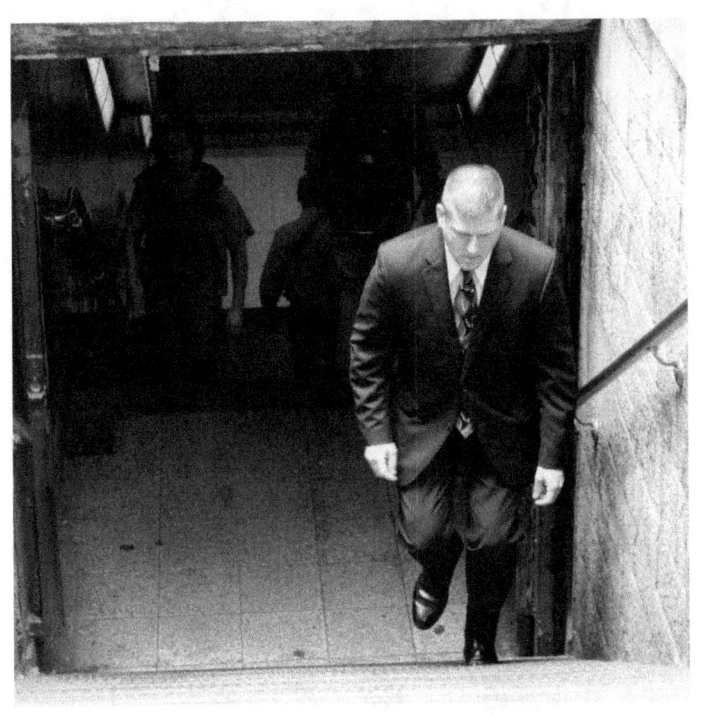

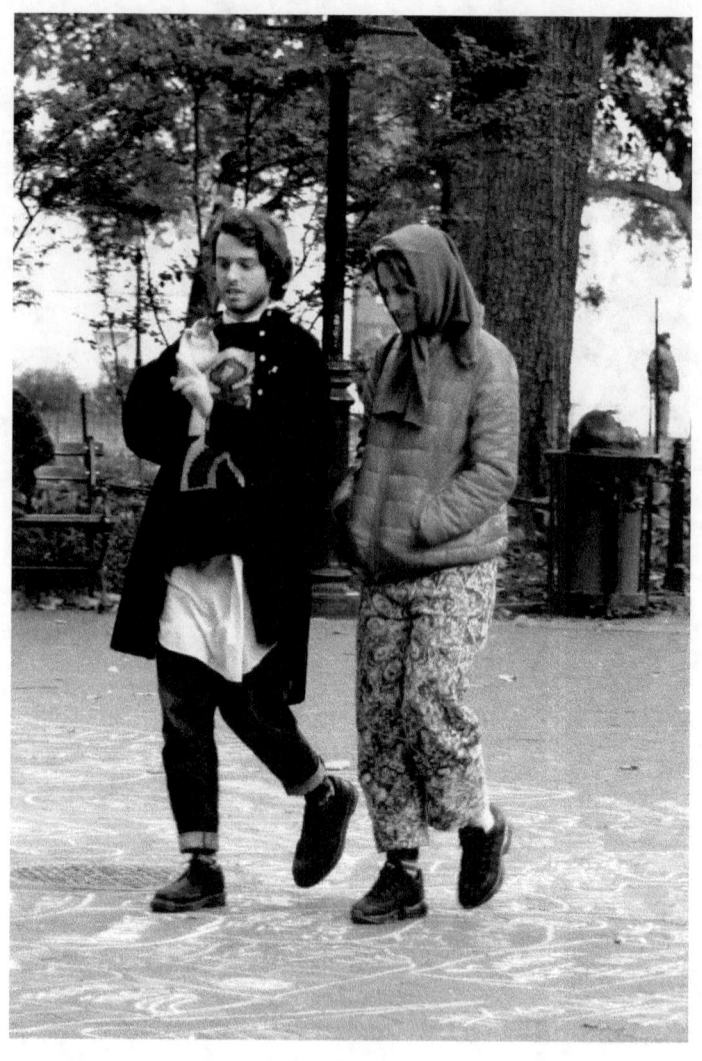

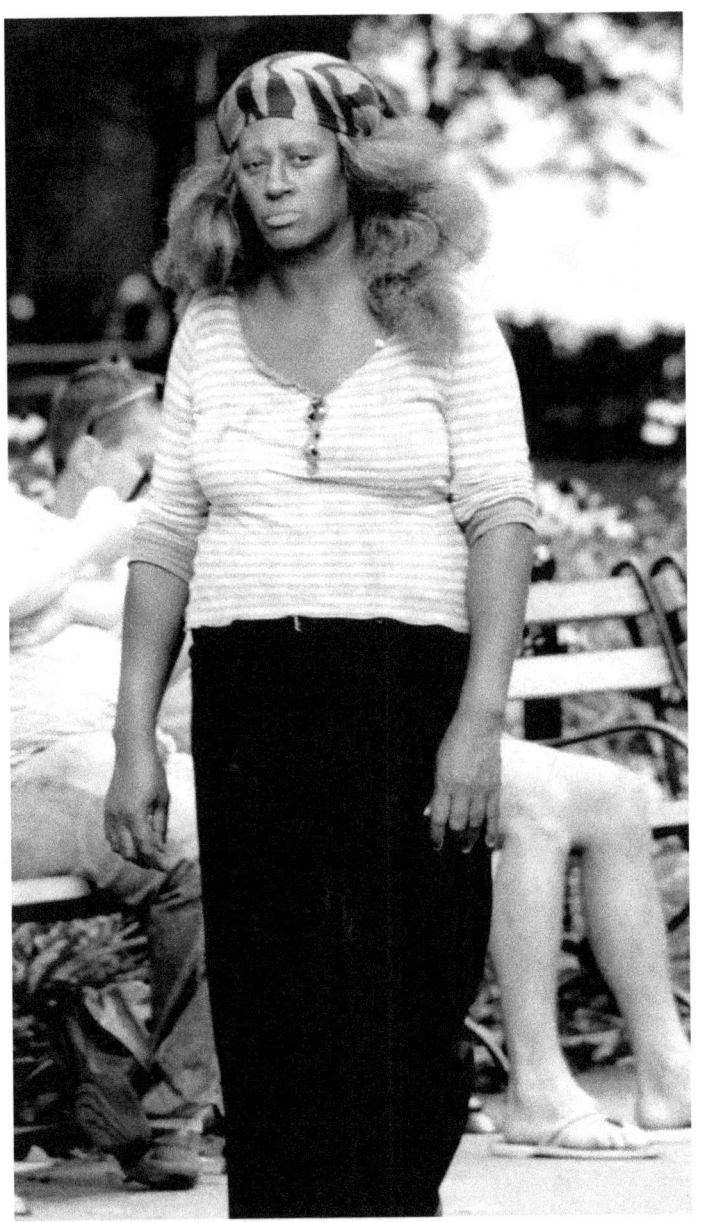

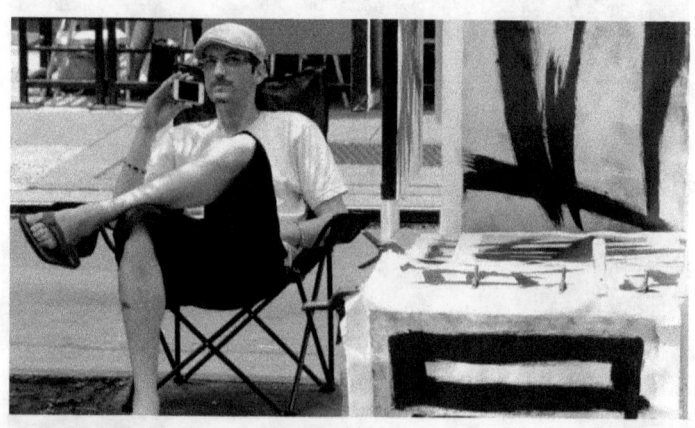

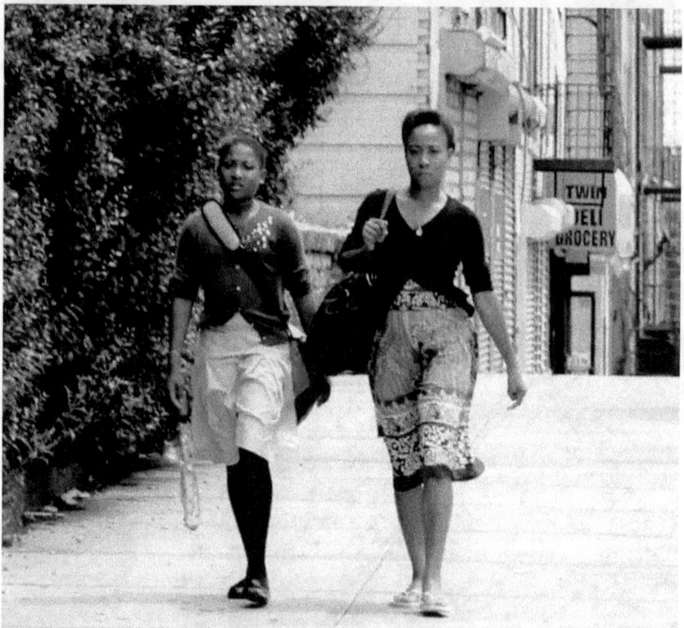

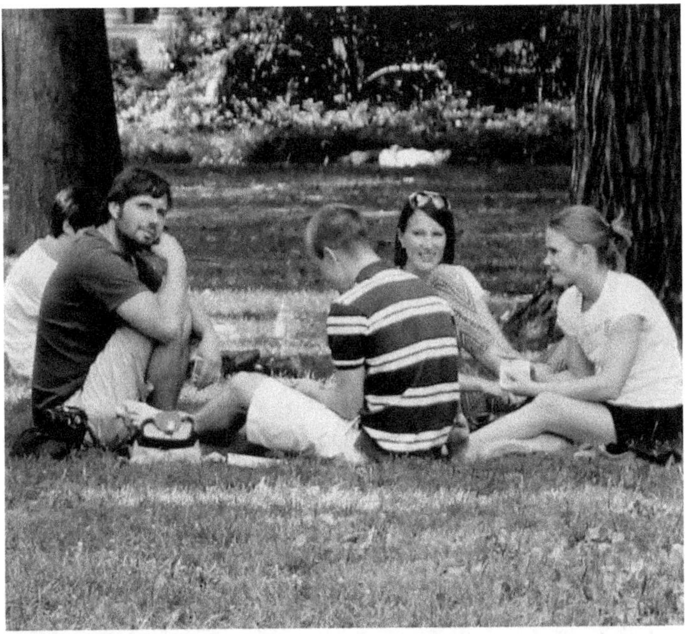

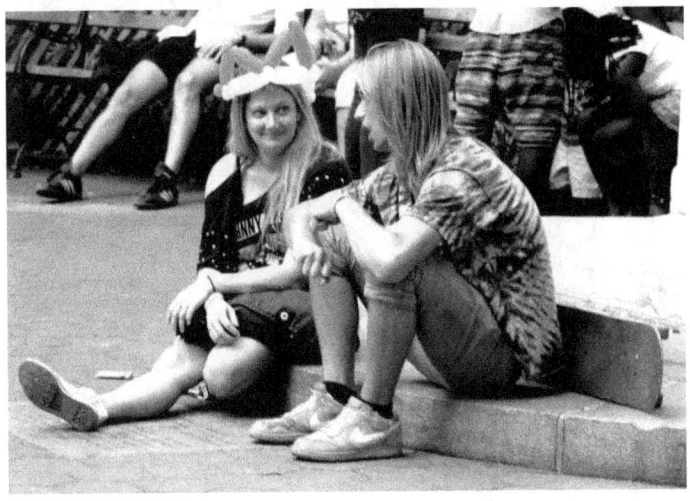

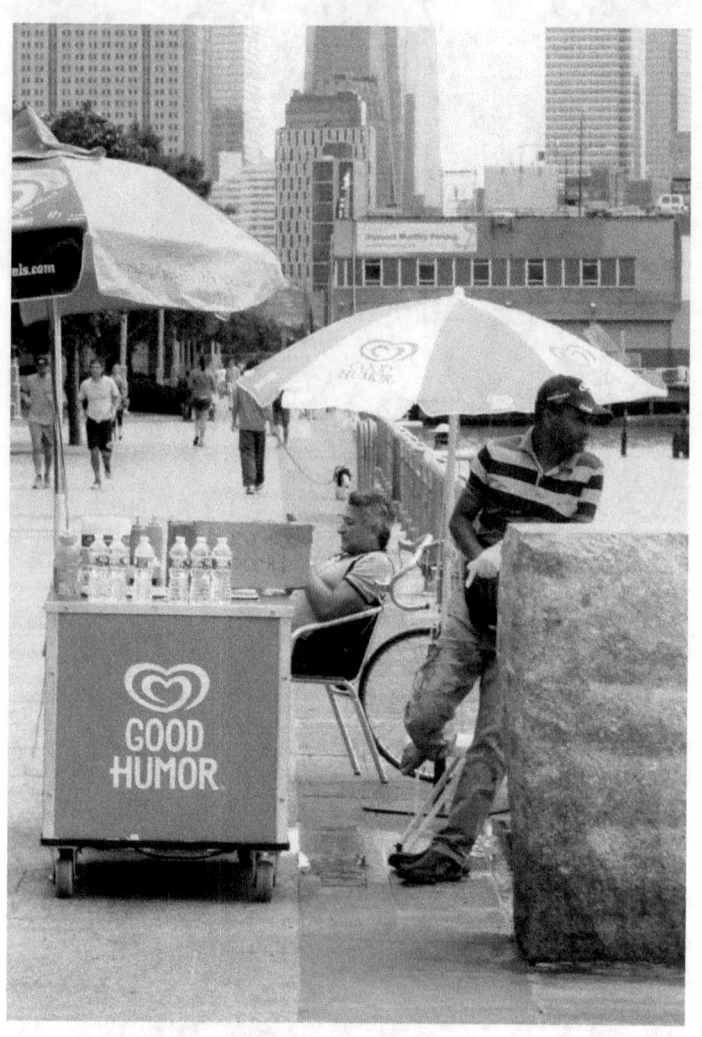

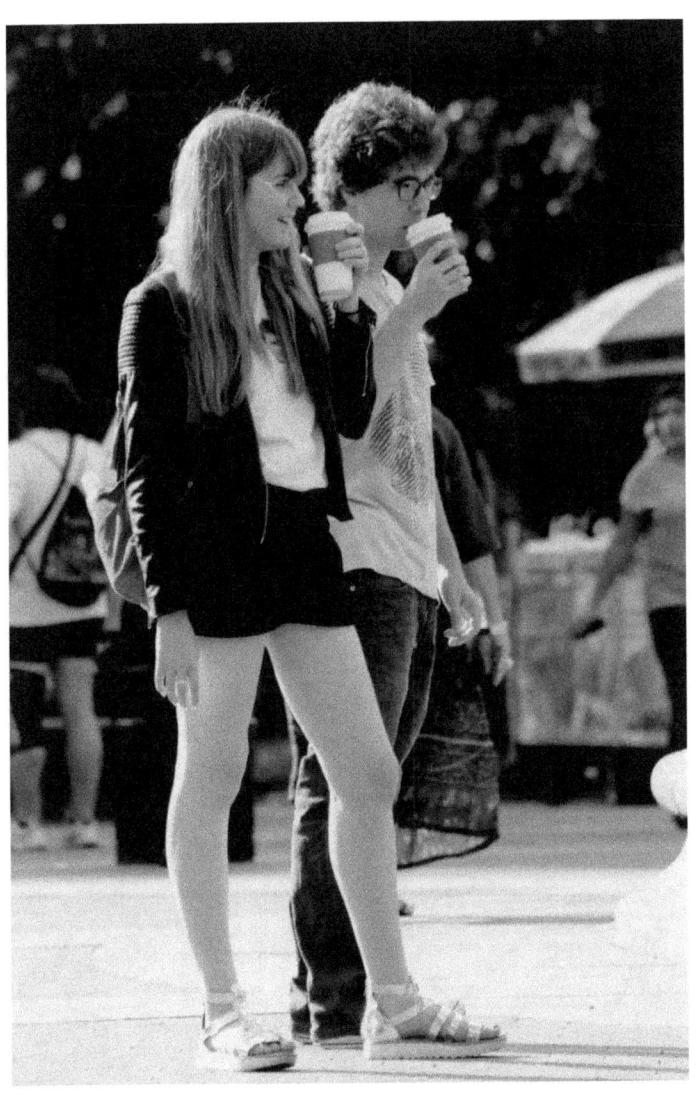

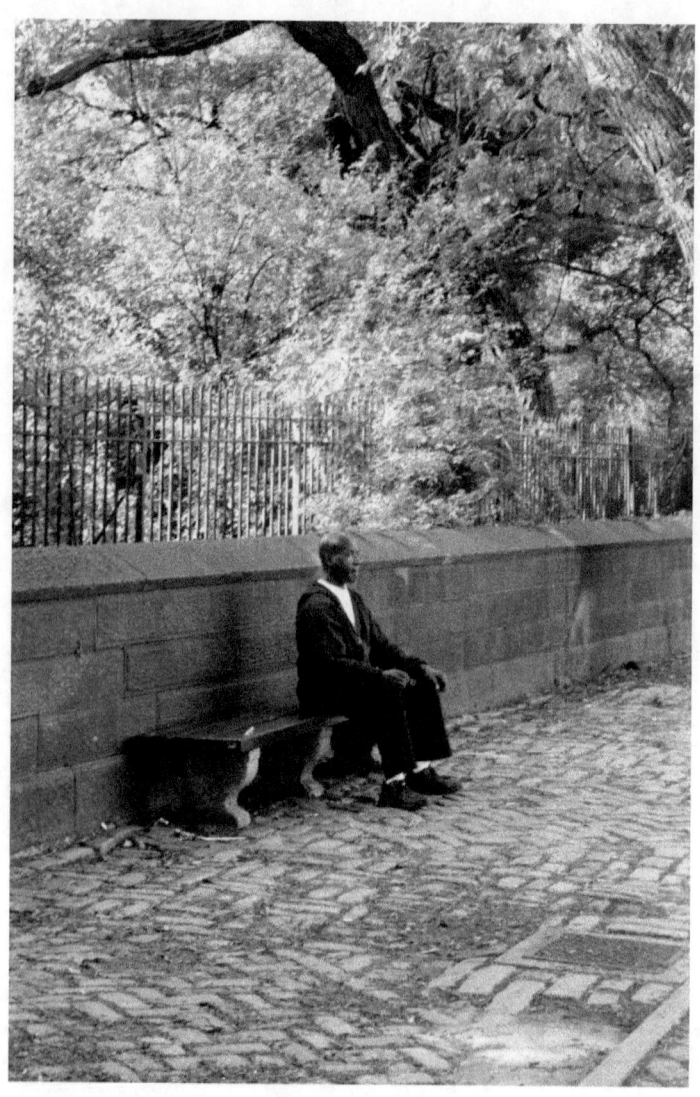

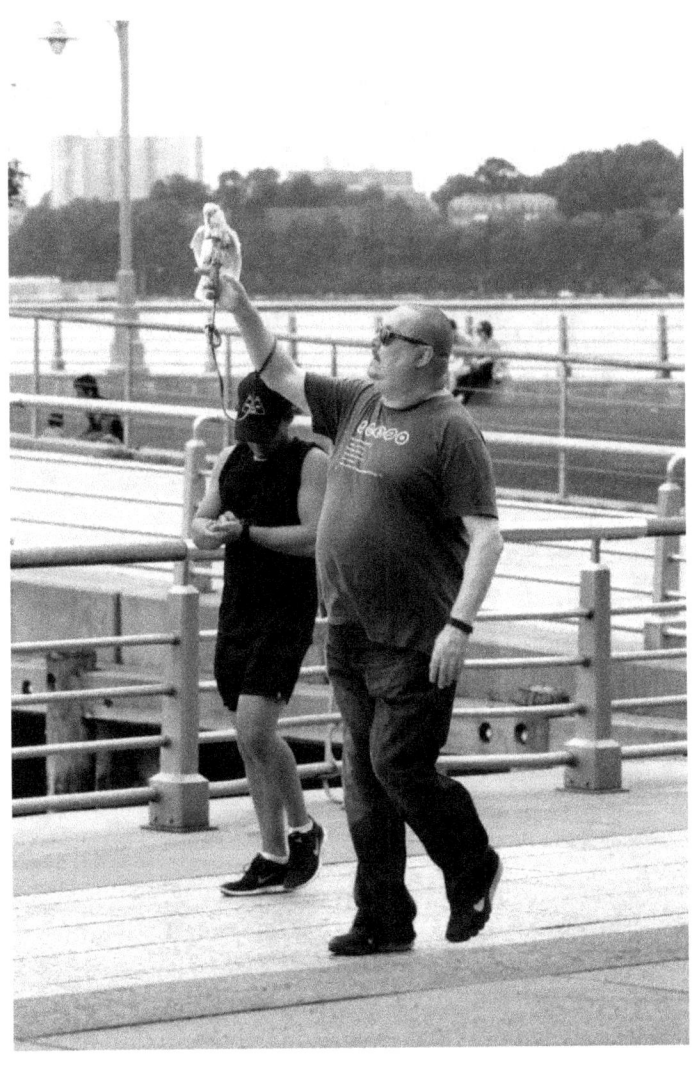

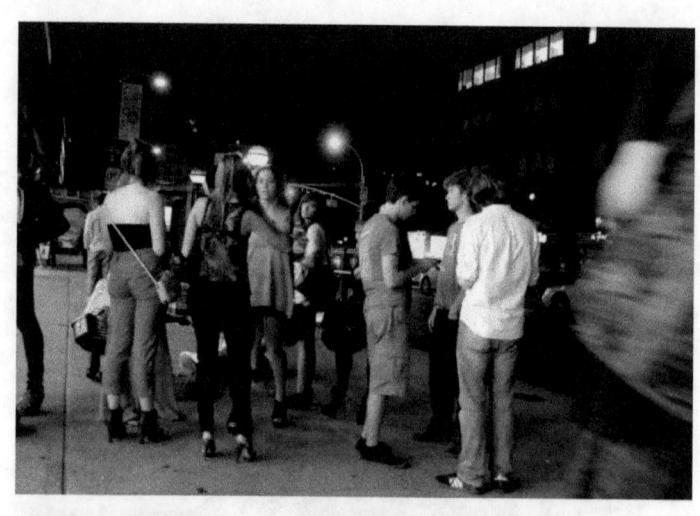

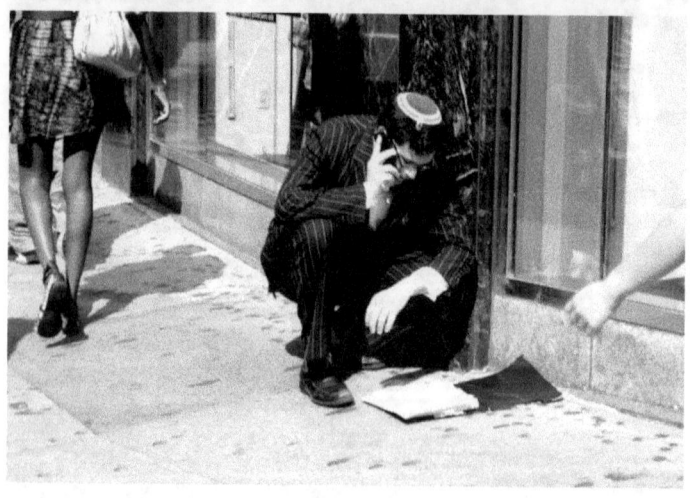

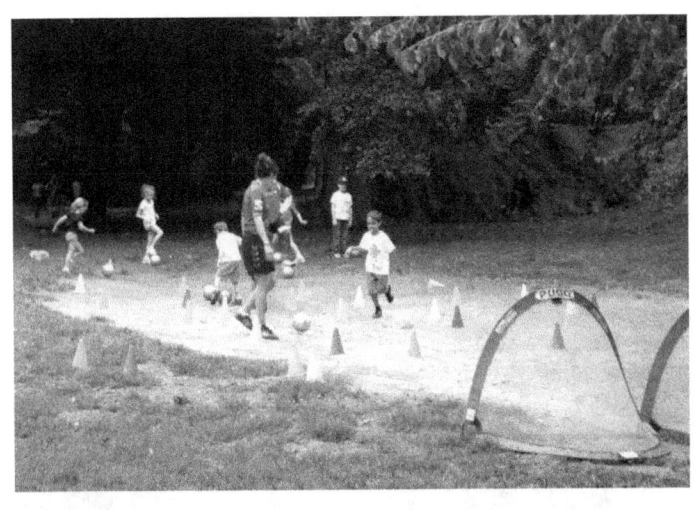

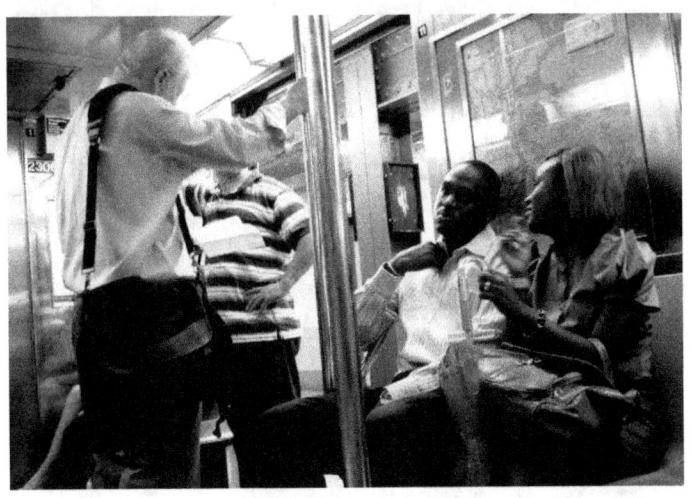

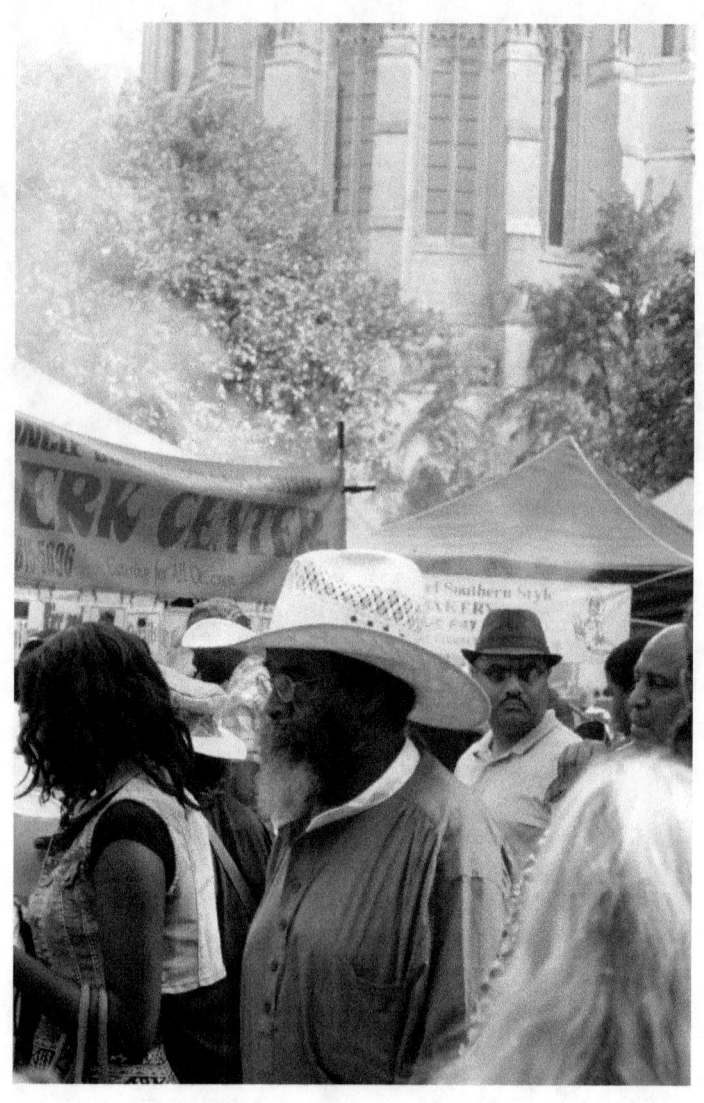

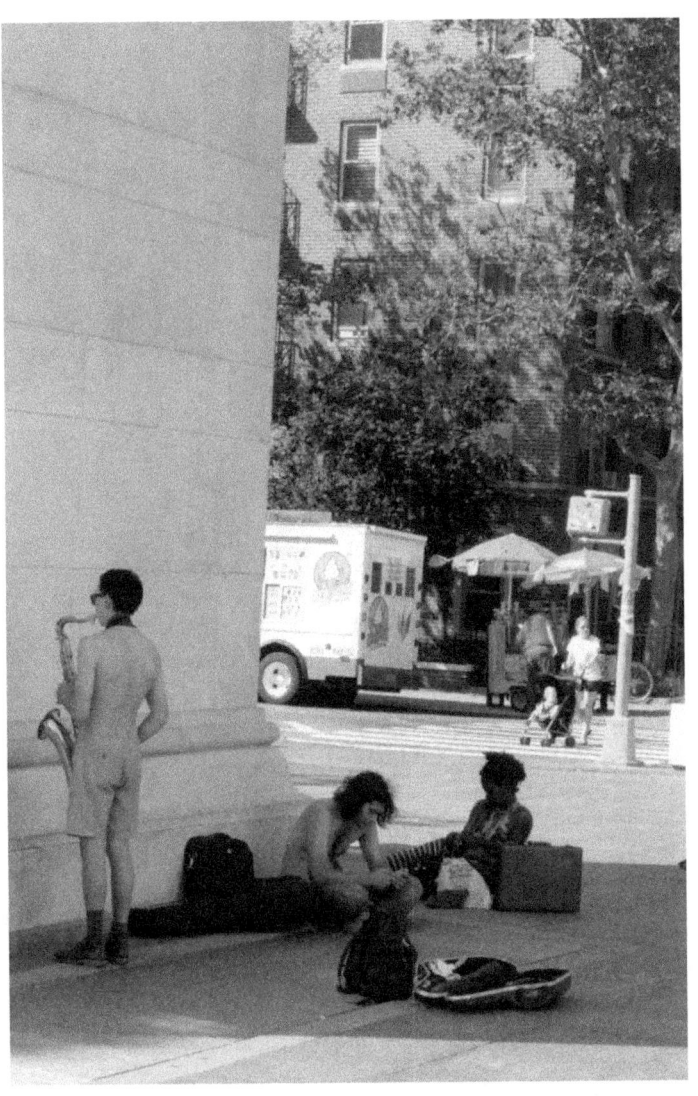

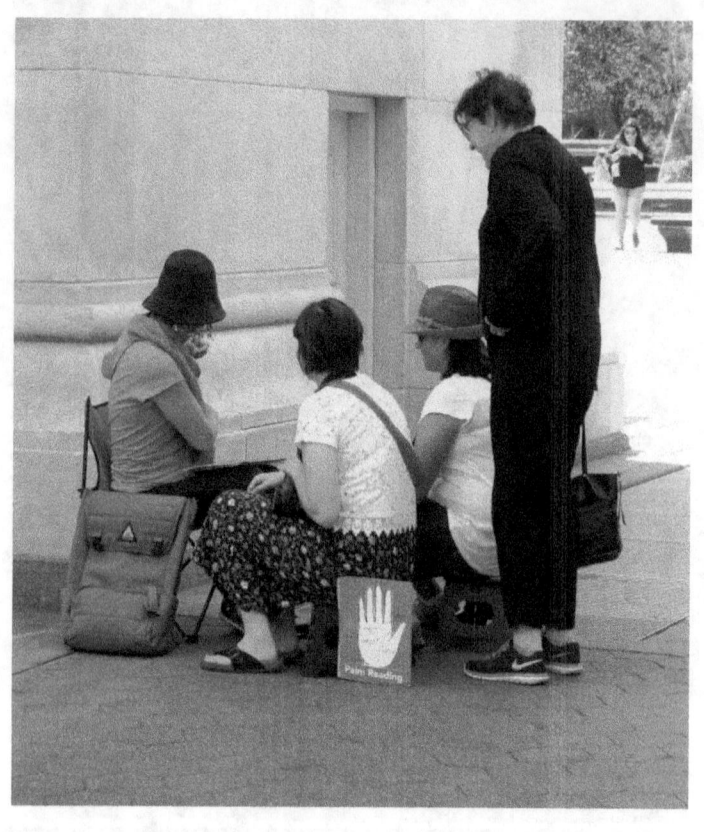

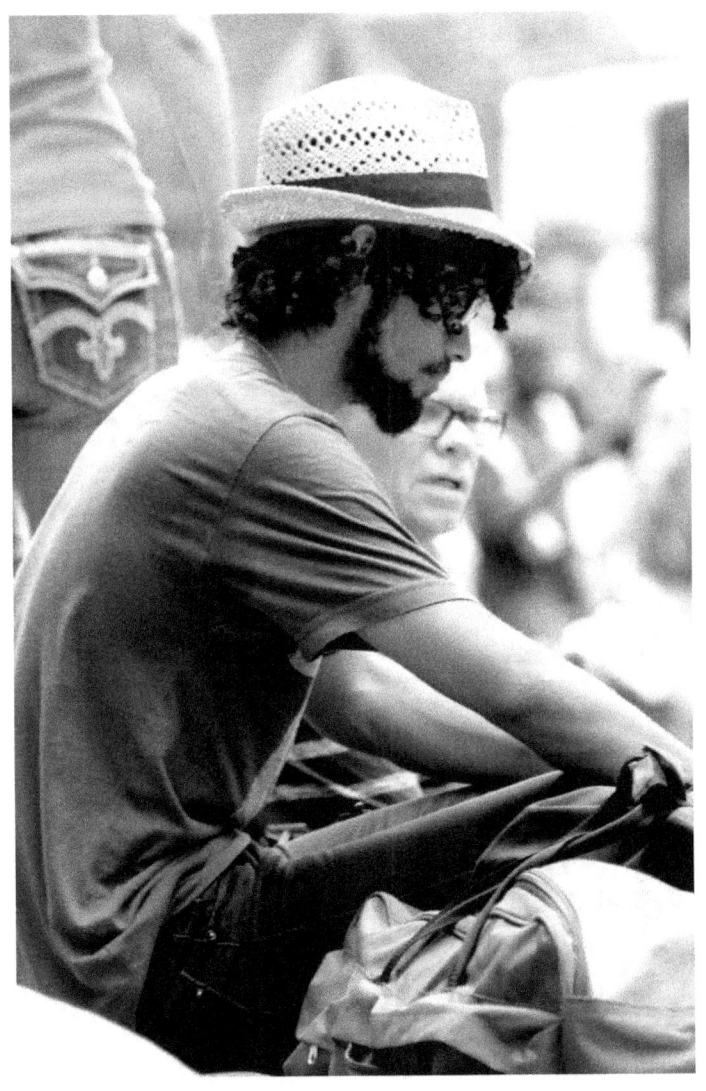

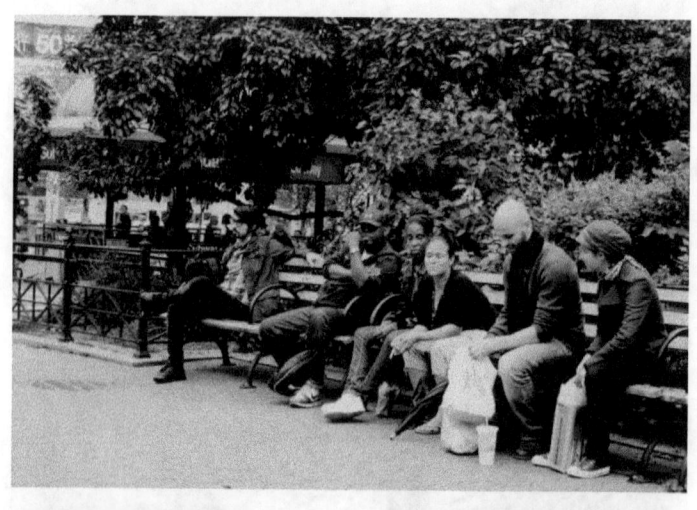

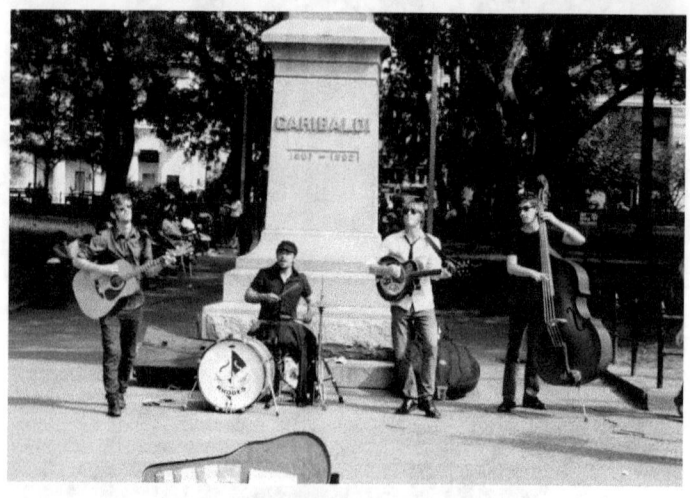

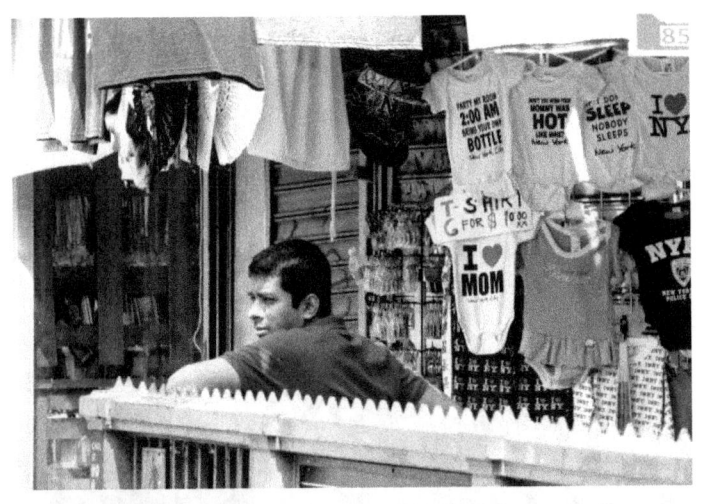

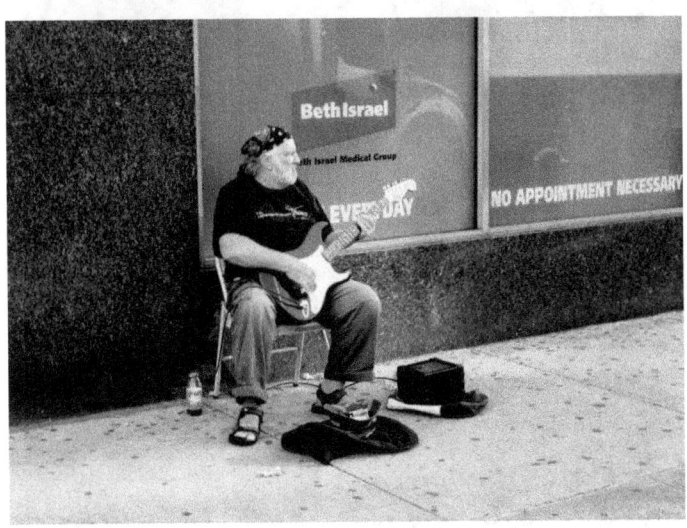

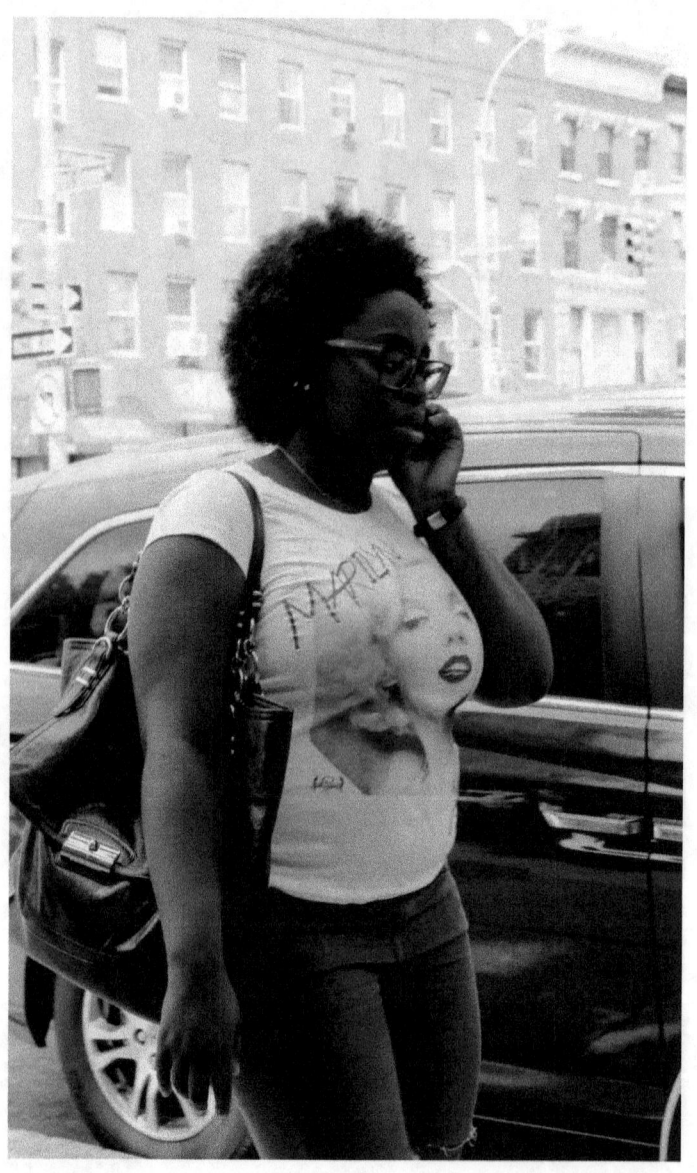

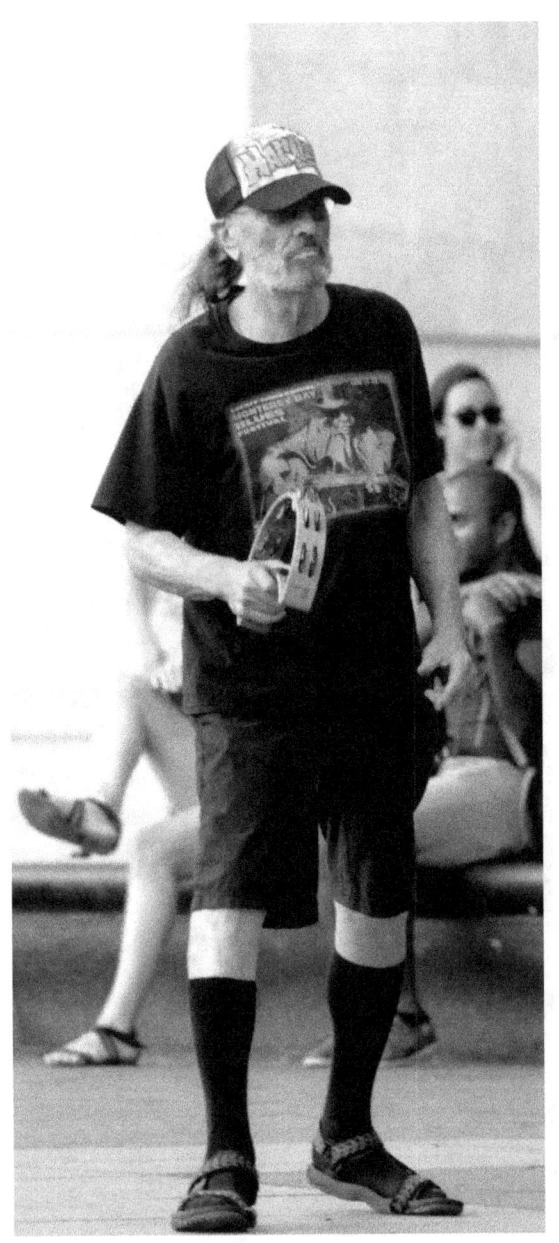

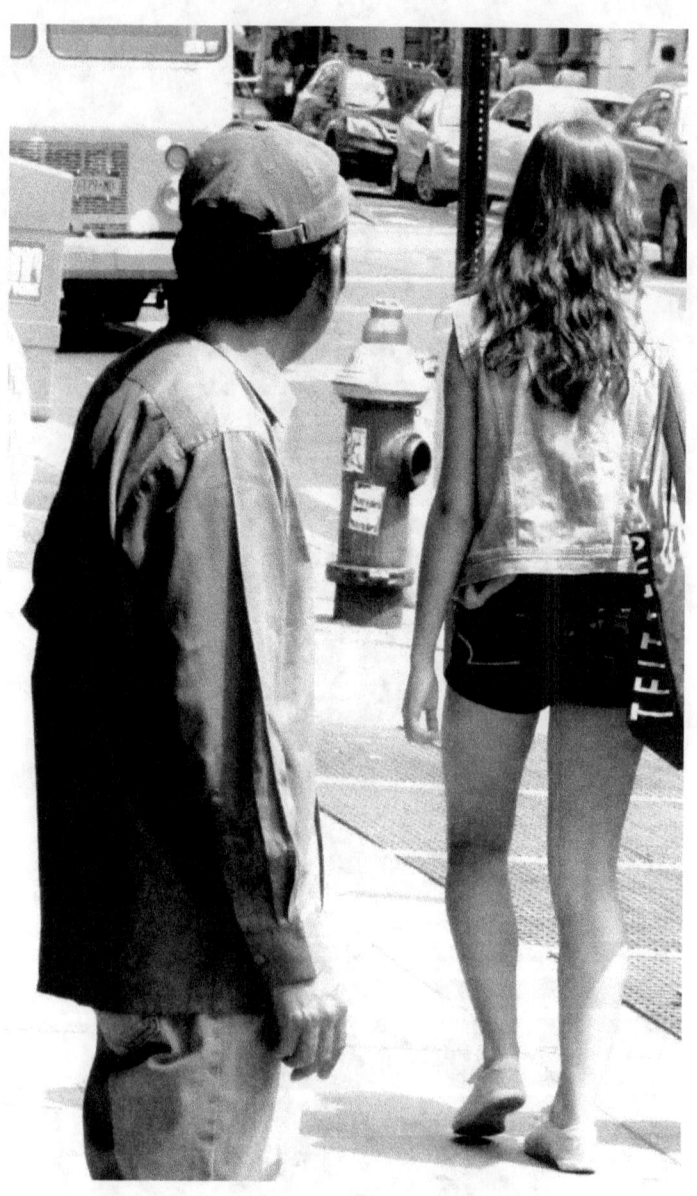

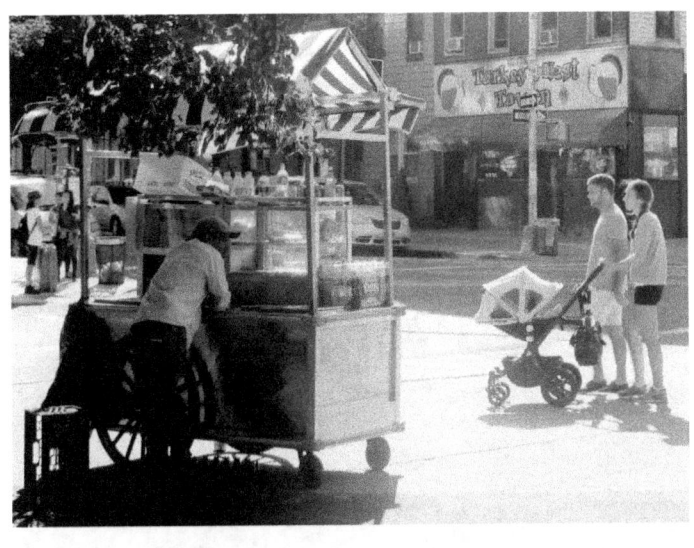

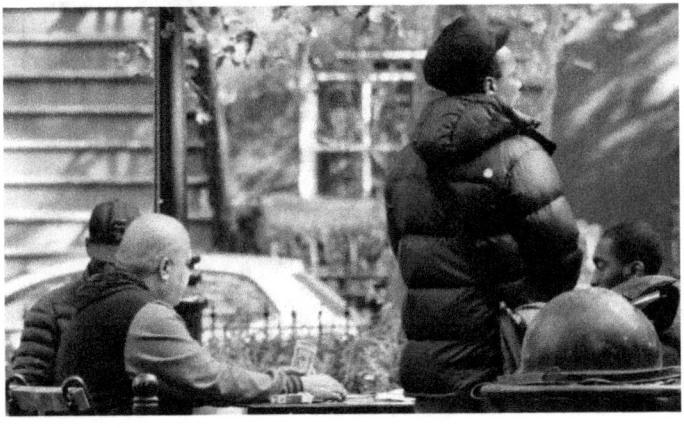

225

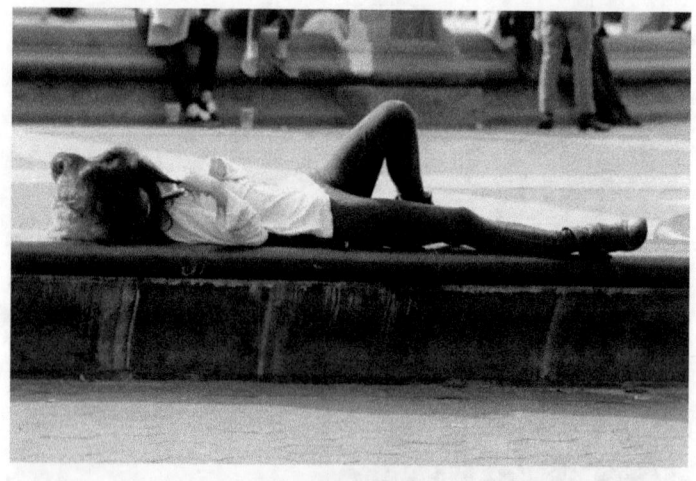

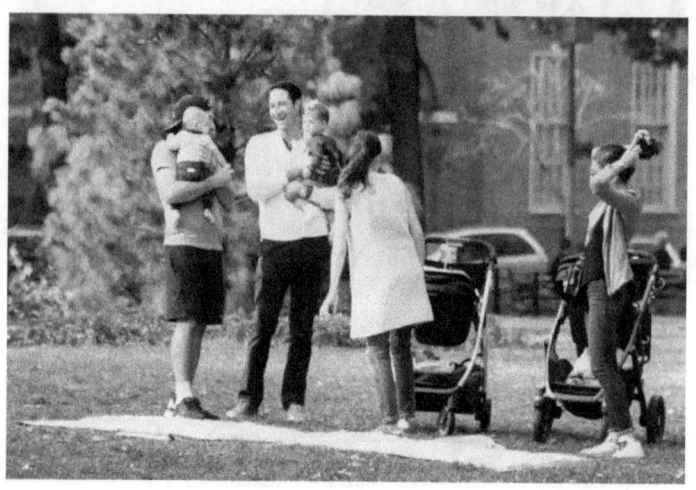

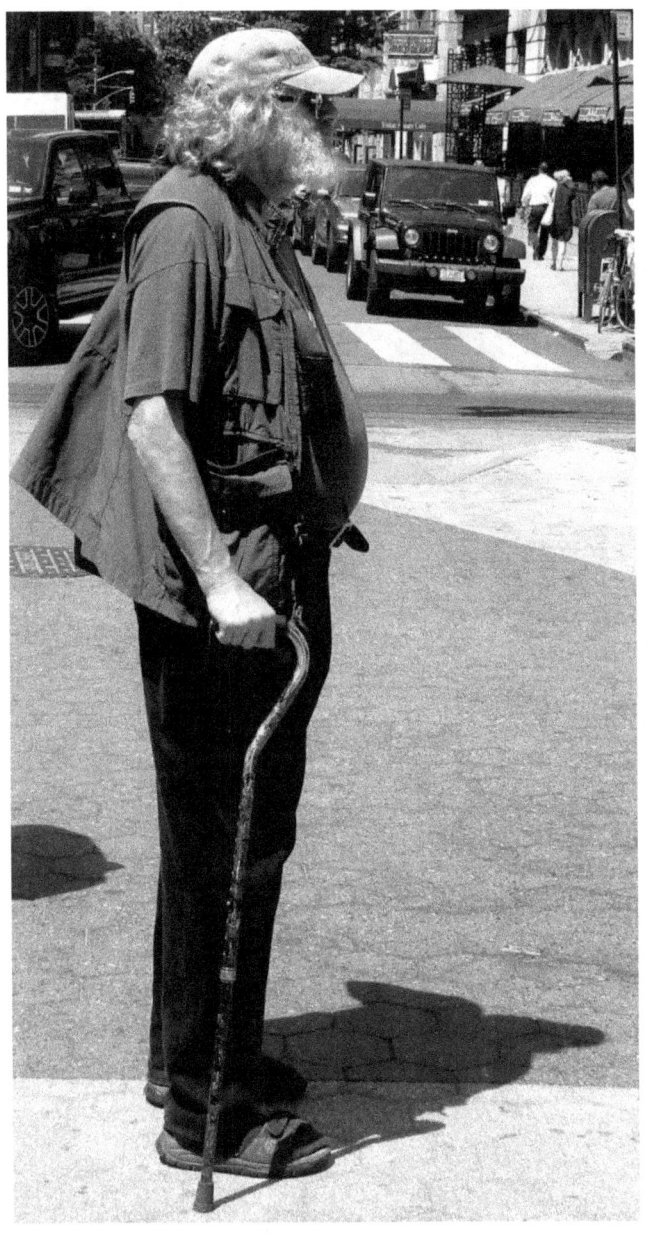

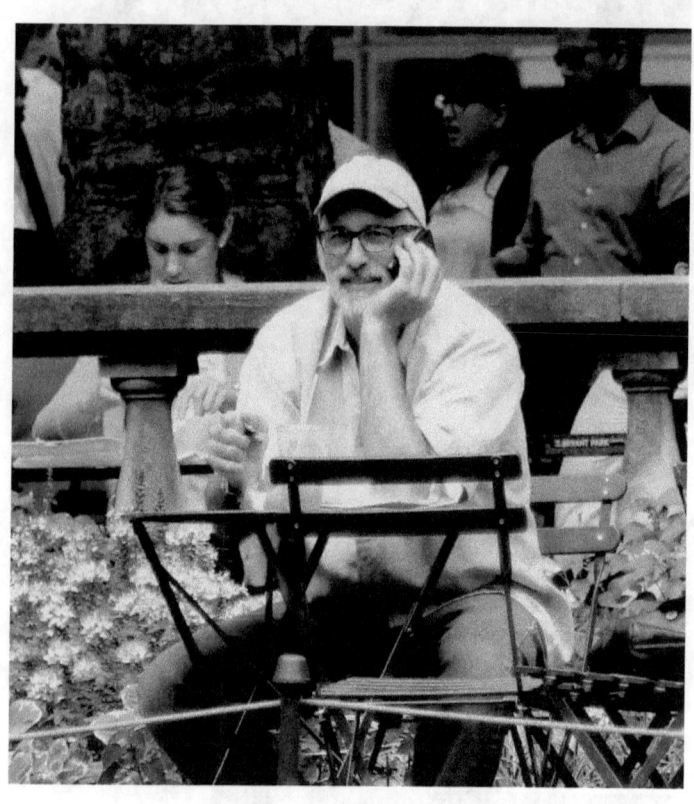

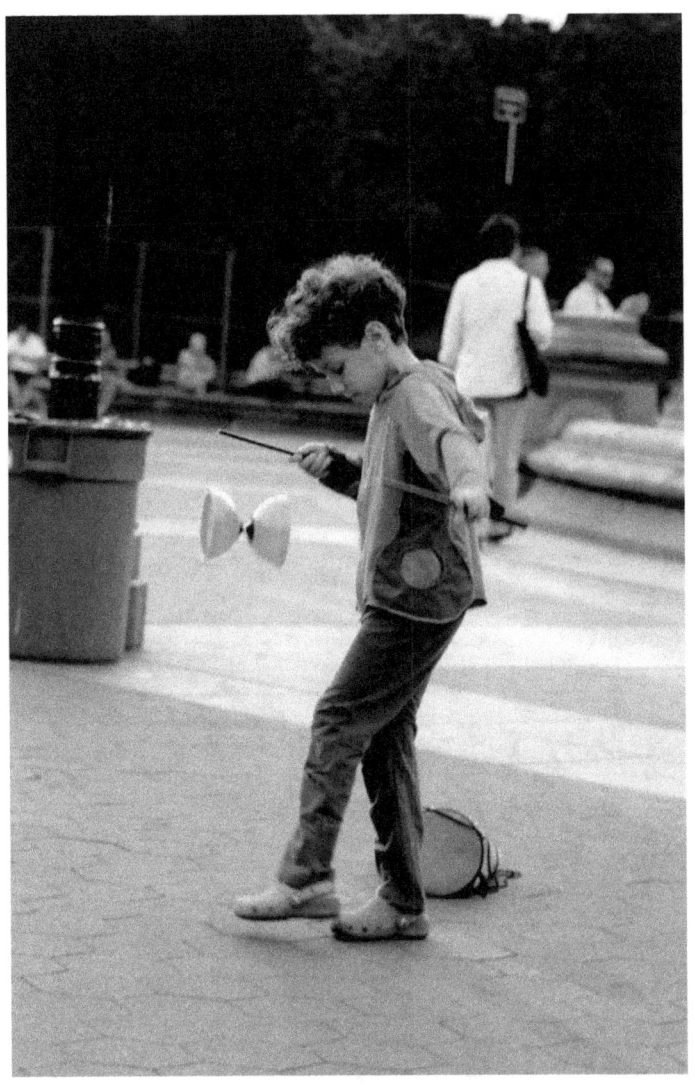

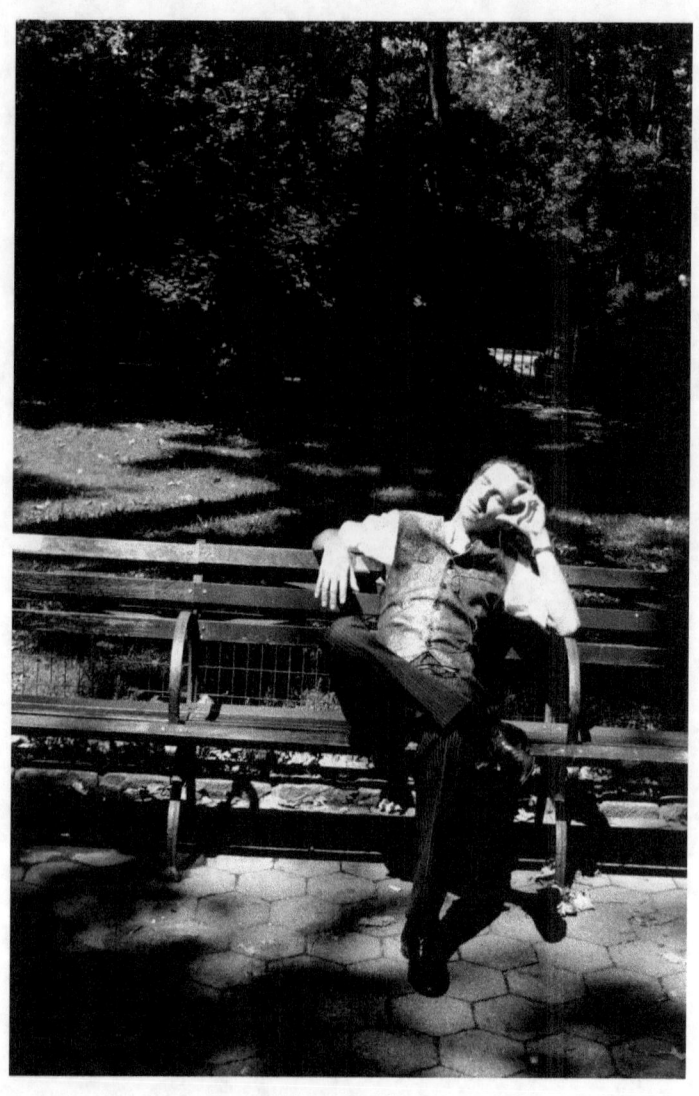

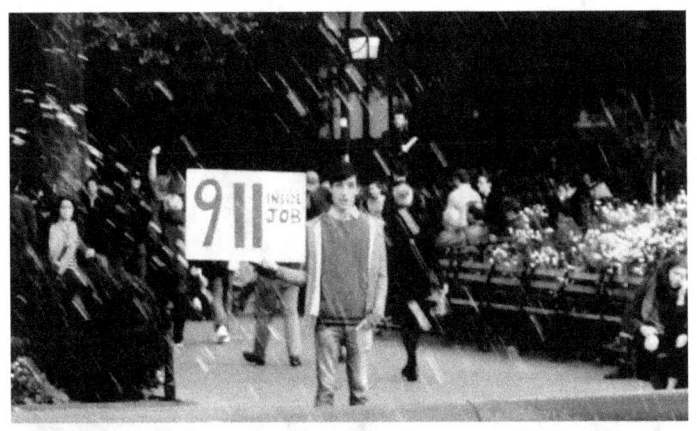

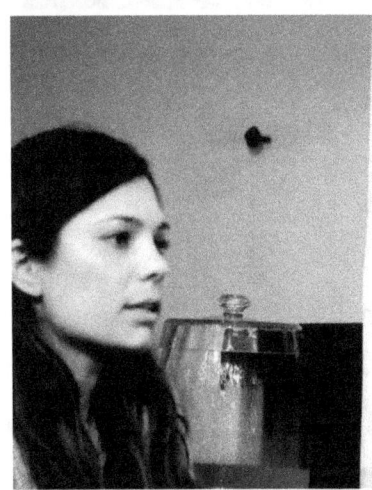

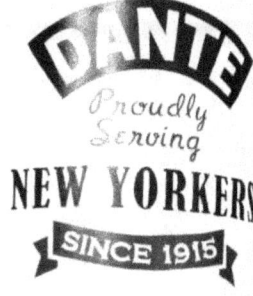

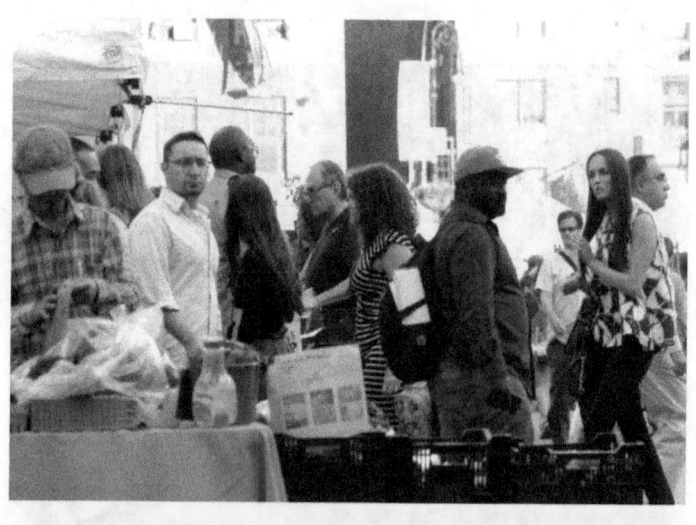

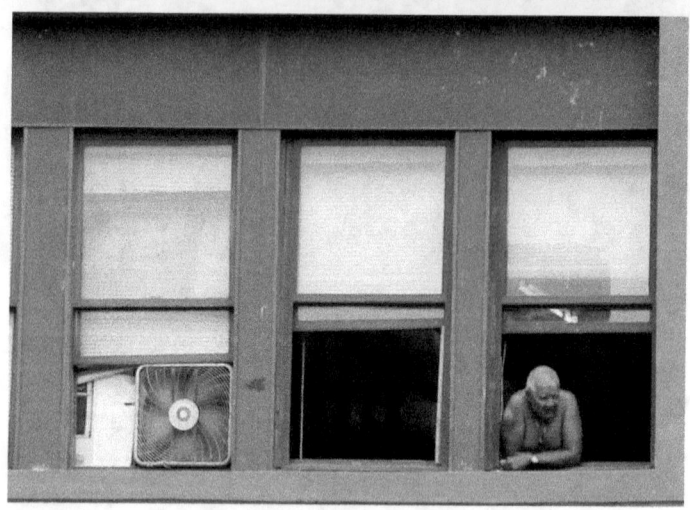

232

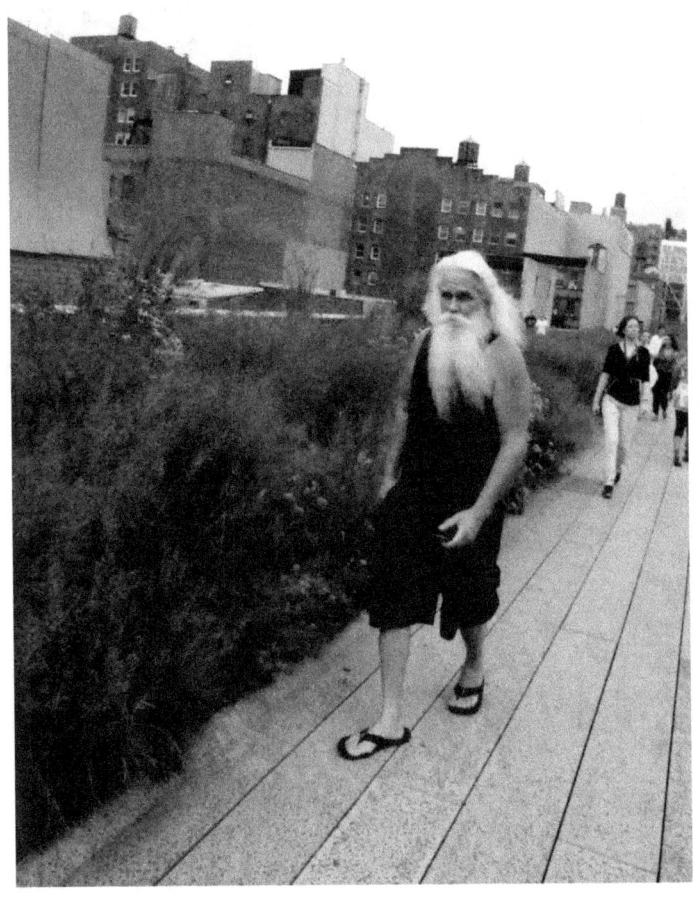

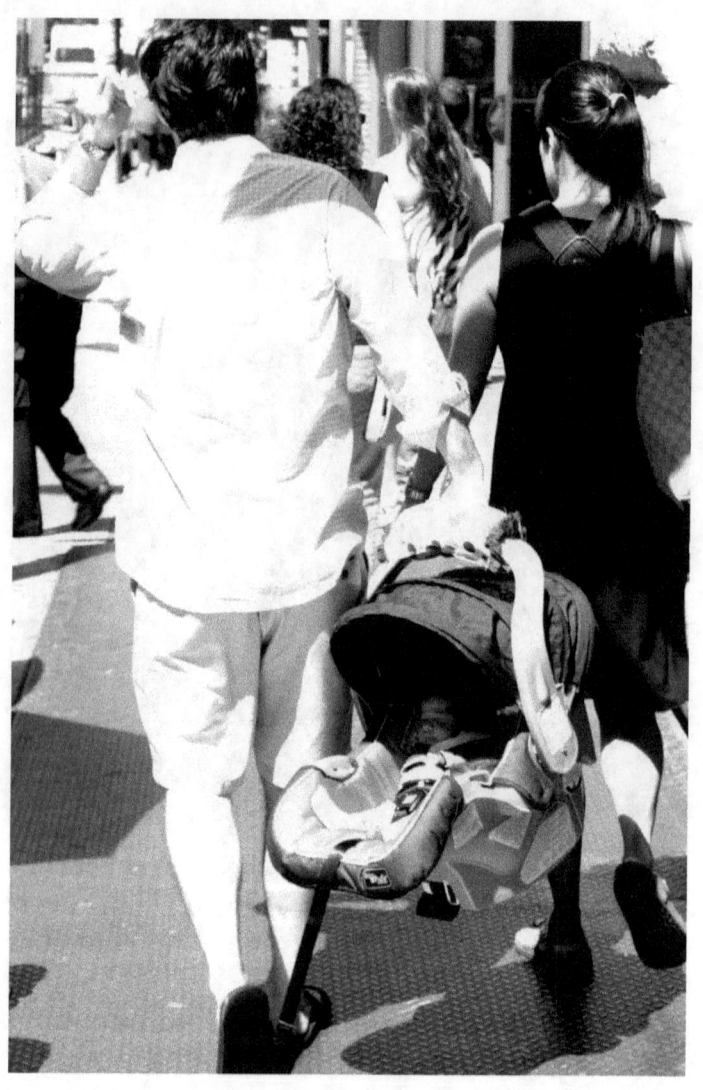

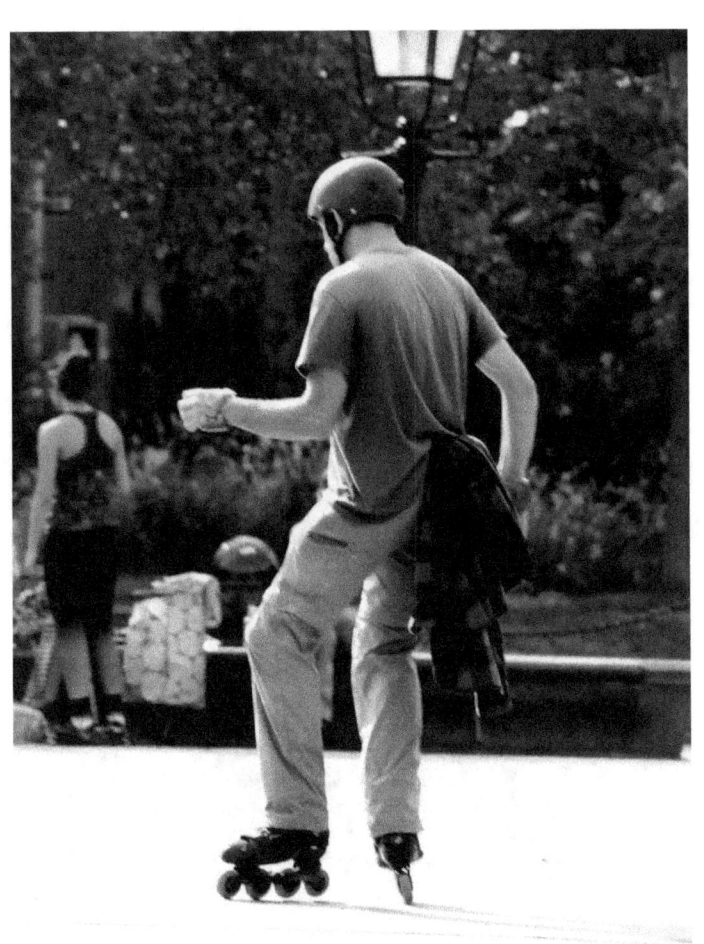

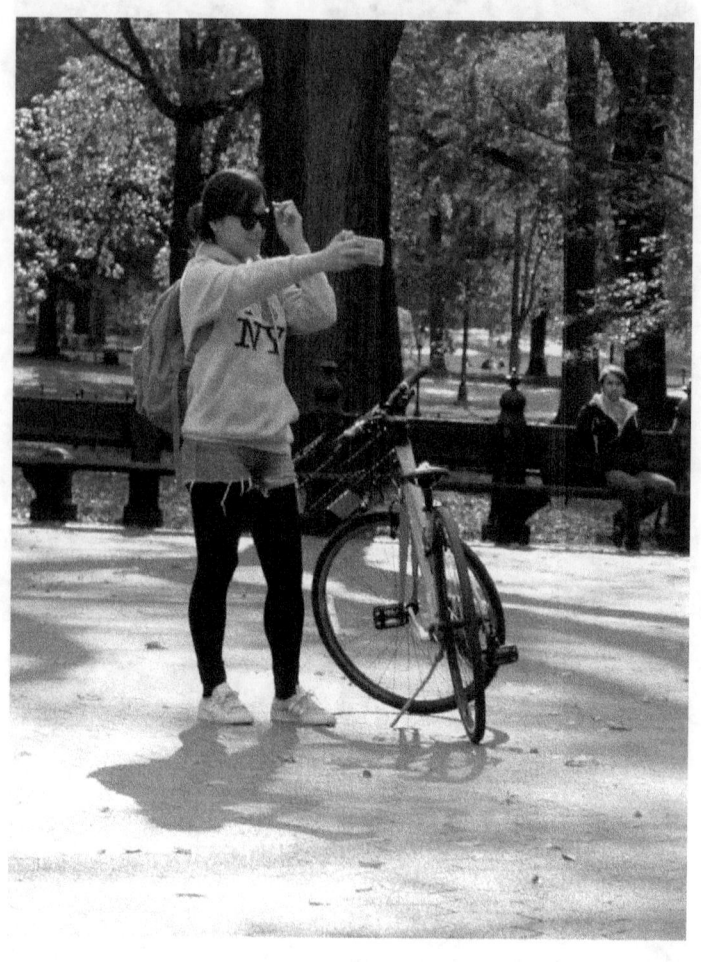

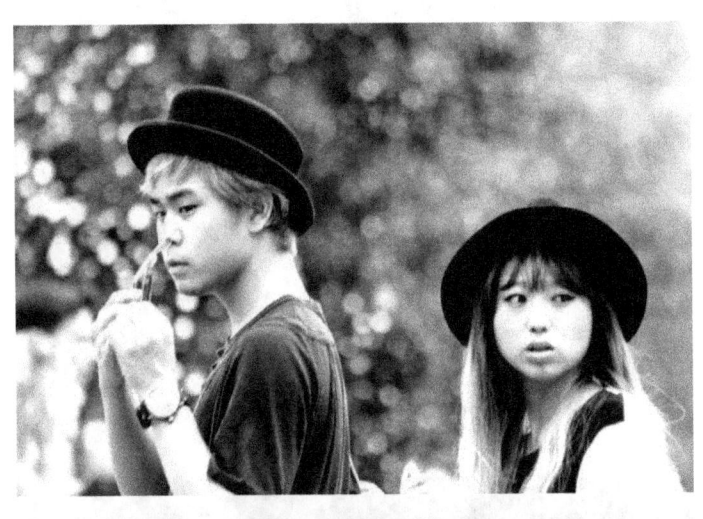

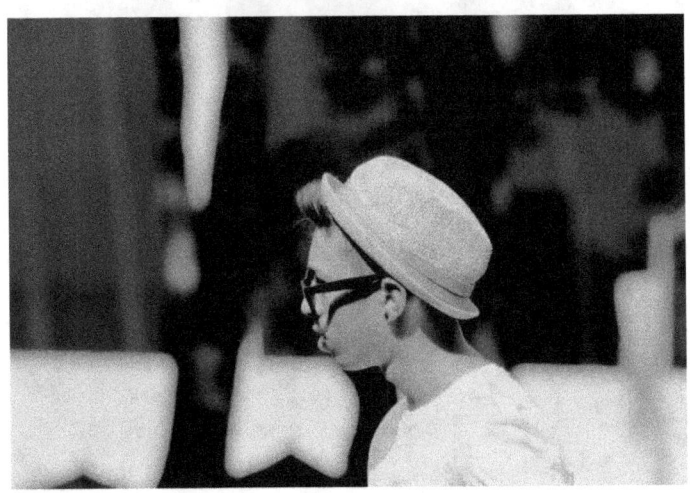

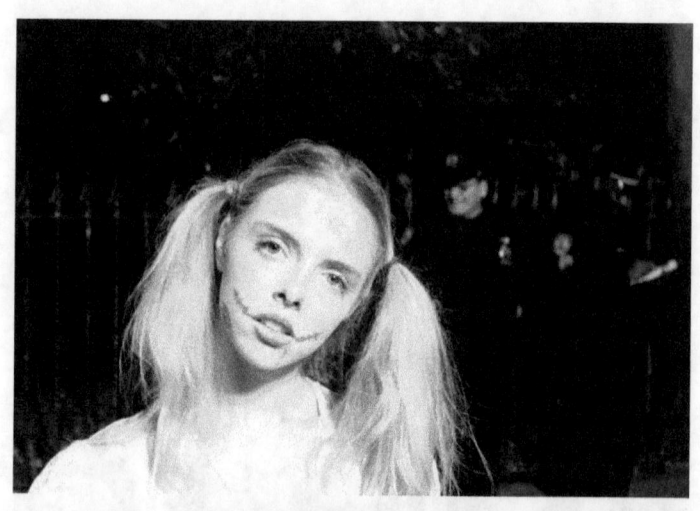

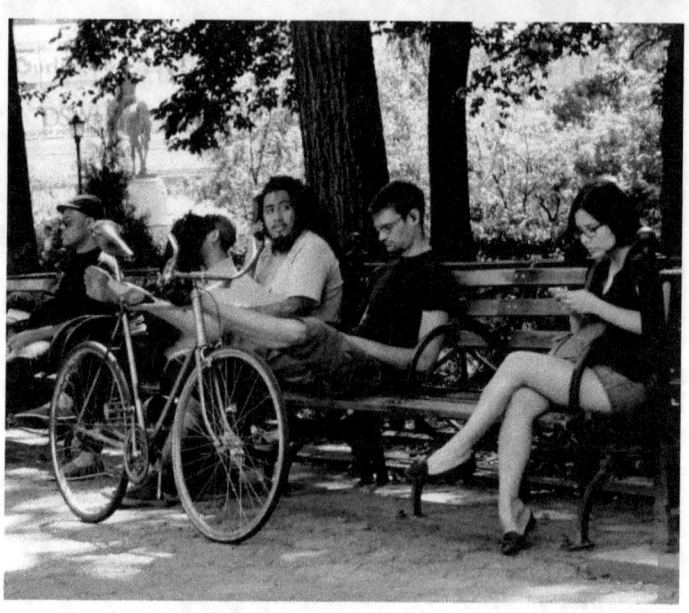

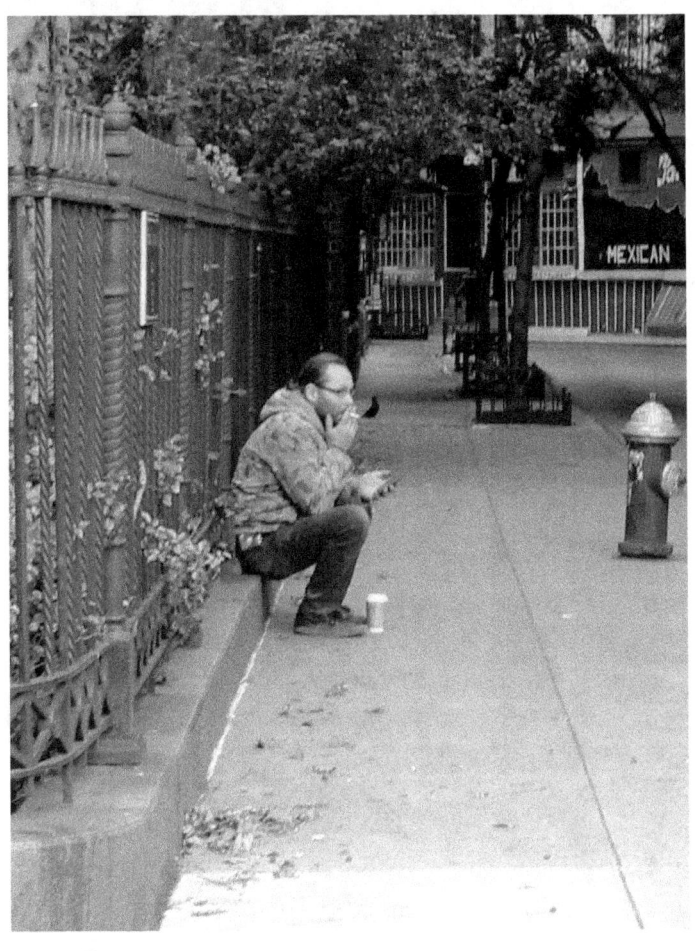

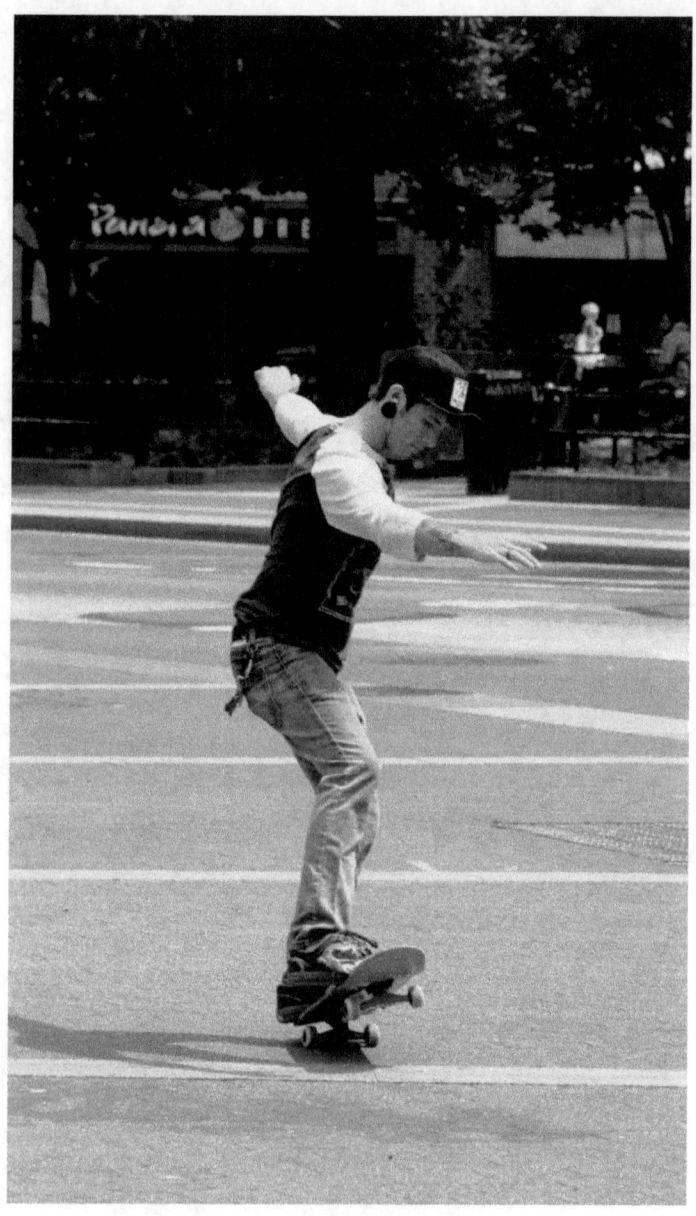

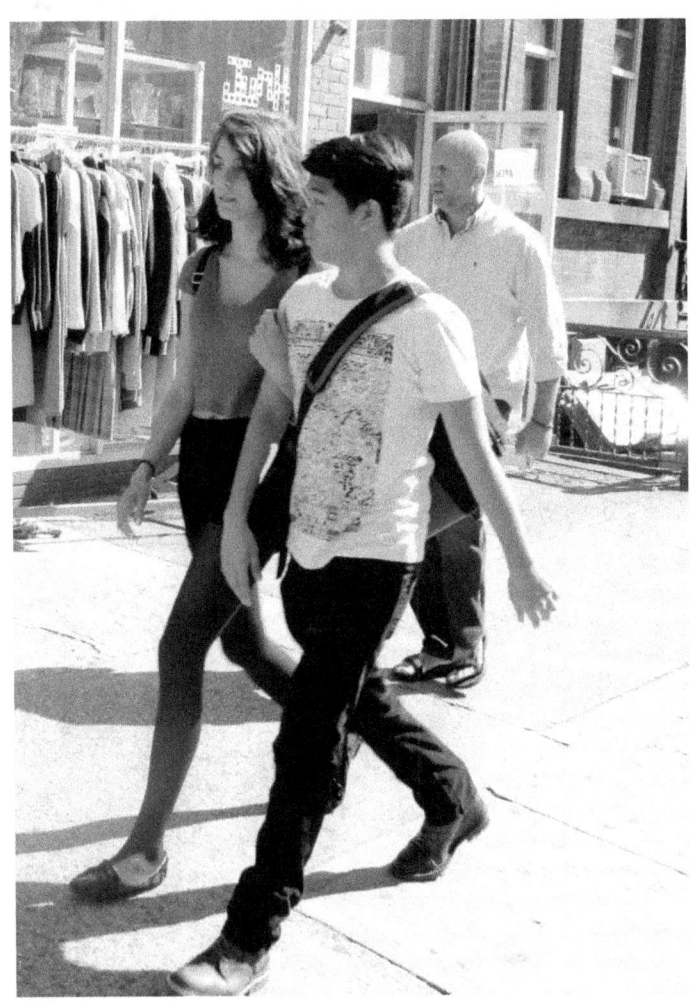

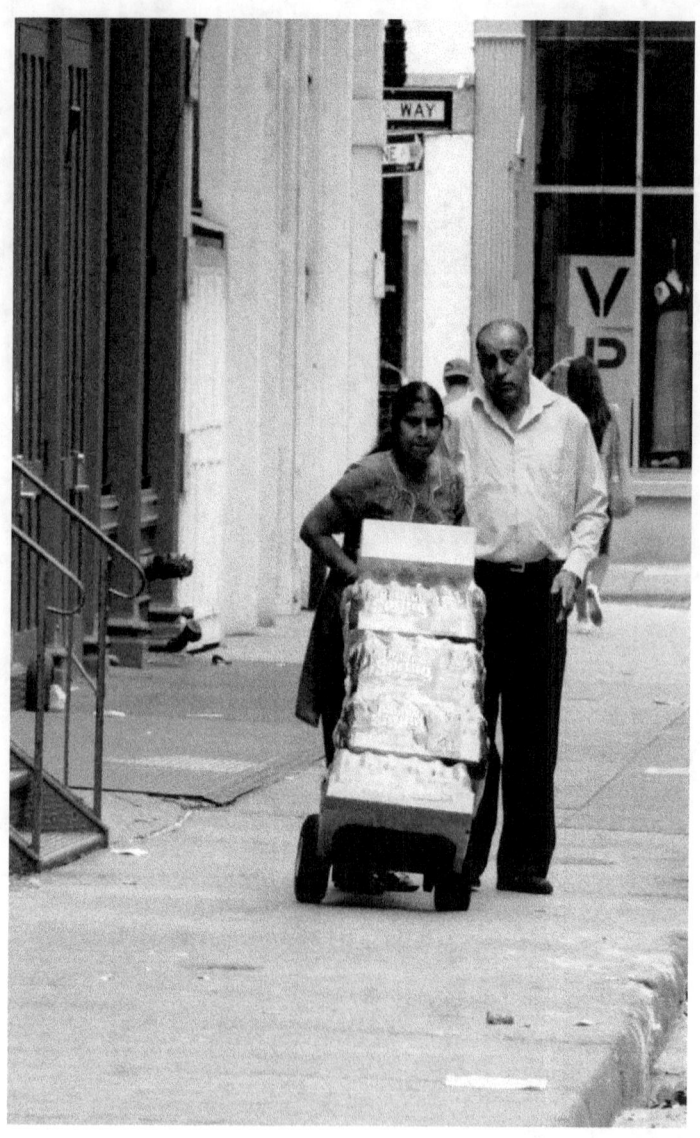

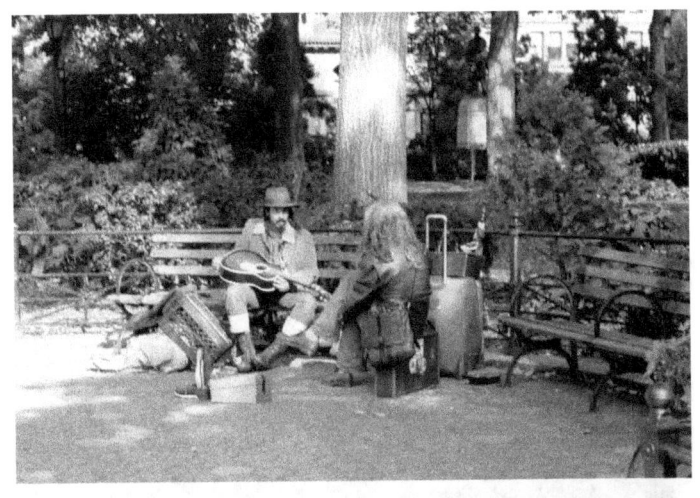

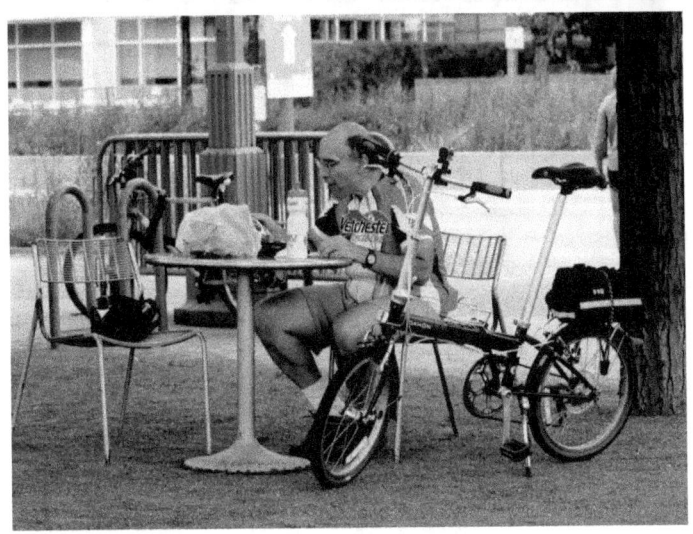

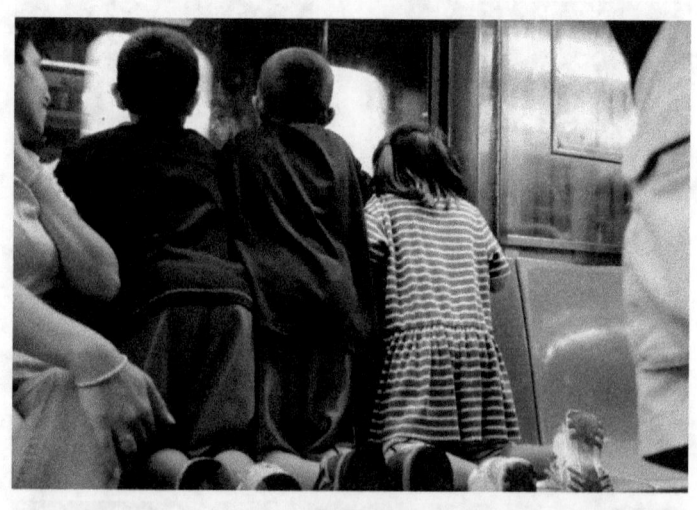

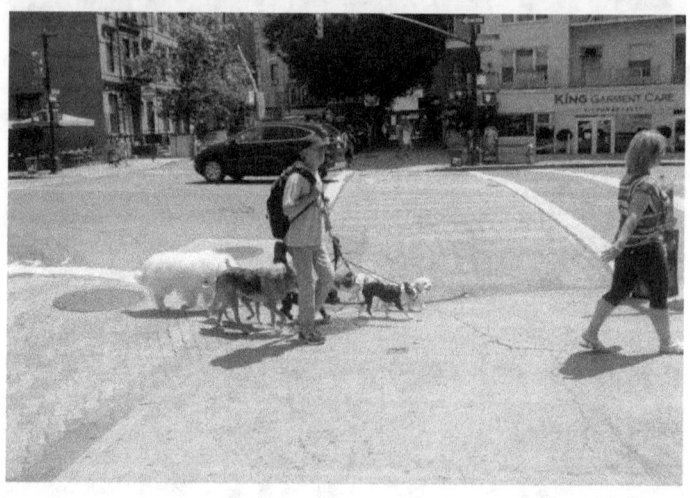

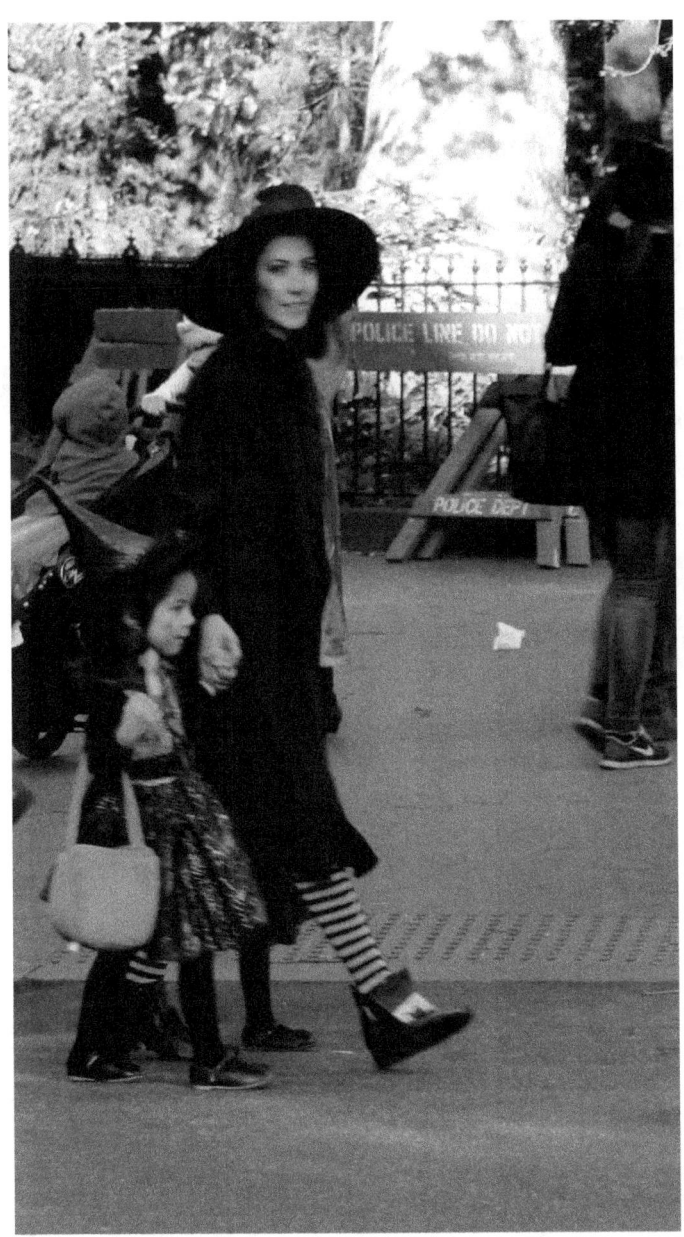

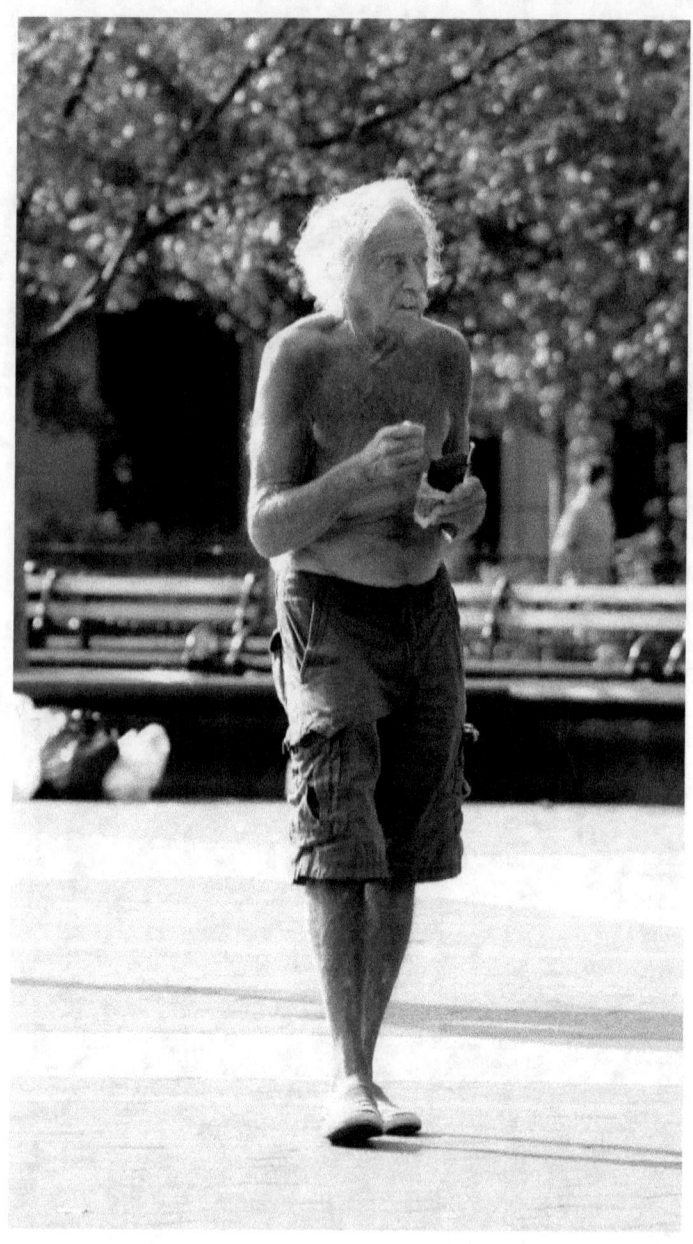

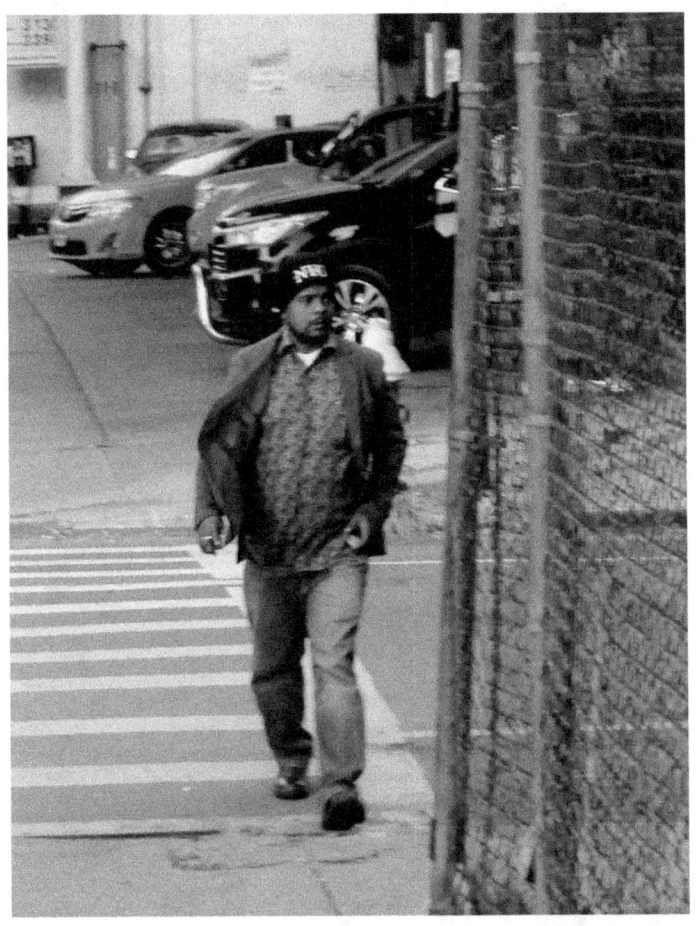

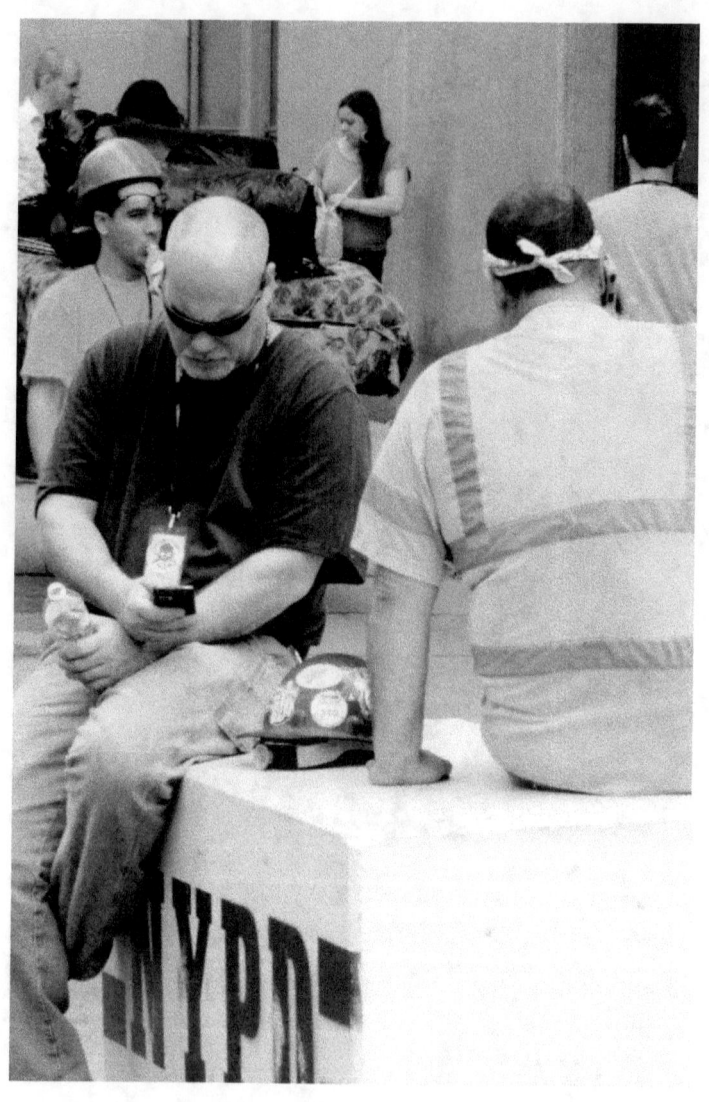